The NORMANS *in* South *Wales,* 1070-1171

By LYNN H. NELSON

T0338976

UNIVERSITY OF TEXAS PRESS, AUSTIN

I dedicate this book to my parents,
Lynn and Helen Nelson

ACKNOWLEDGMENTS

The present work was designed not as a history of the Normans in South Wales but as an extended commentary upon that history. This particular approach was made possible only through the previous efforts of Sir Goronwy Edwards, J. E. Lloyd, T. Pierce-Jones, William Rees, and others. Therefore, the first task of these Acknowledgments must be to record my indebtedness to those scholars upon whose work I have attempted to build.

Whatever new I have brought to this task also I owe to others. Among these are three of my former teachers to whom I feel a special debt of gratitude. Barnes F. Lathrop introduced me to those standards of judgment and performance which make up the historian's craft. What is more, by precept and example he made those standards worthwhile for a man to pursue. Walter Prescott Webb introduced me to a greater breadth of vision by pointing out that History is one great whole and that the arbitrary divisions of time and function of which historians are so fond lead more often to confusion than to convenience. My chief debt, however, I owe to A. R. Lewis, who insisted always that research be something more than the mere collection and arrangement of data. He guided me in undertaking the present work, and offered advice and encouragement at every step. He has been both teacher and friend, and I cheerfully attribute all the virtues of this book to him. The defects I keep for myself.

I have been encouraged and assisted by a host of people, and can single out but a few for special thanks. The Regents of The University of Texas made possible the grant under which I was able to pursue research in England and Wales. The libraries and staff of the Universities of Texas, Kansas, London, and Wales, together with those of the Institute of Historical Research and the British Museum, have been unfailingly kind and helpful.

My friends and associates have been generous with both time and patience. To them I can only say that I hope that my work is worthy of the good will they have shown. Finally, my special thanks to my wife, Carolyn, who has steadfastly refused to be bored by the whole affair.

L. H. NELSON

Lawrence, Kansas

CONTENTS

The Normans in South Wales, 1070–1171

i. The Land and the People

IN THE WEST OF ENGLAND the rich and rolling fields of the Midlands gradually give way to a rougher and less hospitable terrain. By the time one has reached the border shires of Shropshire, Herefordshire, and Monmouthshire, the aspect of the countryside has altered considerably. The rolling slopes and the deep soils of the Midlands have disappeared. Instead, the region consists of a series of low foothills deeply cut by many rivers and streams. The tilled fields which seem so characteristic of the lands lying to the east are here replaced by meadows and by tracts of the ubiquitous oaks which do so much to lend a special flavor to the border shires.

Perhaps the dominant characteristic of the border is the ever-present mass which the Cambrian Mountains rear to the west. This rampart, because of its constant presence, often fades from the visitor's consciousness. And yet, by always lying at the edge of one's vision, and by effectively delimiting the western horizon, these mountains help to maintain a frontier flavor in the region. One seems constantly aware that these shires are the edge of England and that on the western horizon one can see the beginning of another and quite different land.

The country beyond this steep slope in many ways fulfills the promise of its eastern border. It consists of a high plateau upon which massive peaks alternate with deep and narrow valleys. This rugged region forms the mountainous heartland of the peninsula of Wales, today the home of over two million people. The Welsh dairy and sheep-raising industries, together with extensive coal deposits, make a significant contribution to the British economy. A growing tourist trade continues to open up large areas of the peninsula to an even closer and more profitable connection with England. Despite its small size and scanty population, Wales plays a well-integrated and important role in the life of the United Kingdom.[1]

It is obvious to even the most casual visitor to Wales that such was not always the case. The Welsh countryside abounds with fortifications—prehistoric hill-forts, Roman *castra*, and Norman castles. The native heroes—Caratacus, Owen Glendower, and King Arthur—echo this martial note. These and many other things serve to remind the visitor of the long struggle of the Welsh to avoid domination and absorption by their wealthier and more numerous neighbors to the east.[2] It was a bloody and lengthy battle, but it was one in which the Welsh were foredoomed to failure. Although their mountainous isolation afforded them great defensive advantages, it also condemned them to a poverty which made it impossible for them to compete with their more favorably situated neighbors. In the course of time it was inevitable that the superior wealth and numbers of their enemies should succeed in bringing the independence and isolation of Wales to an end.[3]

The final stages of this process began almost nine hundred years ago, when the tide of Norman conquest rolled into the border shires and reached the frontier of the old Anglo-Saxon state. It soon became clear to the conquerors that the existence of an independent Wales posed a serious problem. Sudden descents by the turbulent Welsh tribesmen had terrorized the border for years, and Norman control over the region would never be secure as long as this threat remained unchecked. Nor were hands wanting for the task of subduing the Welsh. For some of the invaders, at least, Wales represented not so much a threat as an opportunity. Beyond the border lay

---

[1] A number of books and articles pertaining to the geography and economy of Wales have been included in the Bibliography. For an excellent introduction to these subjects, see E. G. Bowen (ed.), *Wales: A Physical, Historical and Regional Geography.*

[2] Also included in the Bibliography are some selected books and articles covering the earlier periods of Welsh history. The best general account of the history of Wales up to 1272 is provided by J. E. Lloyd, *A History of Wales from the Earliest Times to the Edwardian Conquest.*

[3] This is not to say that Wales' defeat in this struggle was complete. The Welsh people have managed to retain a high degree of cultural integrity and national consciousness, even in a world dominated by their English neighbors.

WALES 1070–1171 A.D.

ANGLESEY
G
W
Y
N
E
D
D
Snowdonia
●Rhuddlan
●Chester
CHESHIRE

CARDIGAN
SEA

—53°

Dee R.
●Oswestry

Severn ●Shrewsbury
●Cause SHROPSHIRE
Montgomery
ARWYSTLI
●Aberystwyth
P
O
W
Y
S
Offa's Dyke
●Clun
●Wigmore River

CEREDIGION
BUELLT
●Radnor
WORCESTERSHIRE
●Worcester
HEREFORDSHIRE

Cemais Head
●Cardigan
Builth●
BRECKNOCKSHIRE
(BRYCHEINIOG)
●Clifford
Wye ●Hereford

Cilgerran●
Teifi River
D
E
H
E
U
B
A
R
T
H
Llandovery●
River
Usk ●Brecon
Monnow R.
●Ewyas
Harold

—52°
St David's●
Carmarthen● Towy
YSTRAD TYWY
River
Abergavenny●
Monmouth
●Gloucester
GWENT
Wye R.

●Pembroke
●Kidwelly
GWYNLLWG
Caerleon●
●Strigoil
GLOUCESTERSHIRE

Neath●
GOWER
Swansea●
GLAMORGAN
(MORGANNWG)
Glyn Rhondda●
Llandaff●
Cardiff●

▨ Elevation over 600 feet

BRISTOL CHANNEL

0 5 10   20
Scale in Miles

5°   4°   3°

VMB

lands to be had for the taking; lands that were, to all intents and purposes, free and empty. Impelled by twin considerations of political expediency and personal gain, the Norman conquest of Wales began.

The first century of their endeavor was to prove crucial to the invaders of South Wales. During these years the conquerors were forced to adapt to the new circumstances in which they found themselves. The nature of the land, the personality of their adversaries, and even the act of conquest itself all combined to transform the character of the invaders. As the century came to a close, a distinctive Cambro-Norman society had emerged in South Wales. Neither purely Welsh nor wholly Norman, it was a society peculiarly suited to the endemic warfare and incessant land-hunger which characterized the Welsh frontier.

This remarkable process took place in a setting quite different from that which confronts the modern visitor to Wales.[4] The lowlands, which are today the richest and most fertile portion of the peninsula, were untilled and undrained nine hundred years ago. Dense forests and deep swamps covered what are today well-tilled fields. Great oaks dominated the forest growth, except in dales where primroses and bluebells brought a touch of color. The undergrowth was composed for the most part of gorse and bramble, presenting an almost impenetrable obstacle to communication and travel. Much of the region was the habitat of creatures which have long since disappeared from Wales. Beavers, bears, wolves, wildcats, boars, and wild oxen infested the forests, adding to the difficulties the early inhabitants must have faced.[5]

A somewhat less formidable landscape lay along the upper slopes of the interior, where forest growth thinned out under the influence of the increased elevation. Although relatively pleasant, these areas were rather small. The trees came to an end at about a thousand-foot elevation, and above this point lay the moorlands. Here was an environment far different from the forests of the lowlands. The moors and ridges were subjected to the full force of the moisture-laden

---

[4] It must always be remembered in such discussions, that human activity often works great changes, for good or evil, on the land and its capacity to produce. For a well-written essay which illustrates this factor, see Christopher Trent, *The Changing Face of England: The Story of the Landscape through the Ages.*
[5] See Colin Matheson, *Changes in the Fauna of Wales within Historic Times.*

westerly winds. The soil was poor and thin, and the characteristic vegetation of the region was low bracken, gorse, bilberry, and moss. Then, as now, the climate was cool and extremely damp, and the ground was soggy underfoot. Bogs were common, and in the valleys and hollows of the highlands, peat beds were being laid down.

Thus early Wales was composed of two quite distinct environments, and the early inhabitants of the peninsula were forced to choose between them. Both contained great obstacles to settlement. The fertile lowlands were covered by dense forests, tenanted by wild beasts, and blocked by impenetrable undergrowth. The uplands, on the other hand, were incapable of supporting agriculture. In a process beginning in the Mesolithic era, if not earlier, the Welsh chose the highlands.[6] By this choice they determined the direction in which their culture was to travel, and also set a limit on the degree of development they could hope to achieve.[7] They settled the moor and ridges, and only very slowly moved down into the valley floors. They left the potentially rich and fertile lowlands to be the prize of the more complex and dynamic societies which were developing in the lowland zone of Britain and in the plains of northern Europe.

Restricting themselves to their highland environment, the Welsh developed a pastoral society, depending upon the cattle for which the region was suited, rather than upon the agriculture for which it was not. Their basic diet was not bread, but meat, milk, and cheese; and their drink was distilled from the honey their bees drew from the gorse and anemones of the moors. Relying upon their cattle, they

[6] See H. J. Fleure and W. E. Whitehouse, "Early Distribution and Valley-Ward Movement of Population in South Britain," *Archaeologia Cambrensis*, Series VI, Vol. XVI (1916), pp. 101–140; H. J. Fleure and T. C. James, "Geographical Distribution of Anthropological Types Found in Wales," *The Journal of the Royal Anthropological Institute*, XLVI (1916): 35–153; C. F. Fox, *The Personality of Britain: Its Influence on Inhabitants and Invader in Preehistoric Times*, especially page 94.

[7] It seems difficult to dispute the point that the Welsh uplands are incapable of supporting any highly developed material culture. For a general discussion of the role of physical environment in limiting social achievement, see B. J. Meggers, "Environmental Limitation on the Development of Culture," *The American Anthropologist*, LVI (1954), 801–824. This provocative essay suggests some general factors which may well have played a role in determining the overall pattern of the Norman conquest of Wales, especially the Norman failure to take and hold the highlands. See also R. I. Hirshberg and J. F. Hirshberg, "Meggers' Law of the Environmental Limitation of Culture," *The American Anthropologist*, LIX (1957), 890–892.

were self-sufficient in matters of food and clothing, while their simple way of life awakened little need or desire for the importation of foreign manufactured goods.

These free tribesmen were seminomadic herdsmen, reckoning their wealth in cattle, and practicing only the simplest agriculture. Their dwellings were crude and simple, since they served only a temporary purpose. Archaeological excavations have revealed much about the daily life of these people. One series in particular, that on Gelligaer Common, well illustrates the basic patterns of their activities.[8]

There were three houses in this little settlement on the steep slope of the common. These were of the rather common type known as platform construction. The slope had been prepared for the structures by a combination of excavation and terracing which had formed a building platform cut partially into the hill. Upon this platform had been raised a rude wall of unmortared stone, perhaps supplemented with turf or wattle. Roof construction was of the ridgepole type, with interior uprights, and most probably a thatch covering. Two doors pierced the long walls of the rectangular buildings, and there were no windows. The hearth consisted of a flat stone placed near one end of the building, behind which rubbish had been allowed to accumulate. An open fire was the only source of heat for this extensive structure,[9] and smoke was apparently left to escape through the roof. An internal drainage gutter lay along the walls of the upper end of the house, indicating that the buildings were quite damp, in addition to being cold and dark.

The major occupation of the two or three families living here was most probably grazing. Goats, sheep, and cattle could have been maintained, and the woods of the valley below would have provided

----

[8] The results of the excavations were summarized or noted in the following articles: Aileen Fox, "Dinas Noddfa, Gelligaer Common, Excavations in 1936," *Archaeologia Cambrensis,* Series VII, Vol. XCII (1937), pp. 247–268; Aileen Fox, "Early Welsh Homesteads on Gelligaer Common, Glamorgan, Excavations in 1938," *Archaeologia Cambrensis,* Series VII, Vol. XCIV (1939), pp. 163–199; Aileen Fox, "Excavations on Gelligaer Common," *The Bulletin of the Board of Celtic Studies,* IX (1937–1939), 297–299; C. F. Fox, "Dinas Noddfa, Gelligaer Common, Glamorgan," *The Bulletin of the Board of Celtic Studies,* IX (1937–1939), 295–297. The site excavated in 1938, from which most of the information in the text is drawn, dates from considerably later than the period under discussion. All evidence indicates, however, that modes and standards of living remained relatively unchanged for long periods of time in the Welsh highlands.

[9] The largest building at the site under discussion measured sixty feet by eighteen.

excellent pannage for swine.[10] Near the building platforms were found a series of low, wide banks, ranging in length from fifty to two hundred feet. Excavation showed that these banks were composed of loose stones, and that the soil in their vicinity was unusually deep for the area. The conclusion is obvious that these patches represented arable land which had been laboriously created by the removal of the stones which formed the banks. Agriculture must have been important, judging from the labor invested in it, but it could not have been very intensive, even in the small patches. Finally, numerous nodules of low quality iron were found in and about the homestead sites. The inhabitants must have smelted their own iron, but the poor quality of the nodules, and the numerous stone tools found in the same vicinity, indicate that the process was both crude and expensive.

These homesteads on Gelligaer Common were not representative of all Welsh settlements. Permanent peasant communities did exist in some areas where a more intensive agriculture was practicable, but their population was generally restricted to the nonfree tribesmen, or *taeogs*. In time such settlements became a more important aspect of Welsh society, and many free tribesmen settled down to a sedentary existence. During the eleventh and twelfth centuries, however, the typical free Welshman was a seminomadic herdsman, and only the lower classes, who had little choice, worked the soil.[11] Thus the settlement perched on the slope of Gelligaer Common characterizes the life of the mass of early Welsh society—self-sufficient, but lonely, rude, and uncomfortable.

Generally speaking, Welsh society was seminomadic, lacked a firm agricultural base, but was economically self-sufficient. It can easily be seen that these three factors acted against the necessity for, and the possibility of, the growth of any concentrations of population like the farming villages and trading towns which were developing in England. The Welsh lived in scattered pastoral townships, such as that on Gelligaer Common, or even in isolated family homesteads. The activities of life were almost completely restricted to the local level. Thus the factors which discouraged urbanization also acted to protect Welsh society from those forces which elsewhere in western

[10] A. Fox, "Early Welsh Homesteads," pp. 198–199. These woods have long since disappeared, but charcoal remains indicate that the Gelligaer inhabitants had a large supply of oak and hazel nearby. This can only have been in the valley.

[11] E. G. Bowen, *The Settlements of the Celtic Saints in Wales*, p. 144.

Europe were antiquating tribal structures as adequate bases for social organization. The ancient tribal structure of society lived on in isolated Wales, and was fundamental to every aspect of Welsh life.[12]

Property rights, inheritance, citizenship, and marriage were regulated by the kindred, and law was enforced primarily by the family feud. Most other governmental functions were unnecessary in view of the decentralized and primitive character of the society. Despite this fact, much of Welsh life centered around the eighty political bodies into which the country was divided. The fundamental unit in this organization was the *tref*, the residence of a single kindred. Numbers of such *trefs* were grouped into the territorial unit known as the *cantref* (one hundred *trefs*), or, at a later date, the commote (neighborhood).[13]

The commote was much more than simply a territorial unit. It was, to all intents and purposes, the highest element in the Welsh political structure. Regional groupings of commotes did exist, and Wales was traditionally divided into four "kingdoms." In each of these a single leader usually held some ascendancy, but his power was only a matter of force, prestige, or tradition. Real political power lay in the commote, and was there concentrated in the hands of the *tywysog*.[14]

---

[12] Studies dealing with early Welsh political and social institutions are numerous and sometimes confusing. The basis for most treatments is the *Cyvreithiau Hywel Dda*, or "Laws of Hywel the Good." This early codification of Welsh law may be found in *Ancient Laws and Institutes of Wales . . .*, ed. A. Owen. Some important secondary works drawing primarily on this source are H. Lewis, *The Ancient Laws of Wales . . .*, and T. P. Ellis, *Welsh Tribal Law and Custom in the Middle Ages*. Also see William Rees, *South Wales and the March, 1284–1415: A Social and Agrarian Study*. Rees evaluates the "Laws of Hywel the Good," and finds that the picture of Welsh society they reflect is in all probability seriously distorted. The student of early Welsh society must also beware of works which rely on the so-called "Drioedd Dyvnwal Moelmud." These works were long accepted by many as genuine, and were included by Aneurin Owen in his definitive collection. It has been shown that these triads are spurious, and were written by a Welsh antiquarian writing under the name of Iolo Morganwg. See G. J. Williams, *Iolo Morgannwg, a Chywyddau'r Ychwanegiad*, and Lloyd, *A History of Wales*, I, 318–319.

[13] See Lloyd, *A History of Wales*, I, 229–282. Lloyd here attempts to enumerate the various *cantrefs* of Wales, describe them, and define their boundaries. Also see the excellent map included in the second volume of the same work.

[14] For an excellent summary of the position and powers of the *tywysog*, see A. J. Otway-Ruthven, "The Constitutional Position of the Great Lordships of South Wales," *The Transactions of the Royal Historical Society*, Series V, Vol. VIII (1958), pp. 1–20.

This word is traditionally translated "prince," but the translation tends to obscure rather than reveal the true nature of the institution. Welsh law itself defined the *tywysog* as simply the possessor of one or more commotes.

In each of the commotes he possessed, the *tywysog* erected at some central location his *llys*, or court. This court was housed in a great timber hall built to shelter and protect the *tywysog*, his retainers, and bard, and the *teulu*, or armed band, which was necessary to his dignity and safety. Quite frequently the hall and the area around it were fortified against sudden attack. Huddled close to the hall, and often within the fortified area, were the numerous huts and houses of the *tywysog's* servants and administrative officials, the serfs who tilled the nearby fields, and the few artisans required by the economic life of the commote. Here also were located the warehouses in which was stored the tribute which custom required of every *tref*. The *llys* acted as the capital of the commote, and was the nearest thing to an urban center most Welshmen ever saw.

It was here the *tywysog* held his judicial court, and decided all cases, civil and criminal, high and low, which might be referred to him. There was no appeal from this court. In this, as in all other governmental functions, the *tywysog* was the final source of authority within the commote. Within his own territory the *tywysog* exercised all of those powers which are customarily associated with kingship. He might fortify when and where he pleased; his legal competence was all-inclusive; he might conduct war against anyone toward whom he conceived an enmity; and all fee, dues, fines, and perquisites were his to dispense. As long as the *tywysog* remained in possession of his commote, he was truly a king within its precincts and was accorded a large measure of respect outside it.

These extensive powers, however, were entirely dependent upon his continued possession of his commote. Envious brothers, hostile *tywysogion*, and unscrupulous adventurers represented a constant source of danger to the authority and security of the lord of a commote. Any of these enemies could kill or overpower him and thus gain possession of the commote. To all intents and purposes, the usurper then became the rightful *tywysog*, and few questions of legitimacy were ever raised. From the frequency with which such forcible seizures are recorded in Welsh chronicles, one may conclude that plotting and sedition of this sort were endemic to Welsh society. This situation contributed much to the disunity and the shifting

alliances of expediency which formed the characteristic pattern of
Welsh political history.

This instability helped to develop a society in which such petty
warfare became a way of life rather than simply a necessity or a duty.
The free Welsh tribesman was a warrior born and bred. Giraldus
Cambrensis remarked of the Welsh that "The husbandman rushes as
eagerly from the plow as the courtier from his court" at the call of
battle.[15] Since they did not engage in extensive agriculture, the Welsh
were able to devote themselves to year-round military activity if they
chose to do so. As a consequence of frequent opportunities and mass
participation, they became expert in sudden raids and masterly ambushes. Pitched battles and protracted campaigns, on the other hand,
were beyond their capabilities, and the intricacies of siege warfare
were foreign to their experience. Within the limits of their training,
however, and in the terrain in which they operated, there were no
better warriors.

In religion, as in politics and warfare, the Welsh favored decentralization and localism. The center of activity of the Church in Wales
lay in a type of monastic body known as the *clas*. The typical *clas*
consisted of a mixed group of clergy and laymen, living together
under the rule of an abbot, but observing no regular order of discipline. This lack of regulation allowed the development of a wide
range of local usages, and the *clas* was capable of excesses of both
piety and corruption. It is true that a series of episcopal sees existed
in Wales but even these had originally been monastic in character,
and only began to assume their regular episcopal functions under
Norman influence in the twelfth and thirteenth centuries. During
most of the medieval period, the concept of the *clas* dominated religious affairs in Wales. Instead of being the center of a duly organized and regularly functioning parish, the typical Welsh church was
a chapel closely connected with a nearby *clas*.

Wales lay far on the fringe of western Europe, and had been protected by her position and her poverty from the forces of change
which were afoot in the tenth and early eleventh centuries. As a
consequence, Welsh society in the late eleventh and twelfth centuries
was still dominated by institutions of an early and more primitive
era—kindred, *clas*, blood-feud, and the like. These archaic institutions

---

[15] Giraldus Cambrensis, *Opera*, eds. J. S. Brewer *et al.*, Part VI (*Itinerarium
Kambriae*), p. 72.

embodied and perpetuated the decentralization and disorder which characterized Welsh society.

Welsh society was not static, however, and new social and political institutions were evolving. Especially important were the tentative movements toward a political organization which would transcend the localism of the commote. This continuing development can best be seen in the growth of the traditional kingdoms of Gwynedd, Powys, Deheubarth, and Gwent. The name "kingdom" is, in this case, something of a misnomer, for these bodies bore little resemblance to the more fully developed kingdoms of the era. They had few clearly defined governmental institutions and their responsibilities and functions were sharply limited. They were little more than conglomerations of commotes recognizing a traditional affinity. The ties between the commotes were weak and fluid, and the boundaries of the kingdoms were, as a consequence, vague and fluctuating.

Within each kingdom some individual was usually recognized as king, but the title brought with it no grant of authority or jurisdiction. It carried prestige, and little more. The base of the Welsh king's power consisted of his authority as *tywysog* within the commotes he possessed. What additional power he exercised depended primarily upon the support he could obtain from the other *tywysogion* of his kingdom. He had few legal guarantees of such support, and had to secure it as best he could. Military strength, ruthlessness, or personal magnetism could gain him such support, but only continued vigilance and success could maintain his control over his following. While some Welsh kings were able to command and retain much support, and to create at least the semblance of a powerful state, others were kings in name only and were actually weaker than many of the *tywysogion* of their kingdom. The strength of these kingdoms depended ultimately upon the forcefulness and continued good fortune of their kings. A single misfortune could destroy the prestige of the monarch, and the *tywysogion* would withdraw their support of him. The kingdom would then dissolve once again into an ineffectual collection of independent states.

Wales' greatest weakness lay in the fact that there were no stable and effective political institutions beyond the level of the commote. Under this decentralized political system, the Welsh wasted their strength in petty wars, desultory cattle raids, and fruitless intrigue. This weakness made little difference as long as they faced no greater threats than Irish pirates or an occasional band of Scandinavian raid-

ers. The high plateau—the heartland of Welsh society—remained
secure from such attacks, and the Welsh could afford to continue to
defer the development of any real unity. The emergence of a strong
and united Anglo-Saxon state made it quite a different matter; the
question of unity became crucial to the continued independence of
Wales. A growing Anglo-Saxon pressure on the eastern border of
the peninsula was only a forerunner of the crisis the Welsh would
eventually face.

Anglo-Saxon expansion first reached the borders of Wales proper
sometime about the middle of the seventh century.[16] At any rate, the
border regions of Shropshire and Herefordshire were in Mercian
hands by this time. The momentum of Mercian expansion to the west
apparently came to an end with these conquests. Little information
about the period has survived, but the failure of the Mercians to advance further indicates that Welsh resistance stiffened. The Mercians
halted short of the Cambrian Mountains, and contented themselves
with the exploitation of those lands lying in the shadow of the heights.
The barren uplands of Wales were apparently not worth the price the
Mercians would have to pay for them.

This pause created a great problem for the kings of Mercia. Hitherto the Anglo-Saxons had been on the offensive, and the question of
defense had not arisen. They had now reached the natural limit of
their expansion, and possessed a large indefensible border stretching
from the Severn to the Dee. What had been a question of westward
expansion became a problem of frontier defense. This problem was
finally faced by the Mercian king, Offa (757–796). His answer was
to construct a boundary dyke stretching completely across the neck
of the Welsh peninsula. This work generally marked the western
limits of Anglo-Saxon settlement, although numerous later exceptions
might be noted.[17] It seems clear that Offa's Dyke was intended to
define and stabilize Mercia's western border.

This new Mercian frontier policy probably made little actual difference in Saxon-Welsh relations. The Mercians had previously fought
to conquer and to settle; now they fought to terrorize and overawe.
At least this appears to have been Mercian policy in the period
following Offa's death. Raids deep into Welsh territory can be noted
for the years 796, 816, 818, and 822. It was not until the decline of

[16] Lloyd, A History of Wales, I, 195–196.
[17] See C. F. Fox, Offa's Dyke: A Field Survey of the Western Frontier Works
of Mercia in the Seventh and Eighth Centuries A.D.

Mercia's power, and the increase of Viking attacks on England, that this fierce Saxon pressure on Wales' eastern border was relaxed.[18]

By this time the traditional political structure of Wales had emerged. The four kingdoms were gaining prominence, perhaps partially as a result of the pressure and example of the Anglo-Saxons. Even with this somewhat more sophisticated organization, however, the Welsh were still far weaker than their eastern neighbors. Only on occasions when two or more of these kingdoms were united were the Welsh capable of defending themselves adequately. Such occasions were rare, and the hegemonies thus established rarely outlived their founders. Each time such an event occurred, however, the power of the Welsh was increased immeasurably, and the security of the English border was severely threatened.

The first time this happened was in the year 942, when Hywel Dda, king of Deheubarth, succeeded in uniting almost all of Wales under his control. On this occasion, however, English security was not threatened. Hywel maintained close and friendly relations with the English court, and spent his time and energies in attempting to lay the foundations of a stable kingdom. His aims were in advance of his time, and the attempt failed. With his death in 950, the kingdom quickly disintegrated into its constituent parts. Over a hundred years elapsed before the second such hegemony was established; one which was to prove far more dangerous to the security of the English frontier. Its founder was Gruffydd ap Llewelyn, a man who lacked the English affinities which, in Hywel's time, had prevented an open clash. Gruffydd seized the throne of Gwynedd in 1039, and united it to that of Powys. He immediately led the united forces of his two kingdoms against an unsuspecting Mercian army encamped on the Severn. He crushed his enemy completely, and served effective notice that the Welsh were now masters of the border.

Rather than following up the advantage he had gained on the frontier, Gruffydd immediately turned his attention to the conquest of Deheubarth. He was unable to force a decisive encounter with Hywel ab Edwin, king of Deheubarth, until 1041. When the encounter did occur, Hywel was badly defeated, and seems to have lost most of his power within the kingdom. He did manage to retain control of his commotes of Dyfed and Ystrad Tywy, however, and was able to continue to frustrate Gruffydd's plan for the conquest of

[18] Lloyd, *A History of Wales*, I, 201–202.

Deheubarth. It was not until 1044 that the two met in battle once again. On this occasion, Hywel was defeated and killed. Gruffydd was now able to unite the crown of Deheubarth with that of Gwynedd and Powys.

Despite this victory, localism remained strong in Deheubarth, especially in Dyfed and Ystrad Tywy. A leader soon arose to use this localism in an attempt to displace Gruffydd. This man was Gruffydd ap Rhydderch, no less forceful a man than Gruffydd ap Llewelyn himself. The movement soon became dangerous, and the king was forced to conclude an alliance with the English border earl, Swegen Godwinson. The alliance was obviously directed against the southern independence movement, for, in 1046, an allied Welsh and English army invaded Deheubarth, and devastated the countryside. This course of action played into the hands of Gruffydd ap Rhydderch by solidifying public opinion against the northern king. In 1047, Gruffydd ap Llewelyn and his *teulu* were ambushed by the men of Ystrad Tywy, and suffered a crushing defeat. He escaped with his life, but this defeat lost him whatever support and prestige he might have enjoyed in southwest Wales. He retired north, and Deheubarth resumed its independent course of action.

In his place, Gruffydd ap Rhydderch emerged as the paramount leader of the region, and was able to amass a considerable amount of power and support. He proved to be an active ruler, and no better a neighbor to the English than his predecessor had been. In 1049 he struck a bargain with a force of Danish pirates, and led them, together with his native supporters, into Herefordshire. Here he plundered the manor of Tidenham, and slaughtered an English force which the bishop of Worcestershire led against him.[19] He returned to Wales unscathed, and laden with booty. This was but the first of a series of raids into Herefordshire and Gloucestershire—raids which no doubt discomfited their English inhabitants greatly.

It may have been due to this discomfiture and to the exposed position of Herefordshire that a colony of Norman warriors was established in the region. It may, on the other hand, simply have been the result of English royal politics. Norman influences had been prominent in Edward's court for some time, and a number of Norman immigrants had risen to high position with the benefit of royal in-

---

[19] *The Anglo-Saxon Chronicle, According to the Several Original Authorities,* ed, and trans. Benjamin Thorpe, Part I, p. 302.

fluence. A group of these immigrants had established themselves in Herefordshire. Here they distinguished themselves, and gained the hatred of the local populace by erecting the new type of fortress which had been perfected in Normandy.[20]

Norman influence was increased in the area in the year 1051. In this year King Edward found an opportunity to break, at least for a time, the power of the house of Godwine. Earl Godwine and his adherents were banished from England. This sentence included Swegen Godwinson, earl of a border region which took in both Herefordshire and Gloucestershire. His successor proved to be a Norman, Ralph, the son of the count of the Vexin and of Goda, King Edward's sister. Herefordshire had become, to all intents and purposes, a Norman colony.[21]

Earl Ralph apparently continued the Herefordshire Normans' preoccupation with defense. It is recorded that he made an effort to convert his English levies into a cavalry force by ordering them to join combat on horseback, rather than afoot as was their custom. This was later to prove a worthless innovation. The Normans' concern with Herefordshire's defensive strength was well founded, however. A new threat had been added to that posed by Gruffydd ap Rhydderch. Released from his alliance with Earl Swegen, Gruffydd ap Llewelyn was now free to resume his ravages on the border. He was quick to use this new freedom, and advanced into Herefordshire to test Ralph's new forces. The battle, fought in 1052, found the Normans unprepared to meet the impetuous charges of the Welsh. The Normans and English were defeated. Once again, however, Gruffydd ap Llewelyn failed to exploit a military victory. He was content to retire with his spoils and heightened prestige, and to turn his attention to Welsh affairs.

In the following year a number of events were to conspire to place the English borderlands in even greater danger. Gruffydd ap Llewelyn was at last able to eliminate Gruffydd ap Rhydderch, and to reunite Deheubarth to his realms. He soon received a powerful ally from an unexpected source. An exiled English noble, Aelfgar,

[20] For the location and identity of these castles, see J. H. Round, *Feudal England: Historical Studies on the XIth and XIIth Centuries*, pp. 317–331. For an intriguing essay on the development of the Norman castle, see Brian Hope-Taylor, "The Norman Motte at Abinger, Surrey, and its Wooden Castle," *Recent Archaeological Excavations in Britain*, ed. R. L. S. Bruce-Mitford, pp. 223–249.

[21] Florence of Worcester, *Chronicon ex Chronicis . . .*, ed. Benjamin Thorpe, s.a. 1051, I, 205.

had gathered a fleet and army from the Dansk towns of Ireland, and had returned to England to recoup his fortunes. He was quick to strike an alliance with the Welsh chieftain, and the new allies immediately marched on Herefordshire.

This allied Welsh, Danish, and Irish force met the Norman and English defenders of Herefordshire a few miles from the city of Hereford itself. The battle was quickly decided. The chronicles intimate that the Normans, with Ralph at their head, took flight even before battle was joined. In any event, the English levies, unaccustomed to the mounted combat to which Ralph had ordered them, broke before the Welsh attack. The battle became a rout, and Aelfgar and Gruffydd were able to enter Hereford, which they burned and plundered.

The situation on the border had become extremely serious, and Harold Godwinson, a rising figure on the English scene, determined to meet the threat which Gruffydd and Aelfgar had posed. He invaded Wales, but was unable to make headway in a difficult terrain and in the face of powerful opposition. In the interests of peace, he was forced to come to terms with his enemies. Under the terms of this treaty, Aelfgar was reinstated as earl of East Anglia, and Gruffydd appears to have been allowed to keep his border conquests.[22] Gruffydd was content under the circumstances. He had won great wealth, and even greater prestige, and was happy for the opportunity to use both in further consolidation of his Welsh realms.[23] His position became even better in 1057, when Aelfgar became earl of Mercia. As friends, allies, and neighbors, Aelfgar and Gruffydd were powerful enough to meet all threats to their position.

This situation changed drastically in the year 1062. The death of Aelfgar deprived Gruffydd of a great source of strength, and Harold decided to use this occasion to destroy him completely. In the Christmas season, he launched a lightning attack upon Gruffydd's capital of Rhuddlan, and the Welsh leader barely escaped with his life. Harold then put into operation a large-scale plan of attack. While Earl Tostig drove along the northern coast of Wales, Harold ferried a special force of light–armed troops into the heart of Gwynedd itself. Gruffydd was unable to resist the superiority of his enemies and

[22] This is the view of Lloyd, *A History of Wales,* II, 365.
[23] It may well be that it was during this period he added Morgannwg to his conquests. See Lloyd, *A History of Wales,* II, 367.

fled into the heights of Snowdonia. His power and prestige were swiftly declining.

He was allowed no time to recuperate. Harold's light-armed troops followed him into the mountains, harrying him and his supporters. Continued reverses and a mounting English pressure began to tell, and Gruffydd's followers began falling away from him. The end came on the fifth of August, 1063, when his own men turned on him, killed him, and sent his head to Harold as a pledge of their submission. With this victory Harold's immediate aims were achieved. Gruffydd's hegemony disintegrated, and Wales fell back into the disunity which for her spelled impotence. Harold concluded favorable treaties with the lesser figures who succeeded Gruffydd, and a measure of peace returned to the Welsh frontier. With this threat to the security of England ended, Harold was able to turn to the pursuit of his personal designs for power.

These centuries of border warfare provide material for some important generalizations. It is clear that English expansion had halted short of a defensible border. This long frontier could not be adequately defended unless the English were willing to establish strong settlements on the highland plateau which commanded the border shires. Their continuing acceptance of Offa's Dyke as their western boundary makes it clear that the English were unwilling or unable to fight to take and to hold land which had little value apart from strategic considerations. This being the case, England's western border would continue to be vulnerable to Welsh attack.

Little could be done to eliminate the threat of such raids. The Welsh had no effective central government, and hence the English could establish no stable relations with them, short of making a treaty with every free Welsh tribesman. Even if the latter were possible a certain amount of perfidy was built into the Welsh political system. Neither diplomacy nor terrorism could pacify the decentralized and intensely localistic Welsh for any length of time. Peace along the border could not be secured unless a Welsh leader emerged who was strong enough to enforce it among the turbulent tribesmen.

On those occasions when such a leader emerged, however, the peace of the Welsh frontier was threatened in a way far more serious than desultory raids. Firmly united and properly directed, the Welsh were formidable enemies, and were capable of threatening the security of the entire West of England. Thus it was advantageous for the English to maintain the Welsh in a state of disunity. This meant, on the other hand, that Welsh raids would continue to disturb the peace of the border shires. The only effective defense lay in the creation of a strong local force under capable direction and with considerable freedom of action.

This was a dangerous expedient. The alliance of Aelfgar and Gruffydd had shown that a powerful frontier lord and a Welsh king made an extremely formidable combination. Any frontier force strong enough to oppose Welsh attack effectively, could, in alliance with its opponents, threaten the security of the entire realm. The reliability of marcher troops is always doubtful, and so this danger was very real.

This was, in essence, the dilemma of the Welsh frontier. The English had found no solution after having wrestled with the problem for almost three hundred years. They were no closer to an effective and lasting frontier policy in 1066 than in 750. It was to remain a dilemma for the Norman invaders, and much of the history of the Welsh frontier turns upon their various attempts to solve this problem.

ii. The Opening of the Norman Conquest

IN A GENERAL SENSE the Norman Conquest of England represented the final triumph of a continental Latin tradition over the northern Teutonic cultures which had hitherto dominated the island. As such, the Conquest fundamentally altered England's orientation by drawing it firmly into the continental orbit. The English history with which we are most familiar was dominated by factors which arose as a direct result of this new political and social alignment. For students of that history William's victory seems to throw a new light on the English scene. A new orientation and a new and purposive central authority inaugurated an era of change and development. At the same time administrators and scholars following in William's train recorded and expounded upon this development. Small wonder then that later historians have experienced "an instinctive feeling that in England our consecutive political history does, in a sense, begin with the Norman Conquest."[1]

Since English historians have traditionally regarded the Conquest as the watershed of their national development, they have lavished much energy and erudition in investigating and commenting upon the event. The details of the Conquest have been treated so extensively elsewhere that it is unnecessary to elaborate upon them here. The same cannot be said for its more general aspects. The same factors of political, genealogical, and constitutional motivation which prompted the historians to their task inevitably colored their results.

[1] J. H. Round, *Feudal England: Historical Studies on the XIth and XIIth Centuries*, p. 317.

English treatments of their Conquest suffer from much the same partisanship and political coloration as does American historiography of the establishment of the Constitution, and for much the same reason.[2] Another factor also enters the situation. Until quite recently historians have neglected to investigate fully the continental roots of the conquerors. As a consequence, our understanding of the nature of pre-Conquest Norman society is at present undergoing a basic revision.[3] It is well, in this maze of scholarship, to keep in mind a few general points which help to explain something of the development of England immediately after the Conquest.

In the first place, to view the Conquest in terms of a national struggle, as some historians have done,[4] places a great strain on the available data. It is difficult to see any national solidarity in the motley band of Norman, Breton, French, and Angevin adventurers who accompanied William. Little more can be discerned on the English side. Harold seems to have been a usurper himself and was unable to gain the support of the great nobles of the land, such as the earls Morcar and Edwin.[5] As early as 1068 the English people were willing to aid their conquerors in pacifying the rebellious city of Exeter.[6] While the English were to prove a source of strength to William, the early years of the Conquest were to see numerous rebellions among his Norman supporters. The solidarity of the conquering group was apparent only when an identity of interest existed between William and his followers. Rather than being an account of a national struggle, the Conquest of England appears to be the story of a band of adven-

[2] See D. C. Douglas, *The Norman Conquest and British Historians: Being the Thirteenth Lecture on the David Murray Foundation in the University of Glasgow, delivered on February 20, 1946.*

[3] The traditional view of Norman society was developed by C. H. Haskins in a number of works, including *Norman Institutions; The Normans in European History;* "Knight-Service in Normandy in the Eleventh Century," *The English Historical Review,* XXII (1907), 636–649; "Normandy under William the Conqueror," *The American Historical Review,* XIV (1909), 453–476; "The Norman 'Consuetudines et Iusticie' of William the Conqueror," *The English Historical Review,* XXIII (1908), 502–508. Some of the recent publications in this field are *Receuil des Actes des Ducs de Normandie, 911–1066,* ed. Marie Faroux; D. C. Douglas, *The Rise of Normandy;* C. W. Hollister, "The Norman Conquest and the Genesis of English Feudalism," *The American Historical Review,* LXVI (1961), 641–663.

[4] See E. A. Freeman, *The History of the Norman Conquest of England: Its Causes and Results.*

[5] H. W. C. Davis, *England under the Normans and Angevins, 1066–1272,* pp. 5 ff.

[6] See Round, *Feudal England,* pp. 431–455.

turers, predominantly Norman, who took the crown of a disunited land from the hands of a usurper. Neither of the opponents enjoyed any extensive popular support, and national feeling only became apparent at a much later date.

A second point is concerned with the degree to which the Conqueror pursued a conscious and consistent policy in establishing a Norman state in England. We mentioned earlier that British historians regard the Norman Conquest as marking the beginning of the political development of modern England. From this belief it follows that every act of the Conqueror constituted a precedent for later development. It may well be that historians attempt to find in these precedents something of the consistency and planning which some legalists profess to see in the system of law which the precedents ultimately produced. The facts of the Conquest do not support such a view. William's policy appears to have been one of political empiricism, and not of theoretical principles. He acted in response to what must have been three overwhelming pressures: the need to maintain control over a numerically superior and potentially hostile population;[7] the need to maintain solidarity amongst the heterogeneous band of adventurers who had helped him to conquer the country and upon whom he now had to rely to administer it; and, finally, the need to continue a firm control over the turbulent duchy of Normandy, still his major base of power. William succeeded in playing various groups against each other and, by so doing, gained all three goals. That he did so is a tribute to his political genius but does not attest to any conscious and consistent program on his part.

This is perhaps overstating the case, for a certain measure of consistency can be detected in the facts of the Conquest. In another context, the historian William Rees has said:

Invasion may be prompted by other motives than mere lust for conquest and, in spite of apparent exceptions, it may be established as a general rule, that economic expediency rather than political passion is the predominating and guiding principle in conquest, while the minimum of disturbance necessary to attain political subjection constitutes a rude working policy.[8]

---

[7] The military potential of the English is often underestimated. See R. Glover, "English Warfare in 1066," *The English Historical Review*, LXVII (1952), 1–18.

[8] William Rees, *South Wales and the March, 1284–1415: A Social and Agrarian Study*, p. 32.

The second part of this statement appears to describe William's policy of conquest accurately. This factor lies behind his usual tendency to try to return, at least in form, to the state of England in Edward's time. Where it was practical to do so, William simply assumed the position and continued the policy of the kings of England previous to Harold's accession. Where this was impractical, he acted as the situation seemed to warrant. The rebellion of Exeter was treated with benign majesty, while another rebellion in the following year caused the entire North of England to be punished with a ruthless savagery. The situations were different and so too were William's responses. The Conqueror was also left to his own devices where previous policy was lacking or had proven ineffective. Here too he proceeded realistically and empirically toward a solution.

Much more could be said about the Conquest, but a basic thesis is clear. William had no clear-cut and well-developed program of administration in mind when he began to establish the Conquest. Insofar as possible he attempted simply to take over the pre-Conquest structure and to exploit it for his own ends, always trying to satisfy the pressures acting upon him with a minimum of expenditure and loss of personal power. His major concern was with practicality rather than precedent, and with effectiveness rather than theory. This means that when one considers any particular aspect of the Conqueror's activities, it is well to begin with the specific personalities and situations involved before proceeding to the weightier matters of political policy and constitutional development.

In terms of the history of the Welsh frontier, the most important personalities were the three border earls whom William eventually established in the region. These were Hugh of Chester, Roger Montgomery and, of primary importance for the southern frontier, William Fitz-Osbern. Fitz-Osbern was one of the guiding forces directing the course of the Conquest of England, and it was he who set the pattern for the conquest and administration of the Welsh frontier. With his activities in the West of England the conquest of South Wales began.

Fitz-Osbern's youth had not been an easy one. His father was seneschal to Robert, duke of Normandy.[9] When Robert died in 1035,

---

[9] For an excellent account of the establishment and rise to power of Fitz-Osbern's family, see D. C. Douglas, "The Ancestors of William fitz Osbern," *The English Historical Review,* LIX (1944), 62–79. The account is more than genealogical; it is an investigation into early Norman history.

he left his seneschal as guardian of the infant duke, William the Bastard. The office was a dangerous one. Osbern protected the infant duke loyally until 1049 or 1050, when he was struck down in the course of an unsuccessful attempt made by William Montgomery on the life of the duke.[10] With the loss of their respective father and guardian, Fitz-Osbern and the duke fled together to the protection of friends and relatives. As the duke's power grew, Fitz-Osbern emerged as one of his most powerful and loyal supporters, and eventually assumed his father's old post of seneschal.[11] The two worked together to establish and extend the duke's authority, and Fitz-Osbern performed important functions both in court and along the Norman frontier.

In Wace's long epic on the Conquest of England, Fitz-Osbern is pictured as the driving force behind the expedition.[12] If Wace is correct, Fitz-Osbern was in the duke's company when word was received of Edward's death and Harold's seizure of the throne. He took this occasion to be the first to urge upon the duke the plan of an overseas expedition to take England from Harold.[13] His suggestion bore its first fruit when the duke summoned the greatest of his barons to a council on the subject. Fitz-Osbern was prominent in a company which included some of the greatest names of early Norman history.[14] Once the group had assembled at Lillebone, it became apparent that a considerable amount of opposition to the plan existed among the barons. Doubting the possibility of success, and reminding themselves that none of their obligations to the duke entailed overseas service, opponents of the expedition began to unite against the duke's plan. Fitz-Osbern took it upon himself to defend the duke's wishes. His oratory does not appear to have swayed the opposition, but it did impress the assembled barons to such a degree that they asked him to act as their emissary to the duke. According to Wace's account, he created great consternation among the barons by immediately exceeding the authority and ignoring the directives they had given him. Acting as a plenipotentiary rather than as an emissary,

[10] William of Jumièges, "Historiae Northmannorum libri octo," *Patrologia Latina*, ed. J. P. Migne, vol. CXLIX, cols. 847–848.

[11] Wace, *Maistre Wace's Roman de Rou et des Ducs de Normandie, nach den Handschriften*, ed. H. Andresen, ll. 4413–4414, p. 207.

[12] Many scholars emphasize that Wace's account is late, and its reliability is doubtful. See especially Round, *Feudal England*, pp. 399–418.

[13] Wace, ll. 5908 ff., pp. 265 ff.

[14] *Ibid.*, ll. 6003 ff., pp. 265 ff.

Fitz-Osbern assured the duke that the barons would give him full support in the venture, and that each of them would pledge double his normal obligation to the expedition.

The barons immediately objected to this high-handed procedure, and the council broke up amidst dissent and confusion. Fitz-Osbern had achieved his end, however, by preventing baronial opposition from crystallizing and uniting.[15] The barons of Normandy were henceforth able to abstain from the venture, but not to obstruct it. Fitz-Osbern was equally active in gathering resources for the coming invasion and, in the meeting which organized its final details, made one of the largest contributions to the force which was being made ready.[16] If Wace's view is accurate, William Fitz-Osbern not only was responsible for the original conception of the plan to invade England, but was the major cause of its successful organization in the face of a recalcitrant and hostile nobility.

The seneschal appears to have been as active on the battlefield as in council in supporting his lord's pursuit of the English crown. He held no personal command at Hastings but he and his contingent were detached to stiffen the possibly unreliable right wing which consisted primarily of French and mercenary troops under the command of Roger Montgomery.[17]

By 1067 the initial stages of the Conquest had ended in victory, and Duke William prepared to return to Normandy to take care of matters there. He left Odo of Bayeux and William Fitz-Osbern to administer his conquest as wardens of England. The chronicler Florence of Worcester notes that the new warden had already been created earl of Hereford.[18] From other sources we know that Fitz-Osbern's jurisdiction extended far beyond the borders of Herefordshire, and included the entire area of Norman control north of the Thames. His special charge was the great castle which had been

---

[15] *Ibid.*, ll. 6085 ff., pp. 271 ff.

[16] "In Calce hujus libelli in eadem scriptura adjicitur catalogus suppeditantium naves ad expeditionem Willelmi comitis in Angliam," *Scriptores Rerum Gestarum Willelmi Conquestoris*, ed. J. A. Giles, p. 21.

[17] Wace, ll. 7673–7678, pp. 333–334.

[18] Florence of Worcester, Chronicon ex Chronicis . . ., s.a. 1067, II, 1. Also see Orderic Vitalis, "Historiae Ecclesiasticae libri XIII in partes tres divisi," *Patrologia Latina*, ed. J. P. Migne, vol. CLXXXVIII, cols. 330–331. Orderic would seem to indicate that Fitz-Osbern did not receive his earldom until 1070 or 1071. Florence's statement is much more acceptable in view of the fact that Fitz-Osbern died quite early in 1071.

erected at Norwich in anticipation of Danish attack.[19] These wardens were to play an active role in establishing the Conquest in England. A large number of William's troops had been left behind, and special orders had been given to press the construction of fortresses from which these forces could dominate the land.[20] This program necessarily involved the expropriation of property, the impressment of labor, and the maintenance of free access to the various cities of the realm. In short, while the Conqueror had led the Conquest of England, he left to Odo and Fitz-Osbern the task of further subjugation of the land.

It was an exceedingly difficult duty. Perhaps they used overly harsh methods in fulfilling their orders, for the hitherto quiescent opposition soon became active and violent. One would expect the partisan *Anglo-Saxon Chronicle* to stigmatize the Normans' rule as oppressive, just as one would expect William of Poitiers to extoll the virtues of the wardens.[21] Ordericus Vitalis tends to corroborate the English view in a curious passage in his obituary for Fitz-Osbern. He characterizes his subject as "the first and greatest oppressor of the English."[22] The passage refers to the period of Fitz-Osbern's wardenship, and attributes the violent outbreaks to the effects of Fitz-Osbern's arrogance.

Whatever its cause, trouble broke out first in the western frontier, an area commanded by Fitz-Osbern. The English leader of this region, Edric, surnamed "the Wild" by his opponents, had submitted to the Conqueror before the latter's return to Normandy in 1067.[23] The submission was more in name than in deed, however, and Edric's refusal to allow Norman rule in his district quickly led to a series of clashes between his Mercian levies and the Herefordshire Normans. The Normans, led by Richard Fitz-Scrob, a pre-Conquest settler in the shire, repeatedly attacked the Anglo-Saxon rebel, but they could

---

[19] William of Poitiers states that Fitz-Osbern was given command of "Guenta." This has usually been taken as Winchester. For the actual location, see Davis, *England under the Normans and Angevins*, p. 13, n. 1.

[20] Orderic Vitalis, col. 306.

[21] *The Anglo-Saxon Chronicle, According to the Several Original Authorities*, ed. and trans. B. Thorpe, s.a. 1066, Part I, p. 339. Also William of Poitiers, "Gesta Willelmi Ducis Normannorum, et Regis Anglorum a Willelmo," in *Scriptores Rerum Gestarum Willelmi Conquestoris*, ed. J. A. Giles, pp. 156–157.

[22] Orderic Vitalis, col. 355.

[23] *Ibid.*, col. 306.

little afford the casualties he inflicted on their forces.[24] The situation took a turn for the worse in the summer of 1067 when Edric struck an alliance with the Welsh kings Bleddyn and Rhiwallon. The combined Anglo-Saxon and Welsh forces took the offensive, and devastated all of Herefordshire up to the river Lugg.[25] The castles, however, appear to have remained in Norman hands. Little is known about Norman operations against Edric in the two years following this massive raid. It seems clear, however, that they recovered sufficiently to resume their incursions into Edric's territory. It also seems quite probable that these expeditions were used to provide a screen for efforts to rear castles in Shropshire, Edric's home district. At any rate, in 1069 we find Edric and his Welsh allies besieging a Norman garrison which had established itself at Shrewsbury. In the face of these rising threats to Norman rule, Fitz-Osbern hurried to the frontier to raise the siege.[26] He was successful, and Edric was forced to withdraw, although not before burning the town. Edric's resistance was broken either at Shrewsbury or shortly after, for the summer of 1070 saw his final submission to King William.[27]

By the end of 1069, however, Fitz-Osbern had been transferred from England to Normandy to assist Queen Matilda in facing growing threats from Maine, Anjou, and Brittany.[28] New opportunities were soon opened to him in Flanders, where civil war had broken out over the question of succession. The dowager countess, Richildis, offered herself in marriage to the widowed Fitz-Osbern, and he had immediately pledged her his support in the struggle. With a small force, he joined a French column, under the leadership of Philip of France, and moved northward to aid the countess' party. In February of 1071, this Franco-Norman column was met by the insurgents and was signally defeated. William Fitz-Osbern was slain,[29] and his body interred at Cormeilles, one of the two monasteries he had en-

[24] Florence of Worcester, s.a. 1067, II, 1.
[25] *Ibid.*, s.a. 1067, II, 1–2.
[26] Orderic Vitalis, col. 318. Orderic's account seems to send both Brian and Fitz-Osbern to relieve both Shrewsbury and Exeter. It seems likely that the chronicler has confused the operations of two separate expeditions. See Freeman, *The Norman Conquest*, IV, 279, n. 2.
[27] Florence of Worcester, s.a. 1070, II, 7.
[28] Freeman, *The Norman Conquest*, IV, 531, n. 1. Freeman suggests that the transfer was ordered at the midwinter gemot.
[29] Orderic Vitalis, cols. 339–340; William of Malmesbury, *De gestis regum Anglorum, libri quinque; Historiae novellae, libri tres,* ed. W. Stubbs, Part II, pp. 314–315.

dowed on his Norman estates.[30] His Norman holdings were given to his eldest son, William, while Roger, the younger son, received most of his father's English holdings, including the earldom of Hereford.[31]

It can be seen that William Fitz-Osbern's influence upon the Welsh frontier was limited to the period between the beginning of his wardenship in March of 1067, and his death in February of 1071. Even during this four-year period, he was occupied with many things other than his earldom of Hereford. Despite the shortness of his rule and the fact that the majority of his energies were directed elsewhere, he made great strides toward pacifying and organizing the region. Although the details of his administration are hazy, enough can be discerned to indicate that Fitz-Osbern laid down the lines along which the further expansion of Norman power into Wales was to proceed.

One of the first steps he took was to increase the strength of the Norman forces resident in the area. He accomplished this by offering such liberal rewards to his followers that knights were soon flocking to his service. His following assumed the proportions of a private army—one large enough to cause some concern to the Conqueror himself.[32] Fitz-Osbern took additional steps to make Herefordshire an attractive residence for other, unattached soldiers. He did this by strictly limiting the amounts which such men could be fined for infringements of the law. This law in particular set Herefordshire apart from the rest of England. Here the natural license of fighting men was curbed by the threat of fines of only seven shillings. Transgressors in other shires faced fines of from twenty to twenty-five shillings.[33]

These methods seem to have succeeded in attracting enough battle-ready settlers to garrison the region adequately. Enough troops were available for Fitz-Osbern to carry out an extensive castle-building program. A series of fortresses were constructed at various points within the earldom itself and along its western border. Wigmore was built at the point where the river Teme descends from the Welsh

[30] Orderic Vitalis, cols. 339–340. His wife, Adeliza, was already buried at Lyre, the second of the monasteries. See "Ex Chronico Lyrensis Coenobii," *Receuil des Historiens de Gaules et de la France,* eds. M. Bouquet *et al,* XII (1877), 776.

[31] Orderic Vitalis, cols. 339–340.

[32] William of Malmesbury, Part II, pp. 314–315.

[33] *Ibid.,* Part II, pp. 314–315. It is surprising to note that this law remained in effect in Herefordshire as late as the time of William of Malmesbury.

highlands; Clifford arose where the Wye enters Herefordshire; the old fortifications of Ewyas Harold, located at the confluence of the Monnow and the Dore, were restored; Monmouth was built at the juncture of the Monnow and the Wye; and Strigoil was built where the old Roman road crossed the Wye and passed into the Welsh kingdom of Gwent.[34] Fitz-Osbern appears also to have strengthened the defenses of Hereford, and may have been responsible for the first Norman fortifications at Shrewsbury.[35]

Domesday Book provides evidence that small boroughs had quickly arisen around some of these fortresses. There are indications that these settlements were established as part of a consistent program directed by Fitz-Osbern. The first step in this program lay in the erection of the fortresses themselves. These provided a protection that encouraged settlers and at the same time insured a market for merchants and artisans.[36] Thus it seems clear that these towns were intended to be based on trade rather than agriculture. It is also apparent from the examples of Hereford and Shrewsbury that the new boroughs were French, rather than English, in character. Within their environment, the new towns were alien and artificial, and constituted a by-product of the Conquest.

The creation of such centers within a newly conquered area, or along an exposed frontier, was an established practice on the continent. To attract settlers into such new towns, it was customary for their lords to offer liberal terms in the new borough charters.[37] These were extremely important to the success of the ventures, and set the pattern of life the new towns were to follow. Fitz-Osbern chose to grant to the boroughs he established the privileges enjoyed by Breteuil, a frontier settlement in Normandy which had long been in his hands. These customs, which had been devised for a frontier settle-

---

[34] *Domesday Book, or The Great Survey of England by William the Conqueror* A.D. MLXXXVI, fol. 183b, Wigmore; fol. 183, Clifford; fol. 162, Strigoil; fol. 186, Ewyas Harold. This last was refortified by Fitz-Osbern, having been constructed by the pre-Conquest Herefordshire Norman colony. See Round, *Feudal England*, pp. 317–331. For Monmouth, see *The Liber Landavensis, Llyfr Teilo, or the Ancient Register of the Cathedral Church of Llandaff . . .*, ed. and trans. W. J. Rees, p. 266.

[35] Since these fortifications were first mentioned on the occasion of Edric's siege of them in 1069, and since Fitz-Osbern had been in command of this portion of the frontier for two years by this date, it seems not unlikely that Shrewsbury had been garrisoned at Fitz-Osbern's command.

[36] T. F. Tout, *Medieval Town Planning: A Lecture*, pp. 10–11.

[37] *Ibid.*, p. 9.

ment in Normandy, proved just as popular in promoting frontier settlements in England and Wales. The low amercement, moderate rent, and other liberal features of the laws of Breteuil were to become characteristics of the charters granted to the Welsh towns established by the later Norman invaders of Wales, and were carried to Ireland by the descendants of those same conquerors. It is no exaggeration to say that the laws of Breteuil established the pattern for the next century of urban life along the Welsh frontier.[38]

Under Fitz-Osbern's leadership, the Herefordshire Normans took the offensive against the Welsh. Followed by Walter of Lacy and his other troops, he invaded Brycheiniog and met his opponents in at least one decisive encounter. According to one chronicler, he laid low "Risen et Caducan et Mariadoth," all kings of the Welsh.[39] These were apparently Cadwgan ap Meurig, king of Morgannwg, Maredudd ab Owain, king of Deheubarth, and his brother, Rhys ab Owain.[40] It was a considerable victory, and it may well be that Gwent fell into Norman hands as a result of this operation.[41]

Fitz-Osbern did not attempt to displace the Welsh population of the area he had acquired. He appears to have followed a consistent policy of accommodation and absorption rather than complete subjugation and displacement. *Domesday Book* states that he obtained license from the king to grant a group of Welsh villages the same

---

[38] See M. Bateson, "The Laws of Breteuil," *The English Historical Review,* XV (1900), pp. 73–78, 302–318, 496–523, 754–757; XVI (1901), pp. 92–110, 332–345.

[39] Orderic Vitalis, col. 331.

[40] So holds J. E. Lloyd, *A History of Wales from the Earliest Times to the Edwardian Conquest,* II, 375.

[41] This is the view of J. E. Lloyd. It may be that the conquest of Gwent was deferred until the time when Roger of Breteuil, in alliance with Caradog ap Gruffydd, defeated Maredudd ab Owain at the Rhymney River. The pertinent data is as follows:

(1) *Domesday Book* for Gloucestershire (fol. 162) records certain lands in the vicinity of a castle which Fitz-Osbern had granted to Ralf of Limesi. These lands were in Gwent, it is true, but it does not follow necessarily that other areas of Gwent were also under Norman control.

(2) *Monasticon Anglicanum . . .*, ed. W. Dugdale, Vol. VI, Part 2, pp. 1092–1093. This passage records a grant made to the abbey of Lyre of "a half of all tithes between the Usk and the Wye." This gift is almost certainly the gift of William Fitz-Osbern or his son. The later lords of the region of Gwent supported other religious foundations. The scope of this gift indicates that it was made shortly after the conquest of the area.

(3) *Liber Landavensis,* pp. 262–263. Here a passage refers to "the lord of Gwent, Roger, son of Osbern [sic]." In any event, Gwent was in Norman hands sometime before 1075.

tax-free status they had been granted under the Welsh king, Gruf-fydd. These settlements were left under the same Welsh *prepositi*, or *maers*, who had been governing them under the native Welsh princes.[42] This policy was perhaps one which Fitz-Osbern had in-herited from his English predecessors, who had absorbed the Welsh district of Erging, or Archenfield, on much the same terms. Whatever its origin, this approach continued to be a fundamental part of the policy of the Norman conquerors of Wales and led directly to the "Welsheries" of the later marcher lordships. One last piece of infor-mation from *Domesday Book* also shows Fitz-Osbern's care to stabi-lize conditions in his earldom. It is recorded that he made a series of grants to a certain king "Mariadoth."[43] This can only be his one-time foe, Maredudd ab Owain.[44] In this we can see how peace was made with the Welsh chieftain, and how his interests were linked with those of the Herefordshire Normans.

It is difficult to evaluate adequately the significance of Fitz-Osbern's accomplishments along the border. During the years when he was so active elsewhere he somehow managed to transform the southern marches completely. When he first arrived in 1067, Here-fordshire was weak and vulnerable to attack from many quarters. The land itself was prostrate from over a decade of harrying and devastation. Fitz-Osbern established the Conquest in the region, immeasurably strengthened its border defenses, and reduced the Welsh chieftains along the frontier to impotence. Finally, he initi-ated a program of internal development which slowly repaired the damages wrought by the border strife that preceded his coming. Thanks to the security he brought to the region and to his enlight-ened administration, *Domesday* Herefordshire seems comparatively prosperous. It is not the prosperity of a frontier boom, but of a re-gional recovery. The framework for this recovery had been laid by Fitz-Osbern. That even more progress was not made by 1086 should

[42] *Domesday Book*, fol. 162.

[43] *Ibid.*, fols. 187, 187b.

[44] Cf. Freeman, *The Norman Conquest*, IV, 679, n. l. Freeman believes "Maria-doc" to be Maredudd ap Bleddyn. This is unlikely for two reasons. In the first place, Maredudd ap Bleddyn was still very much alive in 1087, and his lands would not have been held by his heir, "Grifin" (*Domesday Book*, fol. 187b). Secondly, "Grifin" later attempted to seize the crown of Deheubarth (*Brut y Tywysogion, or The Chronicles of the Princes*, ed. J. Williams ab Ithel, s.a. 1089, p. 54). This indicates a dynastic claim which could have come only from Maredudd ab Owain. The *Annales Cambriae*, ed. J. Williams ab Ithel, p. 39, shows Maredudd ap Bleddyn to have died in 1132.

not be considered a condemnation of his policies. The fault lay rather with the political incompetence and overreaching ambition of his son, Roger of Breteuil.

Roger took over his father's English lands in February of 1071. At approximately the same time Ralph Guader, a Breton, took command of Fitz-Osbern's old charge of East Anglia. The two young men were apparently good friends, for Roger soon contracted to marry Ralph's sister. The prospect that these two powerful marcher earls should enter into such a close alliance was not to King William's liking. He refused to allow the marriage to take place. The young earls took advantage of William's absence in 1075 to conclude the marriage without royal license. This act was but the symbol of a deeper disaffection, and the bridal feast was used as an opportunity to organize a rebellious conspiracy.

The rebels presented a formidable combination. They both could draw upon strong personal armies stationed along the frontier and they both possessed virtually impregnable private castles. They searched for outside aid and found it forthcoming. Ralph was able to obtain a pledge of support from the Danish court, which still entertained English ambitions. Together, they enlisted the aid of Waltheof, the English earl of Northumbria. The addition of another marcher earl increased the forces and fortresses at their disposal, and they had some hopes that, with Waltheof as their figurehead, the English could be induced to join their movement. The strength and prospects of the rebels were sufficient to cause William's deputy, Lanfranc, no little concern.

Actual rebellion, however, showed the real weakness of the rebels. Waltheof quickly repented, and Ralph and Roger soon found that they could not count on any English support of their cause. On the contrary, when Roger tried to march overland to join Ralph, he found his passage of the Severn blocked by the fyrd of Worcestershire. Another fyrd marched against Ralph, whose Danish support had failed to materialize. The rebellion soon collapsed, and with it the fortunes of the house of Breteuil. Roger and his followers were stripped of their possessions, and Roger himself was sentenced to perpetual imprisonment.[45]

This rebellion forced King William to re-evaluate his system of

---

[45] The details of Roger's rebellion are covered by Orderic Vitalis, cols. 351–356.

frontier defense. In erecting a series of counties palatine along the border—Chester, Shrewsbury, and Hereford—William had, in effect, attempted to follow the same policy pursued by Edward the Confessor in maintaining Harold Godwinson along this same border. William had been guided by considerations of expediency and practicality in choosing his personnel and in establishing their authority. Giving these men sufficient strength to protect the frontier meant allowing them to recruit private armies of considerable size and erect private fortresses of great defensive strength. In order to protect himself from the dangers that such a system implied, William quite sensibly recruited his border earls from those men of whose loyalty he was most assured. Only the wealthier of his followers could afford such a position, however, for the defense of the Welsh frontier required a far greater expenditure than the revenues of the border shires could defray.[46] It was necessary to make the arduous and often costly business of frontier guard attractive to his men. William accomplished this by granting his border earls liberties, prestige, and a certain measure of independence.

As long as loyal followers such as William Fitz-Osbern manned the frontier, the system was efficient, economical, and effective. In the normal course of things, however, thanks to inheritance, King William could not always hope to dictate who would hold these positions and the privileges which went with them. The loyalty of the fyrds during Roger's rebellion must have been gratifying to the king, but his enforced reliance upon them at this critical juncture must have been alarming. William saw the dangers of the frontier system he had established, and did not return to it when the immediate trouble had passed. The escheated earldom of Roger of Breteuil was left vacant under royal administration. Meanwhile he searched for other means to secure peace along the frontier.

Political developments within Wales eventually provided William with a solution to his problem. It was not until 1081 that a measure of order began to emerge from the confusion which had ensued after the collapse of the *Pax Anglicana* which Harold had established following the defeat of Gruffydd ap Llewelyn. The steps by which this unity came about started inauspiciously, with the invasion of Deheubarth by Caradog ap Gruffydd ap Rhydderch.

[46] See W. J. Corbett, "The Development of the Duchy of Normandy and the Norman Conquest of England," *The Cambridge Mediaeval History*, eds. J. R. Tanner *et al.*, V, 506–511.

Caradog, king of the mountainous district of Gwynllwg, was an inveterate opportunist whose power had increased steadily since the elimination of Gruffydd ap Llewelyn. He maintained a free hand by refusing to enter into the system which Harold had constructed. Instead, he struck out at English power as soon as it was practical, and he gained considerable prestige by doing so. In 1065, he plundered a royal lodge which Harold had built in lower Gwent and escaped to the mountains to enjoy his loot.[47] In 1071, some seven years later, he enlisted the aid of the Normans in defeating Maredudd ab Owain, Fitz-Osbern's old enemy, in a battle fought on the Rhymney River, on the western border of Gwynllwg.[48] Sometime about 1073 or 1074, he succeeded in replacing Cadwgan ap Meurig as king of Morgannwg. Now, in 1081, he was moving against Deheubarth.

His sudden attack was so successful that Rhys ap Tewdwr, king of Deheubarth, was forced to take refuge at St. David's. Rhys soon received an unexpected ally in Gruffydd ap Cynan, the deposed ruler of Gwynedd. Gruffydd had sought aid in Ireland and had returned to Wales at the head of a force of Welsh, Irish, and Danish troops, intent on regaining his lost throne. It was only natural for the two to strike an alliance, especially since Traehaearn ap Caradog, the reigning king of Gwynedd, was marching south to join forces with Caradog ap Gruffydd. The two sets of enemies met at Mynedd Carn, and Rhys and Gruffydd were completely victorious.[49] The defeat effectively halted Caradog's climb to power. Rhys gained in prestige what Caradog lost, and by 1081 had emerged as the paramount ruler of the entire region of southwest Wales.

It is at this point that King William entered the scene. Later in the year 1081, it is surprising to note, the Conqueror was moved to pay a visit to the isolated see of St. David's. Contemporary accounts ascribe differing motives for this arduous undertaking.[50] The Welsh chronicle *Brut y Tywysogion* suggests that a pious regard for the great saint of South Wales may have prompted the Conqueror's visit

[47] *Liber Landavensis*, p. 278; *The Anglo-Saxon Chronicle*, s.a. 1065, Part I, p. 330.

[48] *Brut y Tywysogion*, p. 26.

[49] The location of Mynedd Carn has never been determined. See Lloyd, *A History of Wales*, II, 384, n. 2.

[50] For a full discussion of the various contemporary accounts, see Freeman, *The Norman Conquest*, IV, 679–680, n. 3 and 4.

to his shrine.[51] *The Anglo-Saxon Chronicle,* on the other hand, states that William led a fyrd into Wales, and "freed many hundred men."[52] It may well be that both of these sources missed the real point of the event. Modern analysts have suggested that there may well have been a diplomatic purpose in William's actions, and that William used this opportunity to accept Rhys' homage and to reinvest him with Deheubarth as a feudal fief.[53]

This suggestion has much to recommend it. By making such a treaty, William could have hoped to obtain peace along the frontier while at the same time freeing himself to curb the dangerous border barons. Prior to the battle of Mynedd Carn the pattern of political power in South Wales had been such that no potential vassal existed powerful enough to assure William that the peace would be kept. The fact that William's visit followed so closely upon the heels of Rhys' triumph strongly suggests that an agreement with the victor of Mynedd Carn was the actual reason for the Conqueror's remarkable journey.

Such an arrangement would not have been in the least unusual. Ample precedent existed in the oaths of fealty which Welsh chieftains had made to the kings of Anglo-Saxon England. As late as 1063, Harold, acting in the name of Edward, had granted the kingdoms of Wales to Bleddyn and Rhiwallon. Bleddyn and Rhiwallon had then sworn fealty to Edward and Harold, promising to obey their commands and "to pay properly all which the country paid to preceding kings."[54] King William generally attempted to follow the customs of Edward's time, and took great care that his followers enjoyed the same dues and responsibilities as their predecessors. It does not seem likely that he would have failed to pursue the same goal in his own case, and to restore an arrangement which had been acceptable and profitable to Edward the Confessor.

It is not sufficient, however, simply to prove that such a treaty was possible; more positive evidence is required. *Domesday Book* may well supply this evidence when it records the annual obligation of a certain "Riset" to pay forty pounds to the king.[55] It can be noted later

[51] *Brut y Tywysogion,* p. 50.
[52] *The Anglo-Saxon Chronicle,* s.a. 1081, Part I, p. 351.
[53] Lloyd, *A History of Wales,* II, 394; Freeman, *The Norman Conquest,* IV, 679.
[54] Florence of Worcester, I, 222.
[55] *Domesday Book,* fol. 179.

in the same compilation that Robert of Rhuddlan pays a similar sum as the *ferm* of his fief of North Wales. It is tempting, therefore, to infer that "Riset" is Rhys ap Tewdwr, and that his payment is the *ferm* of his fief of South Wales. This suggestion has its opponents, however, and among them is the redoubtable J. H. Round, who states:

> One must not introduce into the text the tempting conjecture that this was Rhys ap Tewdwr, who became king of South Wales in 1079, an event which, Mr. Freeman suggested, might not be unconnected with William's expedition through South Wales not long after, when he is said to have reduced the Welsh kings to submission. The absence of *rex* before "Riset" is against the conjecture.[56]

If Round's argument is correct, a number of problems arise. What was the actual purpose of William's visit to St. David's, and how can one explain the peculiar peace which descended on the Welsh frontier in the years following it? The treaty of 1081, if such existed, would provide the key to the understanding of the history of the Welsh frontier for the next decade. It would be well, therefore, to examine Mr. Round's admonition more closely before rejecting the possibility.

In the first place, Mr. Round argues from silence—in this case, from the lack of the title *rex*. We must first ask ourselves how regularly his contemporaries dignified Rhys with the title "king." The *Brut y Tywysogion*, derived from a contemporary account probably written in the vicinity of either St. David's or Aberystwyth, is likely to have had a most ample knowledge of Rhys. He is mentioned in five entries, but in only one of them is he styled "*brenhin* Deheubarth," or "king of Southwest Wales." In this single instance, moreover, the chronicler was writing his obituary and had every reason for stressing his high station.[57] The *Annales Cambriae* deny him the title even in this instance and call him "*Rector dextralis partis*" instead.[58] Both of these chronicles are drawn from the same contemporary source and may share this source's peculiarities. It must be stressed, on the other hand, that this source was written in Deheu-

---

[56] J. H. Round, "Introduction to the Herefordshire Domesday," *The Victoria Histories of the Counties of England: Hereford*, Vol. I, ed. W. Page, p. 281, n. 109.

[57] *Brut y Tywysogion*, s.a. 1091 [sic], p. 54.

[58] *Annales Cambriae*, p. 29.

barth itself and is more likely than any other to have reflected the
most stringent contemporary usage in this matter. It seems clear that
Rhys' friends and followers did not insist on calling him *brenhin* or
rex. It does not seem very likely that *Domesday* would have scrupu-
lously observed the courtesy.

Mr. Round would probably not have been so concerned about this
lack of title were it not for the fact that *Domesday* uses the title *rex*
in reference to another Welsh leader only a few folios after omitting
it in Riset's case. The problem then is why *Domesday* should use the
title in one instance and not in another. Round's conclusion is that
Riset had no claim to the title. A closer examination of the situation,
however, reveals another possible solution. The passage where *rex*
is used is one describing the Herefordshire estates held by a certain
"Grifin," obviously Gruffydd ap Maredudd ab Owain ab Edwin, son
of Fitz-Osbern's old enemy.[59] *Domesday* here styles the father, "Ma-
riadoc," as *rex* no less than four times. Maredudd's claim to royal
status was valid. He had become king of Deheubarth in the general
reorganization of Wales which had followed the death of Gruffydd ap
Llewelyn in 1063.[60] He ruled this land until his death at the hands of
Caradog and his Norman allies in 1072. The throne then passed to his
brother, Rhys ab Owain, who was killed by the same Caradog in
1078. The throne then fell vacant until taken up by Rhys ap Tewdwr,
a kinsman of Maredudd through their common grandfather, Eineon.[61]
It can be seen that the Herefordshire landholder, Gruffydd, had a
much stronger hereditary claim to the throne of Deheubarth than did
the reigning king, Rhys. It belonged to Gruffydd by the simple appli-
cation of primogeniture. Hereditary claims, however, without the
fact of possession, had little validity in Wales. Only a few years after
Domesday, Gruffydd was killed while attempting to take possession
of the throne to which he was the heir.[62] Here then is a possible explanation of *Domesday's* willingness to grant the title *rex* to Maredudd but not to Rhys. Gruffydd, a substantial tenant of Herefordshire, had every reason to insist on his father's regal status while
denying the same status to Rhys. It may well be that Gruffydd did

[59] *Domesday Book*, fol. 187b. See note 44 above.
[60] Lloyd, *A History of Wales*, II, 372.
[61] *Ibid.*, II, 767.
[62] *Brut y Tywysogion*, s.a. 1089, p. 54. Note that the *Brut* lags two years at
this point. The actual date is 1091.

exactly this, and that *Domesday* simply records the personal prejudices and ambitions of Gruffydd ap Maredudd.

Thus the omission of the title *rex* with reference to Riset does not
prove that he was not Rhys ap Tewdwr. Indeed, it suggests quite the
opposite. The *Domesday* evidence, then, indicates that an arrangement was made between William and Rhys in which Rhys received
Deheubarth as a feudal fief in exchange for an annual render of
forty pounds. Additional documentary evidence supporting this thesis
may be found in the *Brut y Tywysogion*. This Welsh chronicle refers
to William the Conqueror a number of times, and a curious pattern
of titles is used. The entry for 1066 styles him "William the Bastard,
prince [*tywyssawc*] of Normandy."[63] It then continues to describe
his conquest of England. In the entry for 1081 (listed 1079), he has
become "Gwilim Vastard Vrenhin y Saeson ar Freinc ar Brytanyeit."[64]
In the usage of the *Brut*, *Saeson* is generic for all English, while by
Freinc is meant the Normans and not the French proper. Thus his
title has become "William the Bastard, king of the English, Normans, and Britons [Welsh]." This is a title he did not lose. His
obituary reads "Gwilim Vastard, tywyssawc y Normanyeit a brenhin
y Saeson ar Brytanyeit ar Albanwyr." The important point to be
noted is the use of the title *brenhin y Brytanyeit*. The last person,
previous to William, to bear such a title in the *Brut* was Gruffydd ap
Llewelyn, a man who had united all of Wales under his sway.

It seems hardly likely that this title was simply rhetorical or hon-
orific. Both from geographical location and from interest, the *Brut*
was very close to the political realities of the times. The subject
matter of this chronicle consists primarily of accounts of the dynastic
struggles and conspiracies through which men pursue such titles.
One need only note that the last entry stresses that William is king of
the English, but only prince (*tywyssawc*) of the Normans. Again, he
appears as *brenhin y[r] Albanwyr*. William had a good claim to this
title *King of the Scots*, as the result of a feudal arrangement much the
same as that which probably took place between himself and Rhys.

Taken in themselves, the titles accorded to William by the *Brut y
Tywysogion* are perhaps inconclusive evidence of a *rapprochement*
between the Welsh and English kings. Yet they are most easily ex-

[63] *Ibid.*, pp. 44–46.
[64] *Ibid.*, p. 50.

plained by assuming that William actually did receive homage from Rhys during his journey into Wales. Certain other facts also support this theory. The endemic warfare of the Welsh frontier and the Norman raids which had slashed deep into the heart of Deheubarth suddenly came to an end. The remainder of Rhys' reign was marred only by internecine struggles.[65] On the English side of the frontier the occupation of Gwent appears to have proceeded peacefully, and *Domesday* reveals a countryside slowly recovering from the effects of the Welsh attacks which had marked the 1060's. The situation along the border remained peaceful until after the death of Rhys ap Tewdwr, when the Normans burst in on South Wales like a long-pent flood—as if only the existence of the Welsh king had stayed their advance.

When all the evidence is considered, three possible political motives for William's pilgrimage to St. David's emerge. First, he may have felt it wise to reinforce the ascendancy which Rhys had gained at Mynedd Carn and thus maintain in authority a figure with whom it would be possible to deal in stabilizing his Welsh frontier. Secondly, an expedition in force would be useful in impressing upon the Welsh of Morgannwg their now precarious position between two powerful and allied powers. This would do much to curb their adventurous spirit and to heighten the prospects of peace along the southern frontier. His third motive was probably to bring about the personal confrontation which was necessary to perform the solemn act of homage. This relationship would have been far more valuable to William than a simple restoration of the arrangements which Edward the Confessor had made with the dangerous Welsh.

The treaty of 1081 had numerous advantages for William. A strong and loyal Rhys ap Tewdwr made it unlikely that the Welsh would ally with rebellious Norman border lords against the king. At the same time, even a small Norman border force could threaten the comparatively weak, but pivotal, buffer states of Brycheiniog, Gwynllwg, and Morgannwg. Without control of these vital invasion

---

[65] *Ibid.*, pp. 52–55. In 1088, Rhys was driven from Deheubarth by the attack of two sons of the king of Powys. He obtained Danish aid from Ireland, defeated the invaders, and regained power. In 1091, he was attacked by Gruffydd ap Maredudd ab Owain. This latter attack may have been aided and encouraged by Gruffydd's Norman neighbors in Herefordshire, but there is no evidence that they took a direct part in the attack.

routes, Rhys did not present an active threat to the security of the border shires. William's original plan had been to create the border earldoms of Chester, Shrewsbury, and Hereford as semi-independent military buffer states. This policy had proven dangerous. With danger of Welsh attack lessened, the independence and power of the Norman border lords could be safely limited, or at least a start could be made in that direction. Meanwhile, the border shires could continue their slow process of recovery and growth.

iii. Social Classes on
the *Domesday* Frontier

WE HAVE SEEN that the southwestern frontier of England enjoyed an almost unparalleled peace and prosperity in the period following the Norman Conquest. The king had established an effective system of border defense, had chosen the able William Fitz-Osbern to develop and defend the border shires, and had granted him a semi-independent status in performing these tasks. When this system of defense had proven dangerous, the Conqueror succeeded in concluding an effective and durable alliance with Rhys ap Tewdwr, the king of Deheubarth. The wisdom of his course of action is reflected in the fact that the western frontier of England received little mention in the chronicles of the latter years of William's reign. The region apparently continued its recovery and development without any difficulties or setbacks worthy of note. Were it not for the compilation known as *Domesday Book*, our knowledge of this period would be extremely limited. In the pages of *Domesday Book*, however, it is possible to discern much about the somewhat peculiar society which was evolving on England's western frontier.

The ownership of most of the lands of England changed hands during the two decades following the Norman Conquest. V. H. Galbraith points out some of the problems which this massive transfer of wealth and power entailed:

There were already written records in use, but the government was still customary and oral; and it is hardly before the thirteenth century that the government became bureaucratic in character. This is brought home to us by the fact that the great "honours" or complexes of land granted by William to his tenants-in-chief seem to have been made *sine carta*, that is orally and without written records. So too with justice; the transfer of more than half the land of England to a new nobility in this primitive fashion involved confusion, spoiliation, and the seizing of land without title.[1]

The problems which this situation created are readily apparent. Without adequate records, William could have had only a vague idea of the relative strength and wealth of his various barons or of the extent of the resources which still lay under his direct control. Another problem lay in the great change in land values which had occurred since the days of Edward the Confessor. Areas which had once been populous and fertile now lay devastated and deserted, while lands once beyond the limits of English settlement were now undergoing extensive and rapid development. Any rational policy of taxation would have to take into account this greatly changed regional distribution of wealth. Finally, any stabilization of the internal situation in England involved the resolution of the many conflicting land claims which had arisen since the Conquest. These problems no doubt weighed heavily on the Conqueror. At the Gloucester assembly of 1085, he took steps to solve them by ordering a complete assessment of his realm of England. The inquiry was begun shortly after the initial order and, by the time of William's death in 1087, it was substantially complete.[2]

Domesday represents a unique achievement of eleventh-century administration, and its importance as a source for modern students of English history cannot be overemphasized.[3] It must be remembered, however, that the information presented in *Domesday* has distinct limitations. Incidental references may provide valuable evidence for studies of classes and customs in medieval England, but such references are quite fortuitous. Whatever its original purpose and function, *Domesday* was certainly not intended to provide data for future historians. What may appear to be a coherent pattern in its

[1] V. H. Galbraith, *The Making of Domesday Book*, p. 46.

[2] For the conduct of the inquiry, see W. H. Stevenson, "A Contemporary Description of the Domesday Survey," *The English Historical Review*, XXII (1907), 72–84.

[3] Useful bibliographies of the major analyses of this source may be found in Galbraith, *The Making of Domesday Book*, and *Domesday Studies, being the papers read at the meetings of the Domesday Commemoration, 1886*, ed. P. E. Dove.

pages may be nothing but the personal idiosyncrasies of a particular scribe. Even apart from these limitations, one must note that *Domesday* is neither complete nor exhaustive. London, Winchester, Northumberland, and Durham are not included in the survey. It even appears that the figures for the areas which are covered are not always accurate. This means that statistical studies based upon *Domesday* must be especially suspect and their limitations well noted. On the other hand, one must not let the difficulties involved in such studies halt their progress. Even the meticulous J. H. Round recognized this necessity when he noted that "Breadth of view . . . is essential in Domesday study . . ."[4]

In the pages of *Domesday*, the five shires of the Welsh frontier formed a distinct region sharing certain common characteristics which distinguished them from the other shires of England and which bound them closely together into a unit. A number of such distinguishing features could be cited, but perhaps the most interesting are those social classes known to *Domesday* as the *radmanni, radchenistri, bovarii,* and *hospites.* These classes appear within the Welsh frontier, and virtually nowhere else in *Domesday* England. Moreover, their peculiar nature may indicate some of the forces which were helping to shape the character of the region.

The relationship between the first two of these classes—the *radmanni* and *radchenistri*—and the Welsh frontier is most easily presented in tabular form. (Table 1)

Two conclusions may be drawn from this table. The first is that the terms *radmanni* and *radchenistri* were probably regional variations of the same appellation. *Radmanni* is the northern usage, while *radchenistri* is the southern. The distribution of *radmanni* and *radchenistri* within Herefordshire confirms this conclusion by repeating the larger distribution in miniature. Both terms apparently refer to the same status. They are drawn from the same root and have similar meanings, that of "riding man."[5] *Domesday Book* (folio 180) gives additional indication of the identity of the two terms. The record states that the estate of Leominster in Herefordshire had eighty hides and eight *radchenistri* in the time of Edward the Confessor. Twenty years

---

    [4] J. H. Round, "Introduction to the Worcestershire Domesday Book," *The Victoria Histories of the Counties of England: Worcester,* I, 277.
    [5] Sir Henry Ellis adds the information that "Rad-cniht is usually interpreted by our Glossarists *Equestris homo sive Miles;* and Rad-here *Equestris exercitus.*" Sir Henry Ellis, *A General Introduction to Domesday Book . . .,* II, 74, n. 2.

TABLE 1

Location of *Radmanni* and *Radchenistri* in Domesday England

Shire	Radmanni	Radchenistri
Cheshire	145	0
Shropshire	167	3
Worcestershire	33	3
Herefordshire	24	47
Gloucestershire	0	137
Total in the border shires	369	190
Hampshire	0	5
Berkshire	0	1
Total in *Domesday Book*	369	196

later, the same estate had sixty hides and six *radmanni*. The *Domesday* scribe appears to be using the two terms interchangeably in this entry.

The second conclusion which may be drawn from the table is simply that the riding men of *Domesday Book* represent a status or institution almost completely peculiar to the Welsh frontier, at least in the year 1086.

Much information concerning the riding men can be culled from the pages of *Domesday*.[6] In fact, a reasonably detailed, although confusing, picture of them can be constructed. The riding men mentioned in *Domesday* were restricted to rural areas, where they were closely connected with the cultivation of the soil. Unlike the majority of the inhabitants of the border, they enjoyed free status. *Domesday* is incisively clear on this point: "Radchen[istri], id est, liberi homines T.R.E." (folio 166). Together with this somewhat exalted status, many of the riding men possessed substantial wealth.[7] Some variation existed, of course, but the riding men noted by *Domesday* generally appear quite well-to-do. All of these characteristics tempt one to find in the riding men a nascent yeomanry developing along the frontier.

This view becomes somewhat difficult when one considers the obligations which were sometimes placed on some members of the class.

[6] Ellis rehearses much of this information. *Ibid.*, I, 72–74.

[7] *Domesday Book: or the Great Survey of England by William the Conqueror* A.D. *MLXXXVI*, fol. 163. Here nineteen riding men hold forty-eight ploughs.

They were liable to quite heavy dues for the land they held,[8] but such dues were reasonable in view of the extensive holdings of those who paid them. It is somewhat more disturbing to find that the riding men were sometimes liable for boon work.[9] Even this duty is not inconsistent with the idea of a frontier yeomanry, although it would appear somewhat degrading to such a class. They were subject to other exactions, however, which were so onerous as to seem to deny the riding men the free status which *Domesday* ascribed to them. The compilers of *Domesday* wrote, as if they were aware of the inconsistency between the status and obligations of these men, ". . . Radchen[istri], id est, liberi homini T.R.E. qui tamen omnes ad opus domini arabant, herciabant, falcabant, et metebant" (folio 166). The extent of these obligations seems to be great enough, but a later entry states, ". . . omne servitum quod eis iubebatur faciebant" (folio 187).

It is clear that the riding men do not represent a rising frontier yeomanry. Their manorial obligations were too great. It is difficult to determine what their status was, since their obligations were simply inconsistent with the freedom they supposedly enjoyed. This inconsistency is more apparent than real, however, since it exists only in terms of the Norman feudal and manorial systems. The difficulty disappears when one realizes that one is here dealing with an Anglo-Saxon institution. The very derivation of the words *radmanni* and *radchenistri* indicates that the origin of the institution was Anglo-Saxon. Furthermore, the pages of *Domesday* preserve the personal names of nine of these riding men. The names are definitely and without exception Anglo-Saxon.[10] Apparently the riding men formed an institution which remained peculiarly Anglo-Saxon. In a society dominated by the Normans, it was an institution which was fast moving toward extinction. In the riding men of the frontier we see a moribund, not a nascent yeomanry.

It is tempting to view the riding man as a type of *thegn* which had been carried over into the new political and social structure which the Normans were constructing in England. *Domesday Book* tends to support this view in its entry for the vill of Westune in Shropshire.

---

[8] *Ibid.*, fol. 180b. On this estate, for example, the riding men rendered thirteen shillings six pence, plus three *sextars* of honey.

[9] *Ibid.*, fol. 187: ". . . Ibi Radman secebant una die in anno in pratis domini . . ."

[10] *Ibid.*, fol. 174b, "Lefric"; fol. 187, "Ageluuard, Eduuard, Brictmer, Saulfus, Aluuinuis, Godric, Aluui, Ketelbert."

This particular estate was held by six *thegns* in the time of Edward the Confessor. Twenty years later it was held by six riding men.[11] In this case, at least, the terms seem to be interchangeable.

F. W. Maitland went somewhat further and suggested that the institutions of *thegn, dregn, radman,* and *radcniht,* all had a common origin.[12] He suggested that this origin lay in a system which St. Oswald developed, in which church lands were granted to men to be held for three generations ("per spatium temporis trium hominum, id est duorum post se haeredum").[13] The primary obligation of the recipients of these grants was that they were to obey the "law of riding" (*equitandi lex*). The nature of this law was not made clear, but St. Oswald's letter to King Edgar did state some of the specific obligations which this form of grant entailed. The recipients were to pay all customary dues to the Church and were to be subject to the commands of the bishop as long as they held the land. The nature of these commands was quite vaguely expressed. They were to be ready to supply horses and hunting spears when the bishop required them, to supply all other needs of the bishop, and to ride in his service when required to do so. Finally, when the three-generation term had elapsed, it was to be within the bishop's power to regrant the land on the same terms, to retain them himself, or grant them to others. This type of grant clearly exhibits the same combination of high status and extensive obligations which was so characteristic of the riding men of *Domesday Book.*

Maitland suggested that the basic obligations of St. Oswald's riding men were at least partly military, and characterized the "law of riding" as a primitive law of chivalry.[14] He supported his contention by tracing the development of the institution to the *thegns* and *dregns* of Angevin Northumbria. In this region, the characteristic Norman system of tenure by knight-service appeared to have been superimposed upon an earlier semimilitary system. The *thegns* and *dregns,* representatives of this earlier system, fought in support of the king, defended the borders, and took part in expeditions led

---

[11] *Ibid.,* fol. 256.

[12] See F. W. Maitland, *Domesday Book and Beyond: Three Essays in the Early History of England,* pp. 307 ff.; F. W. Maitland, "Northumbrian Tenures," *The English Historical Review,* V (1890), 625–632.

[13] *Codex Diplomaticus Aevi Saxonici,* ed. J. M. Kemble, Vol. VI, No. 1287, pp. 124–126.

[14] Maitland, *Domesday Book and Beyond,* p. 307.

against the Scots. On the other hand, they were subject to a series of menial obligations. They paid rent, rode on the lord's service, helped in the cultivation of his demesne, and even paid merchet.[15] Their obligations correspond so closely to those of the riding men of St. Oswald's day, and of *Domesday Book*, as to suggest that the *thegns*, *dregns*, and riding men were representatives of the same system of tenure. If this is the case, the basic functions of the riding men of *Domesday Book* were semimilitary, and they acted much in the character of a frontier militia.

This view was opposed by J. H. Round, who held that the "law of riding" did not consist of military service, but of providing escorts and performing errands.[16] No specific evidence can be found to support either Maitland's or Round's view, but it is difficult to believe that the riding men were without any military function. The bearing of arms was regarded as necessary to the status of freeman under Anglo-Norman law. One of the laws ascribed to William the Conqueror stated, "Universi liberi homines tocius regni nostri predicti habeant et teneant se semper bene in armis et in equis . . ."[17] While it is hard to believe that all freemen were capable of maintaining a horse, it is obvious from Oswald's letter that the riding men were expected to be able to do so. In view of the law of the land, the riding men of *Domesday* were liable to be called upon to use the spears and horses they were expected to possess.

Even apart from the law, it seems likely that these men, living as they did along the turbulent and dangerous border, were sometimes called upon to defend their lives and property. If the riding men of *Domesday* were truly derived from those of St. Oswald's time, they possessed the horses and arms to defend themselves and their neighbors as well. *Domesday Book*, however, never explicitly states that such military service was one of their regular functions. This should not be too surprising. Whatever *Domesday* is, it is not a customal. The obligations of the English-born burgesses of Shrewsbury furnish proof of this, as well as providing evidence of a function which may be more than fortuitously parallel with that of the riding men.

Domesday suggests that the provision of escorts constituted one of the major obligations of the "better class burgesses" of the town. This class was expected to possess horses and arms. Nothing is said of the

---

[15] Maitland, "Northumbrian Tenures."
[16] Round, "Introduction to the Worcestershire Domesday Book," pp. 250–251.
[17] *Ancient Laws and Institutes of England . . .*, I, 212.

military obligations of this group until the very end of the passage describing Shrewsbury. The compiler notes, almost as an afterthought, that whoever failed to comply with the sheriff's order for an expedition into Wales, was to pay a forty shilling fine.[18] This passage was not included in *Domesday* because of the importance of the military function of these armed and mounted burgesses, but because of the possible source of revenue provided by evasion of this service. This item of information is fortuitous, but the implication is clear. Englishmen in Shrewsbury, possessing much the same equipment and the same obligation of escort duty as the riding men, were regularly expected to provide military service in Welsh campaigns. It is reasonable to assume that the riding men of the rural districts were liable to similar obligations. Whether such service was fundamental to their peculiar tenure is somewhat irrelevant. It seems clear that the riding men of *Domesday Book* constituted a group expected to provide regular military service against the Welsh.

Despite this important function, it would appear that the riding men of the border were declining in both numbers and importance in 1086. It is difficult to find direct data on this point, but a number of facts lead to the same conclusion. The distribution of the riding men of Shropshire has some relevance here. Most of the shire was in the hands of Norman lords by 1086, but a small group of Anglo-Saxons continued to hold about twenty-five hides in the western highland hundreds of Conodovre, Ruesset, and Witentreu. No less than 15 riding men, or about 9 per cent of the total for the shire, resided within this small district. Directly to the east lay the hundred of Recordine, a district almost completely dominated by Norman overlords. If the popularity of the riding men had been as great in Recordine as it was under the Anglo-Saxon lords to the west, *Domesday Book* would have recorded 105 for this district. Only 11 were so reported. It is clear that conditions were such as to make riding men rather unpopular tenants for Norman lords.

This conclusion is supported by a broader picture of the distribution of the riding men within Shropshire. (Table 2)
Generally speaking, where Norman immigration was high, the number of riding men was small by the time of *Domesday*. Again, the distribution shows that the frequency of riding men was highest in the more exposed and poorer hundreds which lay along Shropshire's

[18] *Domesday Book*, fol. 252.

TABLE 2

Distribution of Riding Men within Shropshire

Hundred	Ratio of riding men to hides		Number of *Francigenae*
	Riding Men	Hides	
Ruesset	1	6.3	0
Witentreu	1	3.3	0
Derinlau	1	6.0	0
Recordine	1	9.5	11
Alnodstre	1	8.5	6
Bascherche	1	13.0	6
Patintune	1	8.1	4

western border. If the riding men did provide a mounted militia force, it is only natural that they would have lingered longest in these districts, where the value of such a force was the greatest.

Finally, the distribution of riding men along the entire border again attests to the fact that they were slowly moving toward extinction under the unfriendly administration of the Norman conquerors. The 145 riding men of Cheshire constituted 6 per cent of the total population of the shire. The 170 who resided in the much more populous Shropshire accounted for 3 per cent of the population. Only 71 riding men lived in Herefordshire, constituting only 1.3 per cent of the shire's population. One would expect that Herefordshire, with its long and exposed border would have a relatively higher number of riding men than the comparatively easily defended Shropshire. The fact that it did not can most easily be explained by pointing out that because of its pre-Conquest colony, Herefordshire had been exposed to strong Norman influences for twenty years longer than its northern neighbor.

When one combines all of this information with the fact that the terms *radman* and *radcniht* disappear in the years following *Domesday*, the conclusion is inescapable that the institution was moribund by 1086, probably as a result of hostile Norman influences.

Such then were the men whom the compilers of *Domesday Book* knew as *radmanni* and *radchenistri*. They were free men, pledged to maintain horses and weapons in exchange for grants of land. While often possessing respectable wealth, they were completely bound to the orders of their lord. Their dual character of cavalry militia and agricultural entrepreneurs mark them as the product of a frontier environment, one in which both characters are necessary to the development and exploitation of the land. The frontier which produced this class was not that of the eleventh-century Normans, however, but of the tenth-century Anglo-Saxons. By 1086, the riding men were fast passing out of existence. What was happening to them, it is difficult to say. It is possible that their functions and possessions in the eastern reaches of the border shires were being taken over by the *francigenae servientes* who often appear on the pages of *Domesday Book*. Perhaps some of the riding men moved westward to continue, for a time, an institution which had already become an anachronism.

The *bovarii* were another class peculiar to the Welsh border shires at the time of *Domesday Book*. Of the 737 such men listed, 733 resided in the shires of Cheshire (172), Shropshire (384), Worcestershire (73), and Herefordshire (104).[19] Only 4 *bovarii* were listed outside of these counties, all in the returns for Suffolk. Thus it is clear that the name *bovarius* was restricted to those same areas along England's western frontier in which was found the peculiar status of riding man.

Translators differ in their interpretation of the term *"bovarius."* Some employ "oxman," while others prefer "oxherd."[20] A moment's reflection reveals the impossibility of the second translation. To have warranted a special title, the *bovarius* would have to have been a full-time professional oxherd. Otherwise, *Domesday* would have listed him by status rather than by profession. There were simply too many *bovarii* listed in *Domesday* for them to have found adequate employment as oxherds in the comparatively poor border shires. Indeed, some small manors listed ten or twelve such men.[21] Whatever relation the *bovarius* had to oxen, it was not that of professional herdsman. The translation "oxman" is preferable then. It is true that

[19] Ellis, *A General Introduction to Domesday Book*, II. In Ellis' final tabulation, he counts 749 *bovarii*, but an addition of the totals for the various shires yields only 737.

[20] Both terms are employed in the *Victoria County Histories*. J. H. Round uses "oxman" for Herefordshire and Worcestershire, while Drinkwater prefers "oxherd" in the Shropshire volume. C. H. Drinkwater, "Translation of the Shropshire Domesday," *The Victoria Histories of the Counties of England: Shropshire*, I; J. H. Round, "Introduction to the Herefordshire Domesday," *The Victoria Histories of the Counties of England: Hereford*, I; and Round, "Introduction to the Worcestershire Domesday."

[21] For example, *Domesday Book*, fol. 252b and 253b.

this translation is vague, but this lack of precision allows us to construct our own definition of the term.

A number of peculiarities may be noted in the *Domesday Book* entries concerning these oxmen. In an overwhelming number of entries the number of oxmen noted for a given manor is an even figure—two, four, six, and so forth.[22] In most of those few cases where an uneven number of oxmen are reported, the returns show an uneven number of *servi*, or slaves.[23] This latter is an equally unusual event in *Domesday*. Finally, there are some few cases where the combined total of oxmen and slaves is still uneven. In most of these instances, the entry notes that the demesne contains a half-plough.[24] The implication of this peculiarity is clear.

It is well known that the ploughing of medieval England was a two-man operation, one man to handle the oxen and the other to guide the plough. *Domesday* entries regularly record that the number of oxmen, or the combined number of oxmen and slaves, equalled twice the number of ploughs in demesne. This inescapably suggests that the function of the *bovarii* was that of ploughmen. The data also indicates that the oxmen performed much the same function as did the slaves in tilling the demesne land, and that an oxman was often associated with a slave in this task. This raises the question of whether the oxmen shared the servile status, as well as the function, of the slaves.

It appears reasonably certain that, whatever the status of the oxmen might have been at the time of *Domesday*, the institution had its origins in the servile classes. The distribution of slaves in *Domesday* England gives ample indication of this. (Table 3)

It was long ago pointed out that *Domesday Book* clearly indicates that slavery was much more common in the southwestern shires than it was in the rest of England.[25] Slaves accounted for about 9 per cent of the population of England at large, but percentages ranging around 20 per cent are recorded for the shires of the southwest. Whatever the cause adduced to explain this concentration of slaves, it is difficult to account for the relatively small numbers of slaves

---

[22] Out of eighty-seven such entries for Shropshire, only ten totals represent odd numbers.

[23] An example of such a case is the manor of Piceford in Shropshire, *Domesday Book*, fol. 258.

[24] For example, *Domesday Book*, fol. 256 and 258.

[25] F. Seebohm, *The English Village Community* . . . . See especially the map facing page 85.

TABLE 3

Distribution of *Bovarii* and *Servi* in *Domesday* England

Shire	Percentage of *Servi* in Total Population	Combined Percentage of *Servi* and *Bovarii*
Cornwall	21	21
Devon	18	18
Gloucestershire	24	24
Herefordshire	13	15
Shropshire	17	25
Worcestershire	15	20

found in Herefordshire, Shropshire, and Worcestershire. It can be seen from the table that much of this discrepancy disappears when one combines the totals of *servi* and *bovarii*.[26] The percentage for Herefordshire is still unusually low, but it must be remembered that slavery was a moribund institution under Norman rule, and that this rule had existed in Herefordshire for fifteen years longer than the other shires under consideration.[27] The evidence indicates that the oxmen had at one time constituted a portion of the servile population of the border shires. Whether they continued to do so at the time of *Domesday Book* is another matter.

There exists some evidence which appears to indicate that the status of the oxmen in 1086 was indeed servile. The most telling is found in the *Domesday* description of the manor of Worthen.[28] The compiler records that there are 4½ ploughs in demesne, ". . . *et iiii servi et .vii. villi. et viii bord. cum iii car. et iii bovariis.*" The entry thus clearly states that the villeins and bordars of Worthen owned three ploughs and three oxmen. This interpretation, however, depends upon the single stroke of the pen which transformed the word "*bovarii*" into the ablative plural "*bovariis*." This is a rather weak

[26] The figures presented in Table 3 are those of J. Tait, "Introduction to the Shropshire Domesday Book," *The Victoria Histories of the Counties of England: Shropshire*, I, 303.

[27] See Maitland, *Domesday Book and Beyond*, p. 35; P. Vinogradoff, *The Growth of the Manor*, pp. 332–336. It might also be noted that this situation is analogous to that of the riding men.

[28] *Domesday Book*, fol. 255b. Also see Tait, "Introduction to the Shropshire Domesday Book," p. 302, n. 9. Tait accepted the apparent import of this passage, even though he damaged his general thesis concerning the *bovarii* by doing so.

foundation, and it is tempting to dismiss the passage as a simple scribal error. In the first place, this is the only example of such an entry. Many other entries note the *bovarii* in the same relative position, but the nominative form is used and the meaning is clear. A more important objection can be raised. We have seen that the oxmen and slaves were usually intimately associated in the ploughing of the lord's demesne. If the three oxmen of Worthen were indeed owned by the villeins of that manor, the demesne ploughs were left gravely undermanned, since there were only four slaves available to operate four and one-half ploughs. It might also be noted that the entry for Worthen is one of those unusual cases where the combined number of oxmen and slaves is uneven. There was, however, a half-plough in demesne. It might well be that the passage contains two scribal errors, the second being that of writing *"iiii. car et dim"* for *"iii. car et dim."* This would be the simplest of errors to make. Even if this were not the case, it is difficult to believe that the villeins of Worthen held these three oxmen as slaves. These fifteen villeins and bordars held only three ploughs among them and hardly seem to have been wealthy enough to have afforded to keep slaves. Even if they could have afforded such slaves, it is hard to see what use they could have had for them. The oxmen were ploughmen, and the villeins' ploughs were already overmanned. The bulk of the evidence points toward the conclusion that the Worthen entry is unreliable, and that it represents a simple, or perhaps a compound, scribal error.

Some more reliable evidence does exist in the pages of *Domesday* to indicate that the status of the oxman may have been servile. Five entries record the existence of *"bovarii liberi."* The obvious inference to be drawn from this usage is that the other *bovarii* were not free. This conclusion is not inevitable, however. Ten of the twelve *bovarii liberi* which appear in *Domesday* are found in the single column which describes the Hezetre hundred estates of Ralph of Mortimer in Herefordshire.[29] Thus the *"bovarii liberi"* may represent either the passing usage of the compiler or the result of the system of estate administration which Ralph chose to employ.[30] In any event, whenever the term *"liber bovarius"* appears, it is in contradistinction to

---

[29] *Domesday Book,* fol. 183b. The estates are those of Lenhale, Litehale, and Camehop.

[30] Round, "Introduction to the Herefordshire Domesday," p. 289; also Tait, "Introduction to the Shropshire Domesday Book," p. 302.

servi, rather than other *bovarii*.[31] In no case does a *liber bovarius* appear in the same entry as a simple *bovarius*. They are mutually exclusive. *Domesday* evidence shows no difference between the so-called free oxmen and their possibly unfree colleagues. The sole Shropshire example of a *liber bovarius* occurs on the estate of Ultone, and reads as follows: *"in dominio sunt ii carucae et iii servi et unus liber bovarius et vi villani et iiii bordarii . . ."*[32] Free or not, this particular oxman still tilled the lord's demesne, and in intimate connection with a group of slaves.

It should be clear that the evidence of *Domesday* is inconclusive, but tends to support the conclusion that the oxmen were of servile or semiservile status. J. H. Round reached the conclusion that *". . . Domesday* uses the terms 'bovarii' and 'servi' alternately."[33] This view seems far too extreme. Both terms frequently appear in the same entry. The compilers of *Domesday Book* were intensely interested in compressing their data and would have been more than happy to make one figure serve in the place of two if it had been possible. There must have been very good reason for *Domesday* to make the distinction as regularly as it did. Finally, one might note that in one entry, the word *"servi"* is lined out and the word *"bovarii"* substituted.[34] It is impossible to accept Round's contention; the evidence shows clearly that there existed a significant difference between the status of oxman and that of slave. The nature of this difference is a matter of some dispute.

James Tait has suggested that *Domesday* only uses the term *"bovarius"* in reference to free men who are doing slaves' work.[35] This would mean that the oxmen were, by definition, free men. A number of objections to this hypothesis arise. In the first place, it has been shown that the origins of the oxmen were probably servile. They must have had some connection with the servile classes which this view does not account for. Secondly, if the oxmen were free by definition, it is difficult to explain how the scribe could ever have made the slip which seems to indicate that villeins and bordars could own

[31] W. J. Slack, "The Shropshire Ploughmen of Domesday Book," *The Transactions of the Shropshire Archaeological Society*, L (1939), 32.

[32] *Domesday Book*, fol. 255.

[33] Round, "Introduction to the Worcestershire Domesday Book," p. 276.

[34] *Domesday Book*, fol. 256b.

[35] Tait, "Introduction to the Shropshire Domesday Book," p. 302.

oxmen. Scribal errors are rarely so blatant, or, if they are, are usually noted and corrected. Finally, this hypothesis denies any significance whatever to those passages which refer to the *bovarii liberi* by making the phrase tautological. The evidence does not conclusively establish that the oxmen were servile, but it does indicate that they were not free by definition.

Professor Tait made a second suggestion which appears far more tenable. It may have been that the oxmen occupied a status lying somewhere between that of the slave and that of the bordar. This suggestion better fits the *Domesday* evidence and can easily be tested by referring to certain post-*Domesday* evidence relevant to the *bovarii*. "The Cartulary of Evesham Abbey" refers to certain *bovarii* residing on the abbey's estates in the twelfth century.[36] As at the time of *Domesday*, the abbey's oxmen are associated in pairs and operate the demesne ploughs. The ploughs had been worked, at the time of *Domesday*, by slaves.[37] Evidently, as the system of slavery disappeared, the *servi* tended to work up to the status of *bovarii*. It is difficult to determine how great an advance this represented, since at least some of the oxmen were still regarded as nonfree. The *Liber Niger* of Peterborough Abbey noted that each *bovarius* on its estates was required to pay one penny if he were a *liber homo* and nothing if he were of servile status.[38] The oxmen of the twelfth century were liable to quite heavy labor services, but they had land of their own.[39] This represents a considerable advance over what must have been a servile origin. Some oxmen on Peterborough Abbey's estates held ten acres, and one on the Evesham estate of Blackwell possessed half a virgate. Moreover, the oxmen were closely associated with the *cotarii* in some of their incidental services.[40]

The twelfth-century evidence shows clearly that the oxmen occupied a somewhat vague position between the slaves and the *cotarii*, and that some gradation existed among the oxmen themselves. With this information, Professor Tait's second hypothesis becomes quite tenable. It would appear that the oxmen of the *Domesday* Welsh frontier were men on their way up. They occupied a vaguely defined

[36] British Museum, MS Cotton Vespasian B. XXIV, folios 49d, 53.

[37] Round, "Introduction to the Worcestershire Domesday Book," p. 275.

[38] *Chronicon Petroburgense, nunc primum typis mandatum*, ed. T. Stapleton, p. 163.

[39] British Museum, MS Harleian 3,763, fols. 78d, 79.

[40] Noted by Round, "Introduction to the Worcestershire Domesday Book," p. 274, n. 7.

position somewhere between slave and free—one in which their advance in legal status had progressed much further than the economic
opportunities opened up to them. The *bovarii* represent a stage in
the process by which the slaves of the southwestern shires were
transformed into a free, but regulated and exploited, rural prole-
tariat.

An interesting conjecture may be made at this point concerning
the possible motives behind the creation of this rather peculiar status.
In the official Anglo-Norman manumission ceremonies, the slave was
made free by being invested with the arms of a free man. The climax
of the ceremony was reached when a sword or spear, the *libera arma*,
was placed in his hands.[41] It may well be, then, that the *bovarii* were
armed men. It is interesting to note in this regard that the duties of
the twelfth-century oxmen included the custody of prisoners, a task
which implies the possession of some arms at least.[42] The evidence is
not conclusive, but the possibility exists that the *bovarii* were men
who combined the arms of a free man with the duties of a slave.
Armed men would have been of considerable value along the thinly
settled and dangerous frontier. At the same time, unarmed men
would have represented an actual disadvantage, since their neighbors would have had to protect them. It is only reasonable to assume
that the lords of the border became aware of this situation and took
steps to make the slave capable of defending himself. This required
granting him his freedom along with his arms. The measure of freedom granted was as small as possible under the circumstances. The
result was the creation of a new, and rather anomalous, class—the
bovarii.

The last of the classes we will consider, the *hospites*, is also the
least numerous. It deserves an attention, however, far greater than
its number would appear to warrant. According to the compilations
of Sir Henry Ellis, *Domesday Book* notes only seventeen *hospites*, all
located in the counties of Cheshire (3), Shropshire (7), and Herefordshire (7).[43] An indeterminable number of additional *hospites* are
mentioned in *Domesday*, but their presence is unrecorded by Ellis.
It may well be that he ignored these additional entries because of his
erroneous conception of the nature and function of the *hospites*.

---

[41] *Ancient Laws and Institutes of England*, I, 212, 254.
[42] British Museum, MS Harleian 3,763, fol. 78d for Omberly Manor; fols. 66,
66b for Blackwell.
[43] Ellis, *A General Introduction to Domesday Book*, II, 430, 454, and 481.

Ellis defined the word *"hospites"* simply as "occupiers of houses."[44]
Whatever its rationale, this confused definition obscured for Ellis and
some others who followed him the fact that the essential function of
the *hospites* lay in their relationship to the *land*.

The few *Domesday* passages which mention the *hospites* do not
make this function clear. Some facts, however, do emerge. All of the
hospites pay a money render to the lord of the manor. The only
hospites reported for Cheshire resided on the estate of Hantone. The
estate was of a considerable size, containing 2½ hides. The three
hospites appear to have been the sole inhabitants of the vill, and they
were without possessions (*nil habentes*). Despite this, Hantone was
judged to be worth two shillings and a sparrowhawk annually.[45] This
render must have been a heavy burden for the *hospites* who paid it.
In Shropshire, two *hospites* paid four shillings and eight pence to the
lord of the manor of Letone,[46] while a single *hospes* located at Etone
made an annual render of two shillings.[47] A group of four *hospites* on
the manor of Colesmere paid forty pence,[48] and the seven *hospites* of
Herefordshire, all located at Letune, paid a total of five shillings
yearly.[49]

For what were these men paying? The answer to this question is
found in the *Domesday* entry for the manor of Hope in Herefordshire, which states: "here there are men paying ten shillings and eight
pence . . . *pro suis hospitiis*."[50] The nearby estate of Lyonshall reported
the same situation. Certain men here paid an annual render of one
hundred pence for their hospitality, as long as they wished to have it
(*"quamdiu ipsi voluerunt"*).[51] Although the status of these men is
not stated, it seems clear that they were *hospites*, and that they paid
for their hospitality. Their annual render, then, was a rent.

Domesday gives little clue as to the holdings of the *hospites*, and
is content with merely noting the rent due. Only two of the eight
passages dealing with the *hospites* mention their possessions at all.
One credits seven *hospites* with one plough, and the other notes that

[44] *Ibid.*, II, 94.
[45] *Domesday Book*, fol. 264.
[46] *Ibid.*, fol. 259b.
[47] *Ibid.*, fol. 259.
[48] *Ibid.*, fol. 259.
[49] *Ibid.*, fol. 184b.
[50] *Ibid.*, fol. 184b.
[51] *Ibid.*, fol. 184b.

a group of three had no possessions at all.[52] It is dangerous to draw any conclusions from such a small base of data, but it would appear that the possessions of the *hospites* were few.

The salient characteristics of the *hospites* to be drawn from *Domesday* may be easily summarized. In the first place, they were confined, at least in name, to the western frontier of England. They appear to have been more or less free agents, able to withdraw from their manorial contract at will. They probably possessed little in the way of normal agricultural equipment. Lastly, despite their apparent poverty, these scattered groups were expected to pay substantial rents to the lord of the manor on which they were located.

It is difficult to determine from what pursuits they drew the profits to pay these rents. It is tempting to view them as some sort of industrial workers, but there is nothing in the evidence to support such a view. One group, at least, possessed a plough, suggesting that they were engaged in agriculture. Moreover, if the *hospites* were industrial workers, we should expect part of their render to have been paid in kind, similar to the blooms of iron demanded of the miners and smelters of the Forest of Dean. In view of the evidence, it is most reasonable to assume that the *hospites* were agricultural workers and that their rents were for the use of the land. Their negligible equipment makes it difficult to believe that they were engaged in normal agriculture. It seems most likely that these men were engaged in developing assarts and were paying for the privilege of doing so. This pursuit required little in the way of normal agricultural equipment. After human labor had cleared the land, extremely small teams, often not employing the customary oxen at all, were sufficient to till the light forest soil.[53]

The bulk of the evidence, scanty as it is, supports the conclusion that the *hospites* were settlers who were allowed to assart waste land in exchange for a yearly payment. As time passed, many of the *hospites* no doubt increased their stock and moved up into the class of *liberi homines* encountered in later compilations. Some others must have failed to develop their assarts to the point where their profits justified their rents. These either moved on to new lands or re-

---

[52] *Ibid.*, fol. 184b, 164.

[53] See D. M. Stenton, *English Society in the Early Middle Ages, 1066–1307,* p. 125.

mained where they were, to swell the ranks of the *bordarii* and *cotarii*.

In some respects, the *hospites* appear to have been a response to the peculiar frontier conditions existing along the Welsh border. The region was land-rich and people-poor. Manpower was at a premium, both to defend the land against Welsh attack and to develop the agricultural potential of the region. The lords of the border were no doubt anxious to gain some revenues from the long-devastated estates which lay under their control. It is clear that these lords were willing to offer comparatively easy terms to such men as were willing to settle these estates and provide these revenues. Moreover, there is no indication that the *hospites* were unfree. They must, therefore, have acted to swell the ranks of the fighting men available to defend the region. The Welsh frontier was an area where a man could establish himself with a minimum of capital, and it is apparent that the *hospites* were just such men.

A frontier is, almost by definition, a land of opportunity. It is an area where undeveloped natural resources await only the investment of human labor to yield great profits. Population density, however, is always low on the frontier, and labor is always in short supply. As a consequence, the relative value of each individual is greater here than in less dangerous, more fully developed and more densely populated regions. In this sense the individual is exalted on the frontier; the scope of his activities is greater, his tasks more challenging, and his rewards commensurately greater.

The Welsh border of 1086 was such a frontier. We have observed the processes of immigration and development in full course, leaving their mark on the pages of *Domesday*. We have also seen the opportunities which awaited the immigrants. For the riding men, the frontier was a place where they might for a time retain a privileged status which was quickly passing out of existence. For the adventurous members of such classes as the *villani*, *bordarii*, and *cotarii*, it was a place in which to try their luck as *hospites*, and to carve new and broader fields out of the wilderness. For the less adventurous, the frontier promised freedom from many of the burdensome manorial obligations which blocked the individual's path to personal development. For the slaves, the frontier had a dual aspect. Although it promised arduous labor, here the slave could expect to escape servile status and move up to the slightly higher status of *bovarius*. On the western frontier, unemployed knights could find good pay and the expectation of future rewards in the hire of marcher lords such as William Fitz-Osbern. Common soldiers found land here, and an administration which viewed their peccadillos with a sympathetic and lenient air. Finally, the merchants and artisans of England and Normandy saw a growing market in the west, and found a large measure of freedom under an appreciative government and the liberal laws of Breteuil. The Welsh frontier of 1086 was a land of opportunity for all classes; it had something for everyone.

iv. The *Domesday* Frontier

THROUGH *Domesday* we can see that there was in 1086 a resurgence of English and Norman settlement along almost the entire length of the Welsh frontier. Forests and underbrush were being cleared, and long-abandoned manors were being brought back into productivity. This medieval frontier boom was not a spontaneous process, however, but appears to have been inspired and directed from above. The frontier prosperity of 1086 gives every appearance of having been, for the most part, an artificial development. It was also a selective process. While some areas were the scene of intensive activity, others were neglected or even abandoned. The favored lands were not always distinguished by their fertility or pleasant location. Their primary value lay in their strategic importance or their usefulness in consolidating or improving the holdings of those Norman lords who had emerged as the dynamic force along the frontier.

It was in the direct interests of these lords to populate and develop their estates as quickly as possible. This development would have served the double purpose of increasing their revenues and at the same time providing enough fighting men to render the task of frontier defense much easier. In view of such considerations, it is not surprising that such men as the riding men, *bovarii*, and *hospites* inhabited the border. What is surprising is that there were so few of them.

The *radmanni*, *radchenistri*, *bovarii*, and *hospites* of *Domesday Book* numbered only slightly over twelve hundred men. It is clear that these groups were far too few to have accomplished the extensive reconstruction which was underway in 1086.

An immense task had faced the border shires after peace had been secured in the area. The raids of the Welsh and the forays of Edric the Wild had left large numbers of estates in ruins. In Herefordshire, for example, *Domesday* reported that fifty-two vills completely lacked the teams or men to till their land in 1066. They were, in *Domesday's* terminology, *wasta*. Fifteen other estates were inhabited but had suffered extensive damage and were considered as partly waste.[1] This picture must have worsened in the period after 1066, when the attacks of Edric caused widespread devastation in the northern part of the shire. How great this destruction might have been is difficult to say, but it is certain that additional vills were laid waste, especially in those areas lying near Wigmore and Richard's Castle.

A great deal of progress had been made by 1086. The number of completely waste estates had been reduced to thirty-four. This meant that at least eighteen estates, and perhaps a goodly number more, had been returned to full production. This process was more striking than the statistics would indicate since the waste estates tended to be concentrated in a relatively restricted area. The heavily devastated northwest of the shire had completely recovered, and there were no waste estates in the vicinity of Wigmore. Recovery was almost complete in the area lying between the Dore and Wye rivers. Some waste still existed, but by far the greater number of vills had been returned to cultivation.[2]

Domesday makes it clear that a great amount of capital and a large number of men were succeeding in repairing the damage the shire had suffered. Both men and capital, however, were curiously concentrated in two favored areas—the northwest and the region between the Dore and the Wye.[3] If this process of recovery had been unconscious or undirected, one would expect that the more fertile and protected lands in the eastern part of the shire would have been favored. They were not. This concentration of men and capital suggests that

[1] *The Domesday Geography of Midland England*, ed. H. C. Darby, fig. 32, p. 95.

[2] *Ibid.*, fig. 33, p. 96.

[3] *Ibid.*, fig. 34, p. 97. For a similar treatment of other shires, see the other works of this series.

the process of recovery, in Herefordshire at least, represented a conscious effort on the part of those in authority.

This realization raises some serious questions. Where and how did the Normans acquire the manpower and plough teams which were used in this redevelopment program? We have seen how the frontier protected the riding men and attracted the *hospites,* but neither of these groups were large enough to have contributed significantly to the work that was being accomplished. Again, why did the Norman lords employ this curiously selective approach? Prosperity was not general in *Domesday* Herefordshire. To the contrary, a comparison of the waste vills of 1066 with those of 1086 shows that the greater part of the shire was still distinctly underprivileged. Not only had there been no progress made toward repairing the damage of 1066, but in some areas the number of waste estates had actually increased. This brings us to a third question. From where had these newly waste estates come? It is possible to explain many as the possible result of Welsh raiding.[4] Others, such as those in the relatively well-protected east of the shire cannot be so explained. It is not at all certain, or even probable, that these estates, or even a significant proportion of them, were laid waste as the result of military activity. But even if this were the case, why were these vills, especially those in the hands of the king—immediate overlord of Herefordshire since 1075—left out of the program of redevelopment that was underway?

These three questions are not unrelated. The obvious inference to be drawn is that men and capital were being drained from some regions of the shire in order to be concentrated in others. This suspicion is confirmed by the distribution of slaves as recorded by *Domesday Book.*[5] In the extreme east of the shire, servile elements formed about 25 per cent of the total population. In the fertile central plains, this figure decreased sharply to between 10 and 15 per cent. In the far western part of the shire, along the border but still under direct Norman control, this trend was reversed, and slaves formed between 15 and 20 per cent of the frontier population.

It seems likely that this abnormal concentration of slaves was

[4] *Ibid.,* p. 98.

[5] *Ibid.,* fig. 152, p. 429. These figures avoid the question of whether the slaves mentioned in *Domesday Book* represented the heads of families as did other statuses mentioned. If they should be so regarded, another problem arises; there would be a tendency for unmarried slaves to be concentrated in the dangerous frontier region. This fact would alter the relative percentages somewhat.

caused by their importation, probably from other parts of the shire. The newly waste vills which had appeared by 1086 had not been devastated but abandoned, and their inhabitants used to develop other estates. The slaves were the first to go, since they were completely under the control of their masters and lacked the recourse to customary rights which was open to other classes of society. Other groups must have followed after the slaves had accomplished the first and most difficult labor. Indeed, the very presence of the slaves would have encouraged such immigration. Where slaves, or such men as the *bovarii*, were available to till the demesne, other classes were spared many burdensome duties which otherwise fell on them. It may well be that reduction of such obligations was offered as an inducement to immigration. In any event, later evidence indicates that the villeins of the border were not generally liable to many of the works demanded on estates elsewhere in England. Even their comparatively light duties were replaced by money payments at quite an early date.[6]

It is clear that a general and consistent policy was being pursued in 1086—one designed to redistribute the population of the shire and to direct immigrants into certain areas which had been given a high priority in the process of redevelopment. It is likely that surplus population was being drawn from all the surrounding region. Some areas, however, were contributing an inordinately large number of such immigrants, so great as to reduce their own productiveness. The distribution of waste vills in 1086 shows that the main area so exploited consisted of those estates which the king held in the vicinity of Radnor. It is not surprising that the king allowed or encouraged this, since it was in his direct interest to do so. The security of the interior of the shire and the efficiency of its system of border defense demanded that the border lords be able to develop their frontier estates as quickly as possible. Royal grants of estates along the border were meaningless unless the king provided his vassals the means to defend them against the Welsh. He therefore drew the necessary manpower from his estates in the vicinity, and sacrificed his immediate interests in favor of longer range considerations.[7]

The evidence of *Domesday Book* is tangled and often inconclusive

---

[6] W. J. Slack, "The Shropshire Ploughmen of Domesday Book," *The Transactions of the Shropshire Archaeological Society,* L (1939), p. 34.

[7] An analogous situation apparently existed in Yorkshire. See T. A. M. Bishop, "The Norman Settlement of Yorkshire," *Studies in Medieval History Presented to Frederick Maurice Powicke,* eds. H. W. Hunt *et al.*, pp. 1–14.

and the work that remains to be done to analyze it is immense. The bulk of the evidence, however, points to the conclusion that there existed in 1086 a conscious and effective program on the part of the government to develop the region lying along the border and to encourage immigration into this strategically important area. From Chester to Chepstow, the Welsh frontier was being transformed into an intricate defensive network.

The central portion of this line was under the command of Roger of Montgomery, earl of Shrewsbury and of Arundel. He was the scion of one of the greatest of the noble families of Normandy and his family connections were rather mixed. King William, William Fitz-Osbern, and Ralph of Mortimer were all his cousins. His brothers, on the other hand, were turbulent and disorderly and had brought no credit to the family name. One of them, William, had plotted the assassination of Duke William and had killed Fitz-Obsern's father in the attempt.[8] Roger himself was a firm supporter of Duke William and enjoyed his favor and confidence.[9] Roger's possessions included Montgomery and L'Hiemois, and, through marriage, Bellême, Alençon, and Séez. He was active in support of the invasion of England and distinguished himself at the battle of Hastings. In 1071 he was granted the earldom of Shrewsbury on the western frontier of England. A strong base had already been established in Chester to the north, while to the south William Fitz-Osbern had by this time completed the pacification and organization of his earldom of Hereford. Roger was obviously expected to close up the last gap in a strong western border defense system.

In accordance with the royal frontier policy at the time, Shrewsbury was given what amounted to the status of a county palatine. With certain minor exceptions the entire county of Shropshire was held by Roger as tenant in chief and he enjoyed a wide grant of power. He distributed much of his lands to his followers, and the brunt of the defense of the border naturally fell on them. Prominent among this number was the sheriff. Roger was himself the *vicecomes* of Oximin in Normandy and was apparently fully convinced of the value of a strong and loyal sheriff. He accordingly endowed the office with over seventy manors within Shropshire and some as far afield as Sussex.

---

[8] See chapter II above.
[9] Wace, *Maistre Wace's Roman de Rou et des Ducs de Normandie, nach den Handschriften,* ed. H. Andresen, ll. 4415 ff., p. 207.

The first occupant of this important position was Warin the Bald, whose allegiance had been heightened by his marriage to Roger's niece, Amiera.[10] If the praise which Orderic Vitalis heaps upon him was valid, Warin amply justified Roger's faith in him.[11] By the time of *Domesday*, however, he was dead, and his position, both as sheriff and as Amiera's husband, was occupied by a certain Rainault.[12] R. W. Eyton, one of the foremost historians of Shropshire, identified his place of origin as Bailleul-en-Gouffern, which he had held as a fief, ". . . under Roger de Montgomery, when he was called to fill the more important position of Sheriff of Shropshire."[13]

His new holdings were extensive and somewhat scattered, as we have said. They were concentrated, however, in the hundred of Mersete in the northwestern part of Shropshire. Over 80 per cent of the hundred lay in the sheriff's hands,[14] and he had pushed forward the construction of fortifications in the area.[15] The most important of these was the massive work located at Oswestry, which became the key to the frontier defense of northern Shropshire. From this base of power Rainault was able to extend his power westward into Wales, although he did not succeed in establishing any settlements there. *Domesday* records that two Welsh commotes paid Rainault an annual render of eighty shillings and eight cows as *ferm*.[16]

Immediately to the south of Rainault's holdings in Mersete lay the hundred of Ruesset and the estates of the two Fitz-Corbet brothers, Roger and Robert.[17] Although they held estates scattered over Conodovre and Rinlau hundreds, the main body of their holdings lay in Ruesset and Witentreu, immediately to the south.[18] These lands had

[10] R. W. Eyton, *Antiquities of Shropshire*, VII, 203.

[11] Orderic Vitalis, "Historiae Ecclesiasticae libri XIII in partes tres divisi," *Patrologia Latina*, ed. J. P. Migne, vol. CLXXXVIII, col. 332.

[12] Eyton, *Antiquities of Shropshire*, VII, 205–206. Eyton holds that Rainault was merely exercising the post during the minority of Warin's son, Hugh, to whom Rainault transferred the office and its lands sometime after 1102.

[13] Eyton, *Antiquities of Shropshire*, VII, 206.

[14] J. Tait, "Introduction to the Shropshire Domesday Book," *The Victoria Histories of the Counties of England: Shropshire*, I, 296.

[15] *Domesday Book: or The Great Survey of England by William the Conqueror* A.D. *MLXXXVI*, fol. 253b.

[16] *Ibid.*, fol. 255. The territories of "Chenlei" and "Derniou" probably represent Cynllaith and Edeyrnion.

[17] For this important family of border barons, see the Duchess of Cleveland, *The Battle Abbey Roll: with Some Account of the Norman Lineages*, I, 219–223.

[18] See the Domesday Map of Shropshire in *Victoria Histories of the Counties of England: Shropshire*, I, facing p. 309.

suffered extensively in the disorders which had followed the death of Edward the Confessor. Many, if not most, of the manors of the area showed a considerable decrease in value between 1066 and their acquisition by the Fitz-Corbets.[19] This valuation had risen remarkably by 1086 however. *Domesday* does not mention that any fortifications had been raised in Ruesset. Roger seems to have taken steps to remedy this lack, for Cause Castle was soon erected on a high hill near his estate of Alretone.[20] It seems hardly likely, however, that this was the first fortification in the area. *Domesday* reports that Alretone was occupied by five knights, all vassals of Roger.[21] It is probable that this concentration of military tenants was part of Roger's preparations for the erection of his great castle. A similar concentration of knights was found at the manor of Wrdine (Worthen).[22] It seems more than likely that some sort of fortification also existed here.

To the south of the Fitz-Corbets' holdings, in the hundred of Witentreu, lay the key to the defense of the middle march. Here Earl Roger had constructed his great castle of Montgomery just west of Offa's Dyke. The castle itself was surrounded by over fifty hides of waste land, but not too far away lay eight of Roger Fitz-Corbet's manors. Some agriculture was practiced on these estates, and it may well be that these supplied the immediate needs of the castle's garrison. Three fisheries, an animal trap, and some woods for pannage was the *Domesday* summary of the economy of this rather desolate, but strategically vital area.[23]

South of Witentreu lay the mountainous hundred of Rinlau. The *Domesday* manors of this region were restricted to some few which lay in the valley which the river Clun has cut deeply into the highlands of the forest of Clun. Here too were located the estates of Robert of Sai, or Picot as he was apparently always called in England.[24] Picot's home lay in Argentan, in Roger Montgomery's vice-county of L'Hiemois. It seems probable that, like Rainault, Picot had

---

[19] *Domesday Book*, fols. 255b–256.

[20] Tait, "Introduction to the Shropshire Domesday Book," p. 297; and Eyton, *Antiquities of Shropshire*, VII, 6.

[21] *Domesday Book*, fol. 253b.

[22] *Ibid.*, fol. 255b.

[23] *Ibid.*, fol. 254.

[24] Tait, "Introduction to the Shropshire Domesday Book," p. 297; and Eyton, *Antiquities of Shropshire*, XI, 225.

been brought to the border at the command of his lord.[25] Despite their isolated location, Picot's thirteen manors were well-to-do and yielded about twenty-five pounds annually.[26] They had been worth a good deal more in 1066 but had obviously suffered considerably in the aftermath of the Conquest. Under Picot's management, however, their value had risen greatly by 1086. The center of this compact group of estates lay at the manor of Clun, a vill lying at the fork of the river. A large castle was built here subsequent to the *Domesday* survey. It seems probable that some fortifications already existed, for there was a group of military vassals established here quite similar to those found at Alretone and Wrdine. This settlement at Clun represented the deepest penetration of Norman settlement into the Welsh highlands.

To the south of the estates of Picot lay the Herefordshire hundred of Hezetre. The river Teme ran through this hundred in a sharp arc, cutting across an eastward tongue of the Welsh uplands and forming an extensive pocket of fertile soil. The Teme, together with the Lugg, reached deeply into the Welsh highlands and formed a major route of access from the central plateau of Wales into the heart of Herefordshire. A high and rocky ridge lay along the Teme. A natural cleft ran across the breadth of this ridge, isolating its eastern end and making it a position of great defensive strength. A mound was thrown up on this eastern end, and a timber fortification was built at the command of William Fitz-Osbern. This small fort, replaced by a stone structure early in the next century, became the strong point for the defense of northwestern Herefordshire.

Under the name of Wigmore Castle, it also formed the heart of the holdings of Ralph of Mortimer, a cousin of the earl of Shrewsbury.[27] Near the castle lay a flourishing borough, which paid its lord an annual render of seven pounds. This was not an insignificant sum, considering the liberal terms and low rents the burgesses enjoyed. Near the town and along the banks of the Teme were located a number of manors. These all lay in Ralph's hands, and gave a general air of prosperity and growth. Just to the west lay several manors which had

---

[25] The Duchess of Cleveland, however, identifies Picot with Wace's "Cil de Saie," one of the original conquerors. *The Battle Abbey Roll*, III, 126–128.

[26] *Domesday Book*, fol. 258.

[27] For Wigmore, see G. T. Clark, "Wigmore," *Archaeologia Cambrensis*, Series IV, Vol. V (1874), pp. 97–109.

been held by English thegns under Edward the Confessor, but were now apparently deserted. There is no indication that any effort had yet been made to bring them back under cultivation, and it seems likely that they were mainly used for hunting.

From these waste manors, a great swath of abandoned estates swept southward along what is now the English-Welsh border, centering on a large group of royal manors around Radnor. *Domesday Book* mentions no activity at all in the area except for the fact that Osbern Fitz-Richard claimed eleven manors "on the marches of Wales" which he used only for hunting.[28]

Just to the east of this deserted region lay the hundred of Elsedune, where we can see the basic processes of frontier development well underway. A number of lords held estates in this hundred, but the primary landholder in the area was Roger of Lacy, who held five Elsedune estates from the king and one from the church of St. Guthlac.[29] Progress and intense activity were apparent on all of these manors. The first thing that strikes our attention is the frequent mention of *hospites*. These settlers were found on no less than three of these six estates. New lands were being opened up throughout the area. In the adjacent hundred of Stradford lay the estates of Wibelai and Fernehalle, also in Roger's hands. In the passages describing these estates are found two of the four *Domesday* entries mentioning assarts.[30] This process of agricultural expansion was not restricted to Roger of Lacy's estates. In describing the manor of Wrdeslege, held by Gruffydd ap Maredudd, *Domesday* states that the manor "was waste and still is, except for three acres of land which have been recently cultivated here."[31] It is also clear that labor was in high demand in Elsedune. Roger's manor of Elmelie was being tilled by men from another village, who paid a considerable sum for the privilege. Elsedune Hundred displayed many characteristics of what can best be described as a frontier boom.

Elsedune also shows the early stages of the process which made the marches of Wales a land of castles. *Domesday Book* records no massive fortifications in the hundred, but does mention the existence of

---

[28] *Domesday Book*, fol. 186b.

[29] *Ibid.*, fols. 184b and 182.

[30] *Ibid.*, fol. 184b. It is interesting to note that the other two entries also occur in Herefordshire; on the estates of Marcle (fol. 179b) and Leominster (fol. 180).

[31] *Ibid.*, fol. 187b.

two peculiar establishments each known as a *"domus defensabilis."* One of these was located at Herdeslege and was held from Roger of Lacy by a certain Robert. The land on which it was situated paid no geld, paid no customary dues, and formed an independent region, not a part of Elsedune or any other hundred. It lay in the heart of a deep forest and its population consisted of two serfs and a Welsh-man.[32] After the time of *Domesday*, this small establishment was to grow into the forbidding pile of Eardisley Castle.[33] The second *domus defensabilis* was held by Gilbert Fitz-Turold at Walelege, a manor which had been given to him by William Fitz-Osbern. Only two of the four hides here were geldable. There appears to have been no agricultural activity, and like Herdeslege it was situated in a dense forest.[34] No definite record can be found of the later history of this holding, but it seems likely that Walelege is identical with Lenmore Mount, locally reputed to have been the site of a strong castle.[35] It is easy to see in these two small establishments the earliest stages of the process which produced the permanent fortresses that eventually se-cured the Welsh frontier.

Just to the south of Elsedune Hundred lies the valley of the Wye which here descends from the alpine meadows of Brecknockshire and passes into the heart of Herefordshire. This was a prime invasion route and it was guarded by the great castle of Clifford, constructed by William Fitz-Osbern. At the time of *Domesday*, the castle was in the hands of Ralph of Todeny, brother-in-law of the late earl. Clifford was virtually a sovereign realm. Like Herdeslege, it belonged to no hundred nor did it pay any customary dues. All the tenants of the area held directly from Ralph.[36] These tenants numbered four, named by *Domesday Book* as Gilbert, Roger, Herbert, and Drew. It is not difficult to identify Gilbert Fitz-Turold, Roger of Lacy, and Drew Fitz-Pons, three of the greatest landholders of the shire. Between the three of them, excluding Herbert, they held nine ploughs in demesne and had established the nucleus of a borough which at the time claimed sixteen burgesses.

Ralph himself appears to have taken little interest in Clifford. He

[32] *Ibid.*, fol. 182b.

[33] R. H. Warner, "Eardisley and Its Castle," *The Transactions of the Woolhope Naturalists' Field Club for 1903*, pp. 256–262.

[34] *Domesday Book*, fol. 187.

[35] I. C. Gould, "Ancient Earthworks," *The Victoria Histories of the Counties of England: Hereford.*, I, 226–227.

[36] *Domesday Book*, fol. 183.

held nothing there but one plough and apparently had no men to work it. There was a mill in the castle, but it was not subject to him and was probably not built at his order. As a matter of fact, Ralph had farmed the entire castle to Gilbert, the sheriff of Herefordshire, for an annual render of sixty shillings. Of all of Ralph's extensive holdings,[37] he had chosen to fix his seat at a manor he held in Hertfordshire, rather than in the castle which formed the obvious *caput* of his most extensive holdings. As well as we can judge from *Domesday Book*, Ralph of Todeny took neither interest nor initiative in the development of this major marcher fortress. The credit for improving and garrisoning Clifford, and for guarding this important approach to Herefordshire, must remain with the small group of barons who held of Ralph.

Stretching southeasterly from Clifford flows the river Dore, along a path roughly parallel to, and between, the Wye and the Welsh border. For the first fifteen miles of its length it runs through the narrow valley it has cut in the uplands which tower as much as three hundred feet on either side of the stream. This was the "Golden Valley" into which the English had been pushing since before the time of the Conquest. It was now entirely in Norman hands, but lay exposed to attack from the uplands which stretched along its western bank. The upper valley was controlled by the same Gilbert who held Clifford. The land was almost completely undeveloped and offered Gilbert little revenue except the hawk and two dogs he annually received from the eight Welshmen who were settled on the manor of Bach.[38] Subsequent entries in *Domesday Book* credit the sheriff with holdings totaling fifty-six hides in this fertile valley.[39]

Immediately to the south of Gilbert's manors lay the lands which William Fitz-Osbern had granted to Hugh L'Asne.[40] The center of these holdings was the castle of Snodhill, commanding the northern entrance to the valley.[41] A minor castle was located nearby at Urishay

---

[37] He held estates in Berkeshire, Herefordshire, Gloucestershire, and Hertfordshire.

[38] *Domesday Book*, fol. 187. Also see G. Marshall, "The Norman Occupation of the Lands of the Golden Valley, Ewyas, and Clifford and Their Motte and Bailey Castles," *The Transactions of the Woolhope Naturalists' Field Club for 1936–1938*, pp. 141–158.

[39] *Domesday Book*, fol. 187.

[40] *Ibid.*, fol. 180b.

[41] J. H. Round, "Introduction to the Herefordshire Domesday," *The Victoria Histories of the Counties of England: Hereford*, I, 276.

and acted as an outlier to the major fortress.[42] Three of Hugh's five Golden Valley estates were waste, but the remaining two showed considerable activity. South of these manors lay the holdings of a number of other lords, prominent among them being Roger of Lacy and an Englishman, Alfred of Marlborough.

It is difficult to derive from *Domesday Book* any complete picture of the state of affairs in the Golden Valley. Certain things can be conjectured. Frenchmen and riding men were both common in the valley, and must have made it attractive to the developers because they were able to insure not only agricultural development, but at least some defensive strength. *Bordarii* were attracted by the promise of steady work. One manor records two ploughs in demesne, six *bordarii* and nothing else.[43] The industrious landholder could expect excellent profits from well-developed estates. One of Alfred of Marlborough's estates made an annual render of three pounds.[44] The Golden Valley was fertile, underdeveloped, and strategically important. The men and capital moving into the area would soon plug this gap in Herefordshire's western defenses.

The southern entrance to the Golden Valley was guarded by the castle of Ewyas Harold, perched on a rocky ridge overlooking Dulas Brook.[45] It dominated not only the confluence of the Dulas and the Dore, but also the point where they joined the Monnow about a mile south. This position was of the greatest strategic importance in that, in addition to guarding the valley of the Dore, Ewyas Harold also protected the valley of the Monnow, one of the great invasion routes leading from the highlands of the Black Mountains into the heart of Herefordshire. So important was this position that it is not surprising to note that a castle had existed there before the Conquest, built by the early colony of Herefordshire Normans.[46]

One of the tenants at Ewyas Harold was the same Roger of Lacy whom we have already encountered at Elsedune, Clifford, and the upper Dore Valley. He seems to have been just as active here as he was elsewhere. At any rate, *Domesday Book* reports that, like Rainault in Shropshire, he had managed to establish control over a Welsh

[42] Gould, "Ancient Earthworks," pp. 244 and 254.
[43] *Domesday Book*, fol. 184.
[44] *Ibid.*, fol. 186.
[45] G. T. Clark, "The Castle of Ewyas Harold," *Archaeologia Cambrensis*, Series IV, Vol. VIII (1877), pp. 116–124.
[46] *Domesday Book*, fol. 186. The castle had been refortified at William Fitz-Osbern's command.

commote just to the west of his holdings. The degree of this control is uncertain; *Domesday* merely states that he was to receive an annual render of fifteen *sestiers* of honey and fifteen swine, and was to have the right of pleas over the inhabitants of the area "when the men are there." This last phrase is vague, but it may refer to the seminomadic customs of the free tribesmen. In any event, it is important to note that Roger had made no attempt to plant a colony here. As we have seen, he had no men to spare even in Elsedune. He seems simply to have attempted to gain power and revenue in the area. It may well be that he was simply assuming the position of the local *tywysog*.

To the south of Ewyas Harold and the commote of Ewyas Lacy lay yet another Welsh commote under Norman control. This region, Erging, or Archenfield, had been taken long before by the Anglo-Saxons. *Domesday Book* is vague and incomplete about its status under the Normans. It is clear, however, that no attempt had been made to absorb or displace the Welsh who inhabited the area. They were all regarded as king's men and had certain customary dues and obligations. Beyond this nothing is known of the state of affairs within the area. A strong castle, Goodrich, lay on its borders, and had apparently been there in 1066.[47] Although its original purpose had probably been to pacify the Welsh of Archenfield, it also commanded a vital ford on the old Roman road leading to Monmouth Castle.

Monmouth and Strigoil completed the castle system which stretched clear across the Welsh peninsula. The two were quite similar in a number of important respects: both had been constructed by William Fitz-Osbern, both had, or were soon to have, flourishing boroughs, and both commanded important fords in the Roman road system which linked England with southern Wales. Although both locations were important links in the Herefordshire defense system, Strigoil (or Chepstow) is the more deserving of interest, for it was from here that the Normans made their first permanent penetration of Wales.

At the beginning of the *Domesday* entries for Gloucestershire there is a compact series describing the settlements which the Nor-

---

[47] *Domesday Book*, fol. 181. Rev. Prebendary Seaton, "History of Goodrich," *The Transactions of the Woolhope Naturalists' Field Club for 1901–1902*, pp. 212–225.

mans had made in lower Gwent.[48] On the eastern edge of this region lay the fortress and town of Chepstow, on the western the small colony which William of Scohies had established at Caerleon. The northern limit of settlement was probably defined by those highlands now known as Went Wood. The northernmost place name mentioned is that of Lamecare, which is most likely to be identified with Llanvair Discoed.[49] The southern limit lay along the marshes which stretched south of the line now followed by the railway between Chepstow and Newport. More than likely, this now-fertile region was uninhabited, since the place names of the area are, without exception, non-Celtic. It should be noted that the general area of Norman settlement did not form the spreading wave pattern which might be expected from an undirected advance into a frontier region. It rather formed an elongated westerly thrust, the axis of which was formed by the old Roman road which linked Chepstow and Caerleon.[50]

Within this long and narrow area, the patterns of landholding were sharply differentiated. Generally speaking, the lands of the western portion lay in the hands of the king, and the eastern portion, consisting of lands lying close to Chepstow, was under individual Norman lords. On the royal lands Welsh arrangements were continued with little change. Under Welsh tribal law, homesteads were formed into groups of twelve for the purpose of making food renders to the *tywysog*. *Domesday Book* describes what appears to be a direct continuation of the system under the overlordship of the Norman king. The entry notes that four *"praepositi,"* Waswick, Elmui, Bleius, and Idhel, were responsible for groups of thirteen, fourteen, thirteen, and fourteen vills respectively. Not only was the pre-Conquest Welsh system retained, but it would seem that the native Welsh *maers* were continued in office. In addition to this Welsh group, King William held a few *hardiwicks*, or hamlets. These estates, located at the eastern end of the royal holdings in Gwent, were organized more along the usual manorial lines. Finally, a number of individuals held land from the king in the area. These lands were held freely and without

---

[48] *Domesday Book*, fol. 162.

[49] C. S. Taylor, "The Norman Settlement of Gloucestershire," *The Transactions of the Bristol and Gloucestershire Archaeological Society for 1917*, p. 82.

[50] This road is now followed, along most of its course, by the A48 motor highway.

dues. These men represented a legacy from William Fitz-Osbern's policy of conciliating individuals of dubious loyalty by granting them land, on liberal terms, on the frontier.[51]

The western end of Norman holdings in Gwent was anchored by the castle of Caerleon, located on the western bank of the Usk at the point where the old Roman road forded the stream. This location was one of the most strategically important in southeastern Wales and long before had been the site of the legionary fortress of Isca. The sea was readily accessible from the castle, and a series of Roman roads converged upon the site. These roads, still the best available to the Normans, led west into the vale of Glamorgan, north along the valley of the Usk, and east to Chepstow.[52] The settlement which supported the castle was still quite small in 1086. William of Scohies, one of the more important landholders of Herefordshire, held an estate of eight carucates to the west of the river, and these were held of him by Turstin Fitz-Rolf. There were two serfs and one plough operating on the demesne lands. In addition, three Welshmen had three ploughs and were allowed to continue their Welsh customs (*leges Walensi viventes*). This estate, despite its small size, was valued at the considerable sum of forty shillings. Of lands lying to the north and west of this tiny settlement *Domesday Book* is silent. Apparently, at Caerleon one had reached the very edge of the frontier.

Domesday Book has afforded us an almost uniquely detailed picture of a medieval frontier in operation. Although the account is in many ways incomplete and fragmentary, it is possible to observe many of the processes which we associate with frontier development. Along the frontier an abundance of land was coupled with a lack of manpower. The underdeveloped resources of the region awaited the energies of the exploiter. At the same time, the government was directly interested in having this strategically important area developed and populated as quickly as possible. Under these conditions it is not surprising to see that a frontier boom was underway along the Welsh border in 1086. Land values were rising, population was increasing, and the military security of the region was being assured through the construction of extensive fortifications. Moreover, all of the classes who participated in this process were receiving substantial rewards for their industry.

---

[51] *Domesday Book*, fol. 162a.
[52] R. E. M. Wheeler, *Prehistoric and Roman Wales*, pp. 222–223.

These rewards were not equal, however, and the greatest were reserved for those barons who took up the task of frontier defense. Along the frontier the nobility gained an independence and freedom denied to the barons of the more settled and secure regions of England. The holdings of the border barons were concentrated into relatively compact units, rather than being widely scattered as elsewhere in England. This was true all along the frontier, but was most apparent in Shropshire. This appears to have been the result of a conscious action by the Normans, since such concentrations of holdings were not characteristic of the pre-Conquest Anglo-Saxon system.[53] The military advantages of such a system are obvious, but it should also be noted that this arrangement afforded the border barons advantages which William was loath to grant his other vassals.

In both England and Normandy William made constant effort to limit the building of private castles by his nobility. Along the border, however, the construction of such castles was in the royal interests, since a border defense line could be built in this way with a minimum of royal expenditure. Thus we see numerous examples of castle-building underway along the border. The details of this process are reasonably clear. A certain area was set aside and freed of normal dues. A *domus defensabilis* was then constructed to defend the area while initial development was made. A group of military vassals were moved in as soon as the estate could support them. In the course of time a timber fort was constructed out of the materials which lay closest to hand. Finally, masonry replaced the timber, and the castle was complete. With his compact holdings, and his own castle complete with private army, the border baron was a man of considerable power, and might, if he so wish, defy even the king.

Thus it is clear that the nobility found power and some degree of independence along the frontier. Even greater opportunities awaited them across the border, and *Domesday Book* indicates that at least some of them were taking advantage of them. From their bases of power in England, the marcher lords were slowly bringing Welsh border districts under their personal control. They were not attempting to colonize these areas, but only to control and exploit them. Colonization eventually followed, but it is clear that the leading edge of the frontier consisted of the border barons and their followers, who were striving to extend the peculiar feudal system of the Welsh

[53] Tait, "Introduction to the Shropshire Domesday Book," p. 299.

marches westward into Wales proper. Herein lay a great difference between the Welsh frontier process and the American version with which we are perhaps more familiar. In the American frontier, the dynamic element of colonization and exploitation was the individual—trapper, trader, miner, or farmer. As a consequence the line of settlement moved westward at a faster pace than did political organization.[54] In medieval Wales, however, this order of precedence was reversed. The feudal noble, the embodiment of the political system of the time, provided the active force for westward expansion, and the progress of political organization constantly tended to outstrip that of actual settlement. The results of this peculiarity were to be of some consequence in the development of Norman South Wales.

[54] Land speculation, of course, represents something of an exception to this rule. The normal political institutions of the time—civil law, representative government, and the like—were generally late arrivals to a given area.

v. The Establishment of
the Marcher Lordships

ENGLAND CHANGED RAPIDLY in the course of the eleventh and twelfth centuries. It follows that the institutions with which *Domesday Book* dealt, and the country it described, altered swiftly in the years following the great survey. *Domesday Book* pictures the country as it existed in 1086. This may seem a fairly obvious statement, but it can hardly be overemphasized, especially in regard to the frontier we are discussing. The medieval Welsh frontier was neither a particular geographic location nor a specific group of people. It was a *process*: a process of which *Domesday Book* records only one particular stage. The character of the frontier changed considerably only a few years after 1086. It would have changed in any event, but in this particular case the process was accelerated by the peculiar nature of the royal frontier policy.

We have seen that William the Conqueror finally secured peace along his western border by developing a policy based on balance of power. He stationed a strong group of Norman lords along the frontier to guard against Welsh attack. He then helped to stabilize the position of Rhys ap Tewdwr and used Rhys as a counterbalance to the power of the border barons. As long as both of these antagonistic powers remained intact, each limited the other's freedom of action. It was in the royal interests that this situation be maintained, and William took steps to avoid a decisive clash between the two. It was probably for this reason that he allowed the Welsh kingdoms of Morgannwg, Gwynllwg, and Brycheiniog to retain their independence; they were to act as buffer states. Unfortunately for this plan, these kingdoms never developed sufficient strength to fulfill their roles adequately. Rather than forming a buffer between the Welsh king and the Norman lords, they formed a vacuum. They offered a tempting avenue for expansion, especially for the border barons.

There was little danger that Rhys would attempt to upset this balance of power, for it was in his interests to maintain the situation as it was. Due to the peculiar nature of the Welsh political system, his power was none too secure and he was surrounded by rivals. Any active Norman intervention in the affairs of Deheubarth could have been disastrous for him. At the same time the system worked to Rhys' advantage by eliminating his external enemies. The rival kingdom of Gwynedd was fully occupied with the threat of Robert of Rhuddlan, and the buffer kingdoms were in too precarious a position to entertain any thoughts of westward expansion. The *status quo* was as favorable a situation as Rhys could hope for, and it was in his direct interest to cooperate in maintaining it.

The greatest danger to this balance of power came from the turbulent and land-hungry marcher lords. If the royal frontier policy was to be successful, the border barons had to observe the agreement of 1081 and had to respect the independence of the buffer kingdoms which separated them from Rhys. William was more than equal to the task of ensuring this and he had many advantages working for him. In the first place, he had chosen many of the frontier lords because of their personal loyalty; ties of affection and kinship assured that royal interests along the border would be served. Secondly, many of these marcher lords held estates both along the Welsh border and in the duchy of Normandy. Although rebellion might have gained them a Welsh kingdom, it would assuredly have lost them their ancestral homes. Thirdly, William had granted these men extensive privileges for serving on the frontier. The privileges they possessed may have atoned for the denial of those they coveted. Finally, disobedience to the Conquerer was not a course to be undertaken lightly. He was a ruler without challenger and had concentrated great powers in his hands. Moreover, he used these powers decisively in enforcing his will. While he lived, his authority was supreme and his frontier policy was maintained.

On September 7, 1087, he died and his strong hand was removed from the border. By his wishes, his possessions were divided among his three sons. Robert, the eldest, received the duchy of Normandy, William, surnamed Rufus, became king of England, and Henry was forced to content himself with a sum of money. The balance of power which the elder William had established along the border deteriorated, since his son lacked the power by which he could enforce his will in the region. The border nobility felt no special feelings of loyalty or respect for Rufus. As a matter of fact, many of them had already taken oaths of allegiance to Robert. Nor did Rufus control their Norman estates. These were in the hands of Robert, who quickly became a challenger to Rufus' authority in England. Despite his obviously weak position, Rufus refused to adopt a conciliatory path. On the contrary, he set about to destroy the customary limits which had been set upon the feudal powers of the king, and began to strip the border barons of the privileges they enjoyed. Within a few years he had even resurrected the almost-forgotten doctrine that a fief was a lifetime benefice only, granted at the pleasure of the king. This reactionary point of view must have alienated large segments of the nobility, especially among the border barons. Even this need not have been disastrous, if Rufus had carried out his plans with the determination and pragmatism of his father. These qualities, however, were sadly lacking in him. His personal characteristics were passion, capriciousness, a tendency toward delusions of grandeur and a complete contempt for the basic standards of conduct.[1]

To all of these factors acting against him was added the treachery of his uncle, Odo of Bayeux, who enlisted the aid of many nobles in his attempt to depose Rufus and to place Robert on the throne. The rebellion erupted in 1088, ostensibly over the question of succession. The list of nobles arrayed against Rufus, however, betrays a deeper cause of disaffection. Roger of Montgomery, Bernard of Neufmarché, Roger of Lacy, Geoffrey of Coutances, Robert of Mowbray, Gilbert of Clare, and William of Calais were all prominent among those who took up the cause of Robert Curthose. This was, in essence, a marcher revolt and was directed, no doubt, at gaining these men a greater measure of freedom from the restrictions of royal authority. Despite its powerful supporters, the insurrection was soon quelled by the resolute action of the fyrds and some few loyal barons, all led by the archbishop of Canterbury and by Rufus himself. It is difficult to say whether the movement actually failed, however, since most of

---

[1] For the administration of William Rufus, see E. A. Freeman, *The Reign of William Rufus and the Accession of Henry I*. The complexity of Rufus' character has excited the imagination of many writers. One of the most romantic is H. R. Williamson, in *The Arrow and the Sword* . . . .

the marcher lords who took part appear to have escaped serious punishment. What is more, this rebellion of 1088 coincided with the
apparent disappearance of the royal policy of maintaining a balance
of power along the Welsh frontier.

Bernard of Neufmarché seems to have begun his conquest of
Brycheiniog shortly after the end of the ill-fated insurrection. At
least, in a charter of the same year, Bernard was in possession of
Glasbury.[2] It is thus clear that royal guarantees of the independence
of this buffer state had been allowed to lapse. At the same time the
marcher lords began to probe the position of Rhys ap Tewdwr, and
to seek a means of eliminating him and, with him, the last obstacle
to the conquest of South Wales. It seems clear that the agreement of
1081 still had some force, at least in respect to Rhys, for the means
employed by the border barons were uniformly indirect. In 1088,
Rhys was attacked by the sons of Bleddyn, king of Powys. The at-
tackers may well have enjoyed Norman support in this, the first serious attack on him since 1081. In any event, the attempt failed when
Rhys obtained the aid of a Danish fleet from Ireland. In 1091, another
attack was launched. This time the Herefordshire landholder, Gruffydd ap Maredudd, attempted to assert his claim to the throne of
Deheubarth. The hand of the marcher lords can be seen even more
clearly in this action. Rhys again proved triumphant and defeated
and killed his rival. Despite these victories, however, his position was
rapidly deteriorating. Although he was able to maintain himself
against these Norman-inspired conspiracies, Brycheiniog was slowly
crumbling before the relentless pressure of Bernard of Neufmarché.
In a short time, the independent kingdom of Brycheiniog would
cease to exist, and Rhys would find a strong Norman lordship established on the very borders of Deheubarth. He took the only course
that was open to him when he allied himself with the hard-pressed
king of Brycheiniog. In Easter week of 1093, they moved against the
Norman forces engaged in rearing a strong fortress in the central
plain of Brycheiniog. Rhys had been forced to put himself in the
power of the Normans and, in the ensuing battle, he was killed. With
his death the last vestiges of the agreement of 1081 came to an end,
and the last obstacle to massive Norman invasion was removed. J. E.
Lloyd states:

[2] *Historia et Cartularium Monasterii Sancti Petri Gloucestriae*, ed. W. H. Hart,
Part I, p. 80.

. . . the death of Rhys put an end to a period of orderly, legitimate rule; there was no one who had a rightful claim to the position which he held, and force was to be henceforth the sole arbiter of the affairs of the distracted and unhappy country.[3]

After the death of Rhys, the Norman onslaught began.

Rhys' death was a momentous event for South Wales and ultimately opened the way for Norman domination of that region. Bernard of Neufmarché appears to have been a dynamic figure in the chain of events that led to the demise of the Welsh prince. It was he who led the way in destroying the kingdom of Brycheiniog and forcing Rhys to battle. Finally, it was at the hands of his troops that Rhys died. Despite his importance the accounts of the time are largely silent concerning this marcher lord. Only incidental references, together with the evidence of a few charters, make it possible to discern even the broad outlines of his life. The details of his activities must remain vague.

In his sketch of Bernard, Orderic Vitalis stated that he was a member of the powerful Norman family of Aufay, distinguished by its close connections with, and services to, the ducal house. It had as its *caput* the town of Aufay, a few miles south of Dieppe and on the river Sie. The effective founder of the family was Gilbert of St. Valeri, who established his fortunes by marrying a daughter of Duke Richard. Their son, Richard, continued long in the service of his uncle and was rewarded by being given Ada, the widow of Herluin of Heugleville, in marriage. Richard was greatly enriched by this advantageous marriage. He founded the town of Aufay and gave his colonists the customs of Corneilles.

In 1035, Duke Robert died and was succeeded by the eight-year-old William the Bastard. Normandy entered a stormy period which saw Richard supporting the young duke. His greatest trial came during the revolt of William of Arques in 1053, when, alone of all of the nobles of his district, he remained loyal to Duke William's banner. He garrisoned and held his castle of St. Aubins against the insurgents. Supporting him in this action was his son-in-law, Geoffrey, son of Turketil of Neufmarché. Turketil had acted as guardian of the young duke, and was assassinated while performing this office, per-

[3] J. E. Lloyd, *A History of Wales from the Earliest Times to the Edwardian Conquest*, II, 399.

haps in the same plot that took the life of William Fitz-Osbern's father. Geoffrey now had entered into close contact with his father-in-law's group.

The rebellion was quelled, and the family of Aufay achieved the high regard of Duke William for their loyalty. Geoffrey continued in the ducal service, but with less success than had his father-in-law. He was the lawful heir of Turketil's fortress of Le Neuf-Marché-en-Lions, on the borders of Beauvais. He appears to have been unable to halt the raids of his French neighbors in this region and for this reason lost the confidence of Duke William. He apparently fell far from favor and was finally dispossessed of his fortress for some trivial reason.[4]

Geoffrey had two sons to witness his disgrace in 1060. The one, Dreux, gave up military service and entered the monastery of St. Evroult. He does not seem to have shared his father's disgrace, for his duties consisted of staying with the ducal court and attempting to obtain grants and benefactions for the abbey.[5] The other son was Bernard of Neufmarché, who remained in the service of the duke. Born at the castle of Le Neuf-Marché-en-Lions, he no doubt grew up with the excellent military experience which life on the marches afforded.

There is some question as to whether or not Bernard participated in the invasion of England. Although his name is generally accepted in the lists of the conquerors made by modern compilers,[6] the evidence is somewhat mixed. To support the contention that he *was* present at Hastings, one might point to the fact that he maintained a connection with Battle Abbey so close as to suggest a special regard for the establishment. His name appears on the charter by which William founded the abbey to commemorate forever the battle in which the power of Harold was broken.[7] Bernard later established a cell of this abbey near his castle of Brecon.[8] This evidence is less con-

---

[4] Orderic Vitalis, "Historiae Ecclesiasticae libri XIII in partes tres divisi," in *Patrologia Latina*, ed. J. P. Migne, vol. CLXXXVIII, col. 281. The castle was difficult to defend, and a series of barons appointed by the duke failed in this task. Hugh of Grantmesnil finally defeated the people of Beauvais, and the fief, or a portion of it, was granted to him.

[5] Orderic Vitalis, cols. 455 and 457.

[6] Such as J. G. Nichols, "The Battle Abbey Roll," *The Herald and Genealogist*, ed. J. G. Nichols, I, 202.

[7] *Foedera, Conventiones, Litterae, et cujuscunque Generis Acta Publica . . .*, ed. T. Rymer, Vol. I, Part 1, p. 4.

[8] See *Monasticon Anglicanum . . .*, ed., W. Dugdale, Carta II, 15 Ed. II, n. 8.

clusive than one might think. In the first place, the foundation charter of Battle Abbey must be dated between 1086 and 1087.[9] Secondly,
the Battle Abbey cell at Brecon may have been established as an
analogy to the mother house; to commemorate the battle in which
Bernard broke the power of Rhys ap Tewdwr and delivered South
Wales into Norman hands.

To argue against Bernard's participation in the Conquest, it may
be pointed out that his name is not present in *Domesday*. It is hard
to believe that he would not have received at least some English
lands if he had taken part in the original expedition. While this test
is certainly not conclusive, the burden of proof must rest with those
who wish to include Bernard among the conquerors. The lack of evidence suggests that Bernard did not join William's expedition against
England, or if he did, that he played a very minor role. In any event
the year 1086 found him without English lands, but in attendance at
the Conqueror's court, perhaps in his personal service. The evidence
shows that Bernard's fortunes took a decided turn for the better in the
next two years. His name appears in a charter of 1088 as the donor
of certain lands to the Abbey of St. Peter's at Gloucestershire.[10] The
location of the grants shows that by then he was not only a landholder in Herefordshire, but had already extended his control to
Glasbury, a vill which lay considerably within the borders of the
Welsh kingdom of Brycheiniog. The question arises as to how and
why Bernard had come to the Welsh frontier.

At the time of *Domesday,* Gilbert Fitz-Turold, Alfred of Marlborough, and Osbern Fitz-Richard held the Herefordshire lands
which were later to form part of Bernard's honor of Brecon. Some
few of Osbern Fitz-Richard's lands which later appeared in Bernard's
hands were probably obtained as the dowry of Agnes, Osbern's
daughter, whom he had married sometime before 1088.[11] He also
held the estates of Pembridge, Burghill, and Brinsop, all formerly in
the hands of Alfred of Marlborough.[12] No account can be found as to

[9] It is interesting to note that the name "Willielmus filius Osb'" appears as a
testor to this charter. Since William Fitz-Osbern, earl of Hereford, was long since
dead, it is difficult to discern the identity of this witness.

[10] *Historia et Cartularium Monasterii Sancti Petri Gloucestriae*, I, 80, charters
281 and 282; II, 314.

[11] *Chronicon Monasterii de Bello nunc primum typis mandatum,* ed. J. S.
Brewer, p. 35. For Osbern's Domesday estates, see *Domesday Book: or the Great
Survey of England by William the Conqueror* A.D. *MLXXXVI*, fol. 186b.

[12] *Domesday Book*, fol. 186.

how Bernard gained possession of these estates. The same is true of the estates of Gilbert Fitz-Turold, which formed the greater part of Bernard's Herefordshire holdings. As we have already noted, Gilbert's estates had centered around the vills of Bach, Middlewood, and Harewood, which lay south of Clifford Castle and at the head of the Golden Valley. In addition Gilbert had been entrusted with the border station (*domus defensabilis*) located at Eardisley. By this time he may have commenced construction of the fortifications at Dorestone, Snodhill, and Urishay which were later to connect Clifford and Ewyas Harold to form an unbroken line of frontier defenses.[13]

It has been suggested that the factor that brought Bernard to the frontier was most probably his marriage to the daughter of Osbern Fitz-Richard.[14] Although this is possible, there is no evidence to connect his interests prior to 1088 with those of Osbern. It seems rather unlikely that Osbern would have given his daughter in marriage to a landless knight. In any event, the marriage would not explain Bernard's acquisition of the lands of Gilbert and Alfred. If it is assumed that these lands were granted first, then the factors encouraging the marriage become quite clear. It appears that, for some reason or another, the estates of Gilbert Fitz-Turold and Alfred of Marlborough reverted to the crown and were granted by the Conqueror to Bernard, who was at the time one of his household knights.[15] Once firmly established on the border, he contracted a marriage with Agnes which brought him Osbern's estates of Beryngton and Little Hereford.[16]

[13] I. C. Gould, "Ancient Earthworks," *The Victoria Histories of the Counties of England: Hereford*, I, 236, 244–245, 254–256.

[14] W. H. Hunt, "Bernard de Neufmarché," *The Dictionary of National Biography*. This view is shared by Lloyd, *A History of Wales*, II, 397.

[15] This is substantially the view expressed by W. Rees, "The Medieval Lordship of Brecon," *The Transactions of the Honourable Society of Cymmrodorion for 1915–1916*, pp. 170–172. Rees points out that although Bernard apparently received all of Gilbert's holdings, only a portion of Alfred's estates were granted to him.

[16] It might be well to clear up some misconceptions concerning the identity of Bernard's wife. The Duchess of Cleveland (*The Battle Abbey Roll: with Some Account of the Norman Lineages*, II, 352–353) states that Bernard had two wives, the latter being Nest, the daughter of Llewelyn ap Gruffydd. The duchess apparently derived this information from T. Nichols, *Annals and Antiquities of the Counties and County Families of Wales* . . . . The Duchess holds that it was this later Nest who granted lands to Battle Abbey (see *Chronicon Monasterii de Bello*, p. 35) while suffering "Qualms of Conscience." This is doubtful, since the lands she granted were "*de propria hereditate*," and, at the time of *Domesday* lay in the hands of Osbern Fitz-Richard (*Domesday Book*, fol. 176b), the father

William Rees points out that this order of events is corroborated by the evidence of the charters, which show that the earliest grants made by Bernard were drawn exclusively from those estates previously held by Gilbert and Alfred.[17]

The evidence clearly shows that sometime between 1086 and 1088, Bernard of Neufmarché came into possession of a compact group of estates lying athwart the Wye River. From these estates the comparatively broad valley of the Wye, and the remains of an old Roman military road, led directly into the heart of the independent Welsh kingdom of Brycheiniog. It was perhaps only natural that the energetic Bernard should have expanded along this line.

It is not likely, however, that his first encroachments in this direction took place much before the autumn of 1088. William the Conqueror, as has been said before, discouraged the border barons from disturbing the stability of the frontier. Bernard would not have attempted to circumvent his sovereign so soon after having received the grants which had established his fortunes. William died in September of 1087, however, and the border barons began to organize that rebellion against Rufus which finally crystallized during Lent of 1088. The rebel cause enlisted the aid of virtually all of the families along the border, including the newly arrived Bernard. Together with his father-in-law, he joined the insurgent army which gathered at Hereford shortly after Easter. A rather large force met at this city, where the royal garrison had been recently captured by Roger of Lacy.[18] According to one chronicle, the entire shire of Hereford, the men of Shropshire, and many Welsh joined the expedition directed against the royalist city of Worcester.[19] The rebels were met by the garrison of that city, led by Bishop Wulfstan, and were decisively defeated.[20] By summer the rebellion was quelled, and the major in-

of Bernard's supposed first wife. J. E. Lloyd, considering this matter (*A History of Wales*, II, 397, n. 135), concludes that Bernard's only wife was Agnes, daughter of Osbern Fitz-Richard. Nest, daughter of Llewelyn ap Gruffydd, was the wife of said Osbern, and, hence, Bernard's mother-in-law, not his second wife.

[17] Rees, "The Medieval Lordship of Brecon," pp. 170–172.

[18] Orderic Vitalis, cols. 562 ff.

[19] *The Anglo-Saxon Chronicle, According to the Several Original Authorities*, ed. and trans. B. Thorpe, Part I, pp. 356–358.

[20] Wulfstan's role in saving the threatened city was later magnified into miraculous proportions. See E. A. Freeman, *The History of the Norman Conquest of England: Its Causes and Results*, II, App. D, for a detailed discussion of the development of this tradition.

surgent stronghold of Rochester fell into Rufus' hands. Strangely enough the king's vengeance against the frontier nobles appears to have been quite mild. In the case of Bernard there appears to have been no punishment at all. To the contrary, almost immediately after the collapse of the rebellion he turned to an activity hitherto strictly denied the border barons by royal authority—invasion of the Welsh buffer states lying west of the frontier. By the fall of 1088 he had advanced as far as the vill of Glasbury, and the grant of this estate to the church of St. Peter's of Gloucester may well have been in the nature of a first fruit.[21]

What prompted Bernard to flout a long-standing royal frontier policy by attacking Brycheiniog? J. E. Lloyd, the eminent Welsh historian, suggests that ". . . Rufus could not hold the reins of discipline with the firm hand of his predecessor."[22] This may well be, but it is hard to believe that this was the factor operating in Bernard's case. In the first place, Rufus' power in the summer of 1088 was as firmly established as it was ever to be, and had but recently been impressed upon the marcher lords. Why did the invasion not begin before, or after, Rufus had given "the reins of discipline" such a sharp jerk? Again, it appears to be a general rule that, given a sovereign's weakness, it is the greater, and not the lesser, nobles who are first freed of royal restrictions. Why then was it the parvenu and minor lord, Bernard of Neufmarché, who led the forward edge of Norman penetration, and not the rich and powerful earl of Shrewsbury?

It is far easier to believe that royal frontier policy had been changed, and that the border lords had been given license to attack the buffer states that lay along their borders. Such an interpretation fits well with the facts. It was obvious that the old system of a balance of power had failed to keep the marcher lords from rebelling. Thus the continued protection of the buffer states was of no value to Rufus. At the same time, the restriction was galling to the border barons and had no doubt contributed to the disaffection which they had displayed. Abandonment of Brycheiniog, Gwynllwg, and Morgannwg would have cost the king nothing and would have been useful in restoring the loyalty of the border barons. In this respect it is interesting to note that some of these nobles, including Roger of

---

[21] *Historia et Cartularium Monasterii Sancti Petri Gloucestriae*, I, 80, charters 281 and 282; II, 314. The charter is dated here 1088. It is confirmed by William II in his second regnal year, which did not begin until September.

[22] Lloyd, *A History of Wales*, II, 396–397.

Montgomery, earl of Shrewsbury, had returned to active support of the king by the summer of 1088. It is quite possible that this support was bought by removal of royal restrictions on expansion into the buffer states.

Later events show that, although the king abandoned the buffer states, he continued to honor at least the letter of the royal agreement with Rhys ap Tewdwr. The difference may have been that royal recognition and protection of the buffer kingdoms was *de facto*, but the relationship between the king and Rhys was *de jure* and consisted of a formal and binding contract between the two. Abandonment of Brycheiniog, Morgannwg, and Gwynllwg simply entailed a change of policy while abandonment of Rhys would have required perfidy. On the other hand, the nature of the feudal contract between the Welsh and Norman kings was of a purely personal nature and it is likely that Rufus agreed that Deheubarth was to be regarded as fair game for the border barons after the death of Rhys. Deheubarth, and not Brycheiniog, was the ultimate goal of the Norman lords, and the invasion of the latter appears to have been at least in part a lure to force Rhys to commit himself. Meanwhile, indirect methods were pursued in an attempt to encompass the fall of Rhys. Bernard was the obvious choice to undertake the invasion of Brycheiniog; his lands lay athwart the major invasion route to that unhappy kingdom, and the lands which he might conquer would constitute an adequate reward for his activities.

As we have stated before, Bernard reached Glasbury by the autumn of 1088. Probably with the assistance of Richard Fitz-Pons, lord of Clifford, he advanced steadily for the next two years. Talgarth was reached early in the process, and a castle, Bronllys, constructed at the confluence of the Dulais and Llyfni rivers, probably on the site of the *llys* of the *tywysog* of the commote of Bronllys.[23] He then moved south, along the Llyfni River, extending his control into the valley of the Usk. Moving up the latter, he reached the area where Brecon now stands in about 1091. Brecon was the strategic key to Brycheiniog, and Bernard probably immediately started the fortifications at the confluence of the Usk and Honddu which were later to serve as the *caput* of his honor of Brecon. The topography provided excellent defensive advantages since Brecon lay at the intersection

[23] See G. T. Clark, "Bronllys Castle," *Archaeologia Cambrensis*, Series III, Vol. VIII (1862), pp. 81–92.

of the remains of a number of Roman roads, which were still probably as good transportation routes as could be found.

In the next two years, it seems likely that Bernard continued extending his control over the surrounding countryside, but no record
of such operations remains. The first mention occurs in Easter week
of 1093, when an allied Welsh army led by Rhys ap Tewdwr and
Bleddyn ap Maenarch, king of Brycheiniog, advanced out of the hills
on Bernard's force.[24] The king of Deheubarth had, at last, been
forced to discard the protection of the agreement of 1081 and to
gamble on battle. The Normans met the Welsh force near the new
fortifications, perhaps at the site north of Brecon later marked by
Bernard's donation for a priory of Battle Abbey.[25] The battle ended,
as has been said, with the death of Rhys and the removal of the last
obstacle to a full-scale Norman invasion of South Wales.

Rhys' death, coupled with that of Bleddyn ap Maenarch, allowed
Bernard to extend his power throughout Brycheiniog. His path of
conquest turned down the valley of the Usk, and he advanced in that
direction as far as Ystradyw.[26] Even while this movement was underway, the rest of South Wales was swept by a popular revolt of the
Welsh, who reacted violently to Norman appropriation of their homeland. This reaction, which began in the spring of 1094, at first left
Brycheiniog untouched. In 1095 the Normans of this region attempted to come to the aid of their hard-pressed countrymen elsewhere in South Wales. Attacking through Cantref Bychan and Ystrad
Tywy, the Brecknockshire Normans devastated Kidwelly and Gower,
but without effect.[27] The following year, Brecknockshire itself felt
the violence of revolt, when the Welsh of the area allied with bands
from Gwynllwg and upper Gwent, and apparently gained complete
control of the open country. The Normans sought refuge in their
castles and waited for the flame of revolt to die out.[28]

[24] *Brut y Tywysogion: or The Chronicle of the Princes of Wales*, ed. J. Williams ab Ithel, p. 54. Note that the date given by the *Brut* is 1094.

[25] It may well be that, as Battle Abbey itself was constructed on the spot
where Harold supposedly fell, Brecknock Priory occupied the spot of Rhys'
death.

[26] The bishops of Llandaff complained of this annexation, since it brought the
area into the honor of Brecon, which lay in the diocese of St. David's. See *The
Liber Landavensis, Llyfr Teilo, or the Ancient Register of the Cathedral Church
of Llandaff . . .*, ed. and trans. W. J. Rees, p. 550.

[27] *The Anglo-Saxon Chronicle*, Part I, pp. 361–362.

[28] The various readings of the *Brut y Tywysogion* leave different impressions

Two separate expeditions were mounted in an attempt to relieve these beleaguered garrisons.[29] The first was directed into upper Gwent and experienced no opposition in its advance. It was ambushed, however, on its withdrawal and suffered heavy losses. A second expedition, directed toward the heart of Brycheiniog, was crushed by the men of that region at Aber Llech.[30] The *Annales Cambriae* points out, however, that it succeeded, before its defeat, in performing what must have been one of its major objectives: "Again they came into Brycheiniog and built castles there . . ."[31] There is no further mention of the region in contemporary sources for this period, but it seems clear that the rebellious countryside was slowly brought back under control by the Norman garrisons in the area. The following years were quiet ones for Brecknockshire, in which the settlement of the area was finally established.

Little mention of the processes of the Norman settlement of Brecknockshire can be found in contemporary records. Only the charters help to give some indication of the lines which this settlement followed. Bernard endowed the knights who followed him with extensive Welsh fiefs.[32] The strong fortresses of Tretower, Blaen Llyfni, and Crickhowell were then constructed to guard those passes which offered easy access to the lands south and east of Brycheiniog.[33] This policy of continuing the task of guarding the border of England led to a repetition in miniature of the process which had given birth to the lordship of Brecon. To guard the western frontier of Brecknockshire, Bernard established Richard Fitz-Pons in Cantref Selyff, on the far western border of the lordship. From this base of power Richard continued, on his own, to extend Norman power westward. He moved across the border and, by 1115, was in control of Llandovery

---

of the events of 1094. Most versions read that "the inhabitants remained in their houses, confiding fearlessly, though the castles were yet entire, and the garrisons in them." MS D, however, a corrupt copy dating from the fifteenth century, replaces "fearlessly" with "tremblingly." The former reading is much to be preferred.

[29] Lloyd, *A History of Wales*, II, 406, n. 9. Lloyd is of the opinion that both expeditions originated from the newly conquered region of Glamorganshire.

[30] *Brut y Tywysogion*, p. 58.

[31] *Annales Cambriae*, ed. J. Williams ab Ithel, p. 30 and n. 18.

[32] T. Jones, *A History of the County of Brecknock . . .*, I, 61.

[33] See G. T. Clark, "Tretower, Blaen Llyfni and Crickhowell Castles," *Archaeologia Cambrensis*, Series IV, Vol. II (1876), pp. 276–284; "The Castle of Builth," *Archaeologia Cambrensis*, Series IV, Vol. V (1874), pp. 1–8.

and the surrounding Cantref Bychan.[34] The records state that Richard made this conquest with the express permission of Henry I, and the area was long held in fief by the Clifford family.[35] Richard's achievement offers some indication that the process which led to the creation of the marcher lordships was, to some degree, self-generating.

At the same time that Bernard acted to promote the formation of another dynamic group of Norman border barons, he also created what amounted to a new Welsh nobility by investing the sons of Bleddyn ap Maenarch with some of the more untillable and mountainous portions of his lordship. Gwrgan received parts of Blaen Llyfni and Aberllyfni, while Caradog was granted an otherwise unidentifiable mountainous region. Drymbenog ap Maenarch, Bleddyn's brother, was established in the hills of Cantref Selyff as a neighbor of Richard Fitz-Pons.[36]

It is clear then that the moors and mountains were allowed to remain in Welsh hands, while the Norman conquerors concentrated their activity in the central plains of the lordship. Castles were built on the slopes which overlooked the comparatively fertile valleys of the Usk and Wye. Around Brecon a settlement was established and was granted borough status. Manors were organized, and farming villages soon began to dot the landscape. This agricultural exploitation, one of the more interesting aspects of the settlement of Brecknockshire, was made possible by a combination of circumstances. The land which lay in the valleys of Brecknockshire was, and is, at least partly alluvial in origin. For this reason, the soil has a higher fertility than one might expect from the region. Secondly, although the area is at a comparatively high elevation, it is protected from the extremely heavy rainfall of such altitudes by the high mountains which lie to the west and south. These mountains produce, in the valleys which cut through them, a rain shadow effect which reduces rainfall to tolerable limits. Although these and other factors made agriculture possible to the Normans, the nature of the region is such that it could never have been an easy or very profitable pursuit. In any event, Norman agricultural development was limited to the valley floors, for the

---

[34] Rees, "The Medieval Lordship of Brecon," p. 173; also see the essay entitled "The Family of Ballon and the Conquest of South Wales," in J. H. Round, *Studies in Peerage and Family History*, pp. 181–215.

[35] *Brut y Tywysogion*, p. 122.

[36] Jones, *A History of the County of Brecknock*, I, 62.

slopes were not at all arable, considering the technology of the times. As a consequence, Normanization was restricted to the valleys, where the manors which formed the economic basis of the society could exist. The moors, slopes, and mountains were left to the growth of gorse and bracken amidst which the Welsh pastoralists continued to tend their herds. They took no part in the development of Brecknockshire, other than by paying tribute to their Norman lords, who had established their manors and reared their castles in the valleys far below.

The Welsh of Brycheiniog had lost little through the Norman conquest of the area. For the most part, the Normans could not use the pasture lands which the Welsh valued most highly and made no effort to dispossess the natives of these areas. On the other hand, the land which the Normans had to control to exist were the valleys which the free Welsh tribesmen had little desire to utilize. A peaceful accommodation was possible, in which the Norman lords occupied a dual position. In the valleys, the traditional manorial and feudal structure of Anglo-Norman society was simply transplanted into the new region. In the moors, however, the Norman lords displaced the native Welsh rulers and collected the dues and tributes which hitherto had been rendered to them. The situation was such that the two societies of the region impinged only at the uppermost governmental level, and, by assuming a dual role, the Normans avoided too much contact even here. In discussing the economic aspects of the Norman conquest of Brycheiniog, William Rees states:

> The advent of the Norman . . . did not necessarily imply a violent displacement of the native Welsh. Rather may it be said the Norman agriculturalist of the valley supplemented the Welsh pastoralist of the hills so that economically the area gained by the conquest. The Norman hold on the lowland belt not only weakened the resistance of the Welsh, but also formed a suitable base for expansion into the hill districts from the chief Norman settlements either by force of arms or by the less spectacular but more successful silent diffusion of Norman influences among the Celtic population.[37]

We have seen that Rufus' abandonment of his predecessor's frontier policy spelled the end of the independent buffer states which lay along England's western border. Brycheiniog was the first to fall, and, by 1093, Bernard was actively engaged in transforming that ancient

[37] Rees, "The Medieval Lordship of Brecon," pp. 203–204.

kingdom into his honor of Brecon. The death of Rhys in that year then opened the way for the invasion of Deheubarth itself. The marcher lords were not slow to take advantage of this opportunity. In July of 1093, less than four months after the death of Rhys, Roger of Montgomery completed his preparations and moved down from his mountainous base of Arwystli. In a short time, Ceredigion and Dyfed, the heart of Deheubarth, lay in his hands. If control of this region had truly been the aim of the border baron's activity, then this goal had been achieved; Deheubarth had fallen and the core of Welsh power in the south was broken. But what was the fate of the other two buffer kingdoms, Morgannwg and the mountainous realm of Gwynllwg which lay along its eastern border?

This question is far from easy to answer. The major outlines are clear: the region was conquered by Robert Fitz-Hamon, and was eventually organized as a marcher lordship. With this statement, however, we have presented all that can be definitely said. The silence surrounding the Norman conquest of Glamorgan, and Robert Fitz-Hamon to a lesser extent, constitutes one of the major historiographic problems of the period. The major chronicles, both Anglo-Norman and Welsh, make almost no mention of Glamorgan, one of the richest and most fertile regions of all Wales. The most that can be derived from reasonably contemporary data is a few bits of incidental information which are distorted and often contradictory. To add to the confusion, a series of Welsh antiquarians took it upon themselves to remedy this dearth of information by fabricating some accounts out of equal parts of imagination and popular tradition.[38] The lack of reliable data, the attractiveness of the spurious accounts, and their appearance of authenticity all have tempted scholars to make use of these accounts.[39] Few secondary works are completely free from con-

---

[38] These accounts may be found in the following works: (1) D. Powel, *The Historie of Cambria Now Called Wales* . . ., pp. 88–90. (2) Sir Edward Stradling's account contained in the same volume, pp. 90–107. (3) The "Gwentian Brut" contained in *The Myvyrian Archaiology of Wales* . . ., eds. O. Jones *et al.*, pp. 690–701. (4) The "Brut Ieuan Brechfa," in the same volume, pp. 719–720. (5) "The Names and Genealogy of the Kings of Glamorgan," contained in *Iolo Manuscripts* . . ., ed. T. Williams ab Iolo, pp. 15–16. An English translation of this section is contained on pages 377–382.

[39] E. A. Freeman, for instance, is quite aware of the unreliable nature of these accounts. Nevertheless, he tends to make use of the data and to allow it to color his account. He stated in reference to these accounts that he was "perhaps inclined to put more faith in the general story" than he once thought was justified. See Freeman, *The Reign of William Rufus*, II, 613.

tamination by these sources, and some of the earlier treatments are content to accept this worthless data at face value.

The silence surrounding the conquest of Glamorgan is supplemented by the inadequacy of the data concerning Robert Fitz-Hamon, the leading spirit of this conquest. Poor scholarship has succeeded in obscuring secondary accounts of Fitz-Hamon to the same degree that forgeries have confused the picture of his great accomplishment in Wales. Although the lack of data makes it impossible to construct a detailed picture of Fitz-Hamon and the conquest of Glamorgan, enough material is available to trace the general outlines, and to correct some of the many errors which have crept into treatments of the subject.

Robert Fitz-Hamon was a member of a powerful Norman family who traced its lineage from a close relative of Rollo, the original duke of Normandy. Since the tenth century this family had held the extensive lordships of Thorigny, Creully, Mezy, and Evrecy in lower Normandy.[40] Robert's exact genealogy is a matter of some doubt, but it seems clear that he was a direct descendant of the Haimo Dentatus who was among the nobles slain during the battle of Val-ès-Dun in 1047.[41] It is difficult, however, to decide whether he was the son, or the grandson, of this Haimo. William of Malmesbury states explicitly that Haimo was Robert's grandfather.[42] Acceptance of this source leads to some difficulty, however, in that one is then forced to assign not one, but two sons to Haimo Dentatus. The first of these is Haimo Vicecomes, mentioned in *Domesday* as a tenant-in-chief of lands in Kent and Surry.[43] If Haimo Dentatus is the grandfather of Robert, then Haimo Vicecomes would be his father. This is quite all right, except that a certain Robert Fitz-Hamon appears as witness on certain charters which may be dated as early as 1049, and which are certainly no later than 1066.[44] These are too early for a grandson of

[40] This, and much of the other material in the following discussion is based on T. F. Tout's article "Robert Fitz-Hamon" in *The Dictionary of National Biography*, XIX, 159–162.

[41] Wace, *Maistre Wace's Roman de Rou et des Ducs de Normandie, nach den Handschriften*, ed. H. Andresen, ll. 4037 ff., p. 192.

[42] William of Malmesbury, *De Gestis regnum Anglorum, libri quinque; Historiae novellae, libri tres*, ed. W. Stubbs, Part I, p. 286.

[43] *Domesday Book*, fols. 14 and 36b.

[44] See G. T. Clark, *The Land of Morgan: Being a Contribution towards the History of the Lordship of Glamorgan*, p. 43; M. Pezet, *Les Barons de Creully: Études Historiques*, pp. 21–52; "Chartes normandes de l'abbaye de Saint-Florent

Haimo Dentatus. Thus it would be necessary to assign him another son, one with the name of Robert Fitz-Hamon, to whom the uncomfortably early charters might be assigned.[45]

Some scholars have suggested that Robert was the son, not the grandson of Haimo Dentatus.[46] It is tempting to agree with this view, which would eliminate the need of postulating a shadowy elder Robert Fitz-Hamon. Only the single testimony of William of Malmesbury acts to discredit this suggestion. Furthermore, if one assumes that he was indeed the son of Haimo Dentatus, and was born five years before his father's death, for instance, in 1042, he would have been twenty-four years old at the time of the Conquest, sixty-five at his death in 1107, and of suitable age for all of the charters and the accomplishments which are ascribed to his name.[47]

Whoever his immediate parent might have been, it is clear that he was not an only son. William of Jumièges states that Robert was the brother of Haimo Dapifer, a man whom *Domesday* notes as having been an extensive landholder in Essex.[48] E. A. Freeman goes so far as to identify Haimo Dapifer as the elder brother, but this can hardly have been the case.[49] In a listing of fees held under the church of Bayeux, Robert is credited with ten fees in the honor of Evreux and with the hereditary post of standard bearer for the Blessed Mary of Evreux.[50] Under the system of primogeniture, such family estates and honors normally passed to the eldest son. Since Robert held them, and since no evidence exists to the contrary, Haimo Dapifer must have been his younger brother.[51]

---

près Saumur, de 710 à 1200," ed. P. Marchegay, *Mémoires de la Société des Antiquaires de la Normandie*, XXX (1880), 702.

[45] Tout, "Robert Fitz-Hamon."

[46] Clark, *The Land of Morgan*, p. 19.

[47] Fitz-Hamon probably married Sybil sometime about 1090. This would have made him forty-eight at the time of the marriage. His ability to father four children by her (see *Monasticon Anglicanum*, II, 60) is not unusual enough to present any obstacle.

[48] *Historiae Normannorum Scriptores . . .*, ed. A. Duchesne, 306C; *Domesday Book*, fols. 54b, 100b, and 106.

[49] Freeman, *The Reign of William Rufus*, II, 82–83.

[50] Clark, *The Land of Morgan*, p. 20.

[51] Pezet, *Les Barons de Creully*, p. 20. Pezet makes the same point and, interestingly enough, claims that Richard of Grenville is yet a third son of Haimo. Sources do mention a "Ricardus filius Haymonis" as a Norman lord in 1096. Pezet points out that Grenneville in La Manche was one of the family estates, and that Richard may have derived his name from this place. One must note, however, that Richard Grenville's foundation charter to Neath lists a certain

Fitz-Hamon's early history is just as confused. It seems clear that he was not present in the Norman expedition that conquered England, but even this is disputed. When his biographer, Pezet, considered the evidence, he expressed some surprise that none of the sons of Haimo Dentatus were listed on the Battle Abbey Roll.[52] To this must be added the fact that none of the chroniclers of the Conquest mention Fitz-Hamon as having participated. After having considered the dearth of positive evidence, Pezet was forced to suggest that Robert must have joined the expedition, since most of his immediate neighbors did so. On the basis of this flimsy conjecture, Pezet firmly decided that Robert took an active role in the Conquest of England. Pezet would have been much happier had he read the *Chronicle of Tewkesbury*, which states:

> . . . in the year of our Lord 1066 William, duke of Normandy, acquired England; he who led with him a young and noble man, Robert Fitz-Hamon, lord of Astremerville in Normandy.[53]

One should not place too much credence in this source, however, for it would have been only too easy for the monkish compiler to have attempted to glorify a man who had greatly enriched the monastery, was regarded as its actual founder, and lay buried in an honored position within its walls. In the second place, the records of Tewkesbury appear to have been carelessly kept. In one case, William I is made to confirm the grant of a Welsh church made by Fitz-Hamon. As will be shown later, this seems quite unlikely, and the grant was probably confirmed by William Rufus.[54] Finally, the language of this particular entry is suspect, and introduces the relationship between Fitz-Hamon and the Conqueror much too abruptly to seem an integral part of the passage.

The test provided by *Domesday* is reasonably conclusive. If Fitz-Hamon had taken part in the Conquest of England, we should expect to find his name entered in *Domesday* as having shared in the spoils. His name does not appear, however.[55] This is a very important point, but it has been obscured by Sir Henry Ellis' presentation of

---

Robert Grenville, probably a brother, as a witness. This would add a fourth son, a second Robert, and confuse matters entirely.

[52] Pezet, *Les Barons de Creully*, pp. 274–275.

[53] *Monasticon Anglicanum*, II, 60.

[54] *Historia et Cartularium Monasterii Sancti Petri Gloucestriae*, I, 93.

[55] Pezet (*Les Barons de Creully*, pp. 275–276) states that Fitz-Hamon was listed in *Domesday*. He is mistaken on this point.

MS Cotton Vespasian B, XXIV, especially folios 53 and 55. These folios present an account of those individuals and institutions holding burgages in the towns of Gloucester and Winchelcombe. Ellis presented the list with the suggestion that it may have been one of the original returns which formed the foundation for *Domesday*.[56] Robert Fitz-Hamon appears as a major holder in this listing, credited with twenty-two burgages in Gloucester and five in Winchelcombe. Ellis attempted no explanation of why he appeared in this "preliminary compilation," but not in the finished product. The problem lies in an erroneous dating of the document. Among the names which appear are those of Earl Hugh and Bishop Sampson. The bishop was not consecrated until 1097, and the earl died in 1101. The document dates within those limits and can have nothing to do with the compilation of *Domesday*.[57] The single objection to the *Domesday* test is, therefore, without value.

Pezet was unwilling to accept the obvious conclusion, and, amidst all the rhetoric by which he sought to bolster his contention, he suggested that Fitz-Hamon received a delayed reward for his services.[58] It is true that, a short time after *Domesday*, he did acquire the great expanses of land which formed the honor of Gloucester, which had lain for some time in the hands of Henry, the Conqueror's son.[59] One account, that of the anonymous scribe who continued Wace's narrative, states that he received these lands from the Conqueror himself.[60] The bulk of the evidence is to the contrary, however. The *Chronicle of Tewkesbury* states that William Rufus, not his father, granted these lands to Robert "because of the great labors the aforesaid Robert underwent with his father."[61] Pezet seized upon this passage as proof that Robert earned the honor of Gloucester by his

---

[56] H. Ellis, *A General Introduction to Domesday Book* . . ., II, 446. Unfortunately, Clark accepts this view; see Clark, *The Land of Morgan*, p. 20.

[57] See A. S. Ellis, "Some Account of the Landholders of Gloucestershire Named in Domesday Book, A.D. 1086," unpublished, British Museum, number 10352.h.12, p. 5.

[58] Pezet, *Les Barons de Creully*, p. 275. ". . . on peut être certain que sous l'une des armures de ces nobles hommes portant la gonfacon et la lance, de ces cottes de mailles, de ces longs et larges boucliers dont la tapisserie de Bayeux contient la représentation battait le coeur du baron de Creully . . . . Il ne fut point de recompenses dont il gratifia ses vaillants compagnons."

[59] The transmission of these lands is considered in some detail by Freeman, *The Norman Conquest*, IV, 761–764.

[60] *Chroniques Anglo-Normandes* . . ., ed. F. Michel, I, 74.

[61] *Monasticon Anglicanum*, II, 60.

activities during the Conquest.[62] One wonders why, in that uncertain age, Robert would have been willing to wait twenty-one years for his share of the spoils.

It seems far more likely that Rufus rewarded Robert, not for services rendered to his father twenty-one years before, but for services rendered to himself quite recently. The revolution of 1088 had been quelled by the combined force of the English fyrds and that small band of barons who remained loyal to the king.[63] Fitz-Hamon had been pre-eminent among this group of loyal nobles. In view of this, it is not surprising to see the lush lands of the honor of Gloucester placed in Robert's hands. They had proven difficult to defend during the rebellion, and Rufus had been forced to abandon them while he pursued the siege of Rochester. By placing Robert in Gloucester, he not only rewarded a faithful follower, but also took steps to strengthen the defenses which barred the routes to London to the powerful, faithless, and turbulent frontier nobility.[64] Thus it was the expediency of royal politics, rather than the lure of the frontier or his accomplishments during the Conquest, which first brought Fitz-Hamon to the Welsh border.

He soon cemented his position there by marrying Sybil, the daughter of Roger of Montgomery and sister of Robert of Bellême. After his marriage, a blanket of silence descends upon his activities as earl of Gloucester. Pezet, in his customary attempt to exalt the position and activities of the baron of Creully, held that he joined Robert Curthose in the First Crusade.[65] This seems unlikely for a number of reasons. In the first place, Fitz-Hamon, a close confidant and supporter of William Rufus, would not have joined forces with a man who had a counterclaim to the throne. We should expect that Curthose received no more support from Fitz-Hamon than he did from Rufus. Robert's supporters were not Fitz-Hamon's friends. Secondly,

---

[62] Pezet, Les Barons de Creully, p. 278.

[63] The Anglo-Saxon Chronicle Part I, pp. 356–358.

[64] One need not believe, as does G. T. Clark (in The Land of Morgan), that the purpose of this grant was to provide Robert with a strategic location for the invasion of Glamorgan. No indication can be found that Glamorgan presented either a danger or an attraction for William Rufus. The events of 1088, on the other hand, had shown clearly that the marcher lords did present a danger. Only Wulfstan had stood between Rufus and the armies of the border.

[65] Pezet, Les Barons de Creully, p. 283. Pezet's only authority for this remark seems to be the testimony of L. de Masseville, Histoire Sommaire de Normandie, I, 246–249. De Masseville gives no indication of the sources from which he drew his list of the companions of Curthose.

Fitz-Hamon had much at home to occupy his attention. Probably by now he had occupied Glamorgan, and was engaged in the immense task of organizing and developing his new acquisition. Moreover, a general Welsh insurrection had broken out in 1094, and the Welsh of Brycheiniog, Gwynllwg, and upper Gwent were in arms by 1096. It is unlikely that he would have left his newly won domains surrounded by powerful enemies.[66] A third point is that no contemporary account of the crusade mentions Fitz-Hamon. Fourthly, as Pezet himself points out, Curthose was still on his return trip from the Holy Land when he received word of Rufus' death.[67] Robert, on the other hand, was in England, and in Rufus' company, on the very day Rufus was to die.[68] Finally, Fitz-Hamon joined the forces of Henry in the confusion following the death of William Rufus.[69] If he had spent the previous four years under the command of Curthose, it is difficult to explain his rapid espousal of the duke's rival.[70] It is clear that Robert Fitz-Hamon did *not* join the First Crusade; the close of the eleventh century found him ensconced on the marches of Wales, consolidating the conquest of the Welsh kingdom of Morgannwg.

In the struggle between Henry and Robert Curthose, Fitz-Hamon took an active part on behalf of the former. He engineered a truce between the two; but it failed, and armed conflict broke out. He gathered followers from his paternal estate in Normandy and attacked the nearby town of Bayeux, held by Duke Robert's supporters. The attack failed, and Fitz-Hamon himself was led captive into the town.[71] This defeat stung Henry into action, and he attacked Bayeux. He forced the liberation of Fitz-Hamon and then devastated the town. Fitz-Hamon accompanied Henry in his successful attack on Caen, and was active during the subsequent siege of Falaise. In this

[66] Lloyd, *A History of Wales*, II, 406. Lloyd refers to Norman expeditions directed against the Welsh in 1096. If his inference is correct that these forces came from Glamorgan, they may well have been led by Fitz-Hamon himself.

[67] Pezet, *Les Barons de Creully*, p. 284.

[68] William of Malmesbury, Part I, p. 333. This is not too telling a point, however, since Robert was notoriously slow in relinquishing the delights of his triumphal return. Fitz-Hamon could have decided to precede him. William of Malmesbury does picture Fitz-Hamon as transmitting to Rufus the warning vision of a *monachus quidam transmarinus*. However, this says only that the monk was foreign, and not that he was in foreign parts when communicating this vision to Fitz-Hamon.

[69] William of Malmesbury, Part I, p. 394.

[70] Pezet, *Les Barons de Creully*, pp. 284–285. Pezet suggests a falling-out between Fitz-Hamon and the duke.

[71] Wace, ll. 11,125 ff., pp. 469 ff.

last struggle, he suffered an injury which deprived him of his reason and forced his withdrawal from active life.[72] He was returned to England, where he lingered for a time, before dying in March of 1107, without male issue. His body was then interred at Tewkesbury, the abbey which he had done so much to enrich and glorify.[73]

Very little more is known of the life of Robert Fitz-Hamon. The striking lack of information concerning him makes every account of his life more or less unsatisfactory. Unless new information is found, the only aim of the biographer can be to clear away the structure of error which contradictory evidence and ill-founded conjecture have reared about the man. Much the same is true of the story of Fitz-Hamon's great achievement: the conquest of Glamorgan. We have already remarked on the dearth of data concerning this event and mentioned the spurious accounts perpetrated by the Welsh anti-quarians. Although the falsity of this narrative has long been known, many of the older works on the subject, otherwise quite respectable, have been contaminated. For this reason, it is well for the student of the subject to be acquainted with the details of this rather romantic tale.

According to this tradition, the conquest of Glamorgan occurred in the following manner.[74] Cydifor ap Gollwyn, a great chieftain of Deheubarth, died in the year 1091, and his two sons, Eneon and Maredudd, rebelled against the authority of the reigning king, Rhys ap Tewdwr. The brothers allied themselves with Gruffydd ap Mare-dudd ab Owain, a claimant to the throne of Deheubarth. The allies met Rhys at Llandudoch, and in the ensuing battle were defeated, with Gruffydd being killed. So far, the account of the antiquarians agrees quite well with contemporary narrative. From this point on, however, the antiquarian tradition presents events for which no contemporary source can be found.

According to this narrative, Eneon survived the battle, and fled to the court of Jestyn ap Gwrgant, king of Morgannwg, who had also opened hostilities against Rhys.[75] Eneon was well received at the court, perhaps due to the fact that he had "served in England before,

[72] At Falaise, and not Tinchebrai as Clark states in *The Land of Morgan*, p. 43.

[73] *Monasticon Anglicanum*, II, 60.

[74] For the source of this tradition, see note 38 above.

[75] Jestyn was probably an actual person. Although no contemporary evidence of his existence can be found, his name appears immediately after the conquest as the patronymic of certain Welsh lords in Glamorgan.

and was well-knowen and acquainted with all the English nobilitie."[76]
He was given the promise of Jestyn's daughter in marriage and, in
exchange, offered to secure the services of a Norman army in
Jestyn's struggle against Rhys.[77] He obtained the aid of Robert Fitz-
Hamon, twelve other knights, and a sizable force of Norman men-at-
arms. The contingent sailed for Glamorgan and landed at Porthkerry
early in 1093. Jestyn and Fitz-Hamon made a concerted attack on
Dyfed, devastating the region. Rhys struck back, and met the allies
in battle at Bryn-y-Beddau, near the border of Brycheiniog. The
allies were victorious, and not only Rhys, but his two sons, Goronwy
and Cynan, were killed. The triumphant Jestyn paid the Normans
their promised rewards; and Fitz-Hamon's force returned to their
ships. Jestyn was not so faithful to the bargain he had struck with
Eneon. Having been scorned, Eneon pursued the departing Normans,

and when he came to the shoare, they were all ashipboard; then he
shouted to them, and made a signe with his cloake, and they turned againe
to know his meaninge.[78]

Eneon spoke with Fitz-Hamon, and urged him to attack the faithless
Jestyn. The Normans

were easilie persuaded, and so vngratefully turned all their power
against him, for whose defense they had come thither, and at whose hands
they had been well intertained, and recompensed with rich gifts and great
rewards. At first they spoiled him of his Countrie, who mistrusted them
not, and took all the fertile and valey ground to themselves and left the
barren and rough mountains to Eneon for his part.[79]

The battle was fought at Mynedd Bychan, near Cardiff, where
Jestyn himself was killed. Eneon, henceforth surnamed *fradwr*, or
traitor, received the lordship of Senghenydd as his portion. The
various accounts of the conquest of Glamorgan then end with a listing
of the twelve knights who followed Fitz-Hamon.[80] These lists agree in
recording the names of Londres, Stradling, St. John, Turbeville,
Grenville, Humffreville, St. Quentin, Soore, Sully, Berkeroll, Syward,
and Fleming.

[76] Powel, *The Historie of Cambria*, p. 89.
[77] *Ibid.*, p. 92. In Sir Edward Stradling's account, Eneon appears simply as a
follower of Jestyn—"a Gentleman of his."
[78] *Ibid.*, p. 89.
[79] *Ibid.*, p. 89.
[80] That is, Powel's and Stradling's accounts so end.

These accounts can be directly verified in only two respects: in their account of the death of Rhys ap Tewdwr, and in the genealogies appended to the texts. In both instances contemporary data cast doubts on the narrative. In the first place, these Elizabethan versions ascribe the death of Rhys to the allied force of Jestyn and Fitz-Hamon. Genuine records which refer to this event make no mention of such an allied army. To the contrary, they explicitly state that Rhys met his death at the hands of the Normans of Brecknockshire.[81] In addition to this, the genealogies are clearly in error. While some of the names are probably those of original conquerors, the Stradlings, for instance, did not settle in Glamorgan until considerably after the conquest of the region.[82] The completeness and romantic detail of the accounts found in Powel's *Historie* create distrust by their very richness. The well-developed narrative seems to be more a literary endeavor based perhaps on local tradition than a sober history based upon now-inaccessible evidence.[83]

The narratives found in the *Historie*, however, were corroborated by data presented by more recent Welsh antiquarians. In the *Myvyrian Archaiology* and the *Iolo Manuscripts*, Edward Williams presented what he said were transcripts which he had made during his distinguished career, from original manuscripts.[84] They verified the earlier narrative in all essential points. For this reason, many were more disposed to accept the Elizabethan narrative than before. More recent scholarship, however, has branded the "transcriber" of these "documents" as having been guilty of numerous forgeries.[85] Thus, all accounts which have presented this rather romantic account of the conquest of Glamorgan have proven to be of the most dubious validity. Since almost nothing contained in the Elizabethan narrative can be corroborated, it must be regarded as conjecture, or at the most as representing a sixteenth-century popular tradition.

The genuine data is extremely limited and appears to be rather untrustworthy. The evidence as to the time at which the conquest was made can be briefly summarized as follows.

(1) *The Annals of Margan* states: "... and the city of Cardiff was

---

[81] Lloyd, *A History of Wales*, II, 402, n. 9.

[82] Clark, *The Land of Morgan*, p. 187; Freeman, *The Reign of William Rufus*, II, 613.

[83] Clark makes this same point: Clark, *The Land of Morgan*, p. 18.

[84] *The Myvyrian Archaiology of Wales*, pp. 719–720 and 690–701.

[85] G. J. Williams, *Iolo Morgannwg, a Chywyddau'r Ychwanegiad.*

built, under King William I."[86] This would indicate that Norman power was established in Glamorgan by 1081. This period, however, is prior to the founding of Margan, and the account contained in the annals is clearly a conflation, probably of a Winchester chronicle and some other source. Since the *Annals* make no mention of William's visit to South Wales in this same year, it seems unlikely that the sources from which they are drawn were well acquainted with affairs on the Welsh border at this time. If this is true, the Margan annals may represent only a popular tradition, or, at best, a transitory aspect of William's visit to Wales.

(2) A somewhat more impressive piece of information may be found in the *Cartulary of St. Peter's of Gloucester*. This cartulary records a confirmation by William the Conqueror in the following words:

In the year of our Lord 1086, I, William, King of the English, upon the petition of Serlo, abbot of Gloucester, and certain of my nobles, concede to God and to the church of St. Peter in Gloucester possession of [those] lands which archbishop Thomas held of the same church. To wit: Lecche, Otidona, Standisse; and also the church of St. Cadoc, with the lands which Robert Fitz-Hamon gave to the same abbey.[87]

If the dating of the document is correct, this passage would indicate that Robert Fitz-Hamon held Welsh lands under William I, and hence prior to 1087.[88] Few scholars would be willing to assign such an early date to the conquest of the kingdom of Morgannwg. The objections which might be raised are many. In the first place, there is the silence of *Domesday* on this point. This compilation minutely records the composition of the small outpost the Normans had established on the banks of the Usk. It is silent concerning any acquisitions further west. It is difficult to believe that a permanent Norman settlement in Glamorgan would completely have escaped the notice of these compilers. Secondly, it seems unlikely that Fitz-Hamon could have undertaken such an extensive task as the subju-

---

[86] *Annales de Margan*, ed. H. R. Luard, p. 4. MS D of the *Brut y Tywysogion* agrees, but its editor characterizes it as "very carelessly constructed, the facts in many instances perverted and the language frequently obscure." See *Brut y Tywysogion*, p. xlvi.

[87] *Historia et Cartularium Monasterii Sancti Petri Gloucestriae*, I, 334, *i.e.*, fol. 85 of the cartulary. Serlo was abbot of the monastery from 1072 to 1104.

[88] See Freeman, *The Reign of William Rufus*, II, 84, n. 2. Freeman suspects that an erroneous date has been given by the cartulary.

gation of Morgannwg without possessing an equally extensive base of attack from which to draw the manpower and revenues necessary to support the operation. The conquests begun by other border lords illustrate that this was the normal procedure. Bernard of Neufmarché possessed considerable lands in Herefordshire from which he advanced into Brycheiniog, as did Roger of Lacy. Roger of Montgomery, the conqueror of Deheubarth, was, of course, earl of Shrewsbury. Even Braose's conquest of Buellt was based upon his early grant of lands around Radnor.[89] More instances could be adduced, but it is clear that the conquerers of South Wales generally launched their attacks from extensive landholdings near the object of their attack.[90] Fitz-Hamon did possess such holdings, but he did not acquire them until after the death of William I.[91] If Fitz-Hamon undertook the conquest of Glamorgan before he received his vast Gloucestershire holdings, his achievement was quite unique in character and represented a radical departure from the general mode of Norman operations in the region.

The evidence concerning the conquest of Morgannwg is thus not only scanty, but apparently untrustworthy, and assigns a date to the conquest which is far too early. Some scholars would place the conquest of Glamorgan after 1093 in order to make it accord with the general Norman onslaught which followed the death of Rhys ap Tewdwr.[92] This is not a necessary supposition, however, since Morgannwg, like Brycheiniog, was a buffer kingdom. The forces which acted to protect Rhys and Deheubarth ended in 1093, it is true, but the policy protecting the buffer kingdoms ended as early as 1088. Brycheiniog was invaded in that year, and there is no reason to assume that the invasion of Morgannwg was much delayed.

It is impossible to draw any conclusions from the scanty and fragmentary evidence which has survived. It can only be stated that at some time, very probably after the accession of William Rufus, Normans under Robert Fitz-Hamon occupied the lowland region of Glamorgan. Various features of this occupation strongly suggest that the attack was launched across the Bristol Channel, rather than overland.

[89] Chartes normandes de l'abbaye de Saint-Florent près Saumur, de 710 à 1200," p. 14, n. 2.

[90] Freeman, *The Reign of William Rufus*, II, 73–74.

[91] See the discussion of this point earlier in this chapter.

[92] Lloyd, *A History of Wales*, II, 398–399; Clark, *The Land of Morgan*, pp. 18–19.

The most natural invasion route for the Normans to have followed consisted of the Roman road leading from Caerleon to Cardiff and then through the vale of Glamorgan along the line now followed by the A48 highway. If this were the route used, we should expect the conqueror of Glamorgan to be also the lord of Gwent. He was not, but was, rather, the lord of lands lying directly across the Bristol Channel from the region invaded. It is clear that, although the Via Juliana had acted as the axis of early Norman penetration into Wales, this route was abandoned by Fitz-Hamon and his colleagues. Glamorgan was invaded from Gloucestershire, Gower from Somersetshire, Carmarthenshire from Devonshire, and Pembrokeshire from the north. The cause of this new departure can easily be seen in the topography of Glamorgan. On the eastern and western borders of the country, tongues of highland project southwards from the upland mass of central Wales, and extend to within a short distance from the sea. In these two places, Avon in the west and Senghenydd in the east, the Roman road runs at the very foot of the mountains. At these two points the overland route of South Wales clearly lay under a constant threat of Welsh attack. The efficiency of the road seems not to have been worth the expenditure which would have been necessary to fortify these points adequately. As a matter of fact, Fitz-Hamon not only neglected to fortify these places at all, but actually left the highland regions in the hands of native Welsh chieftains, and made no effort to extend any direct Norman authority there. Even now these two upland areas are among the least anglicized of the county of Glamorganshire. He could have afforded such a negligent policy only if the Via Juliana held no strategic value for him. Furthermore, the road could have been without strategic value only if Fitz-Hamon were assured of secure sea communications with less threatened Norman-held lands, most probably those which he held in Gloucestershire.

The conquest of Glamorgan by sea in itself represents a radical innovation in Norman methods of invasion. It seems to have been a rather dangerous policy in view of the continuing strength of the sea raiders who had long dominated the region of the Irish Sea. Numerous indications exist that the threat of attack by such raiders influenced the policies of the Norman conquerors. When Gower was occupied, for instance, two castles would have been quite sufficient to defend the peninsula from attack by the mainland Welsh. Far more than two castles were constructed, however, and most of them were located in positions of no value except as defense from sea-borne attack.[93] Fitz-Hamon appears to have ignored this danger when embarking on the conquest of Glamorgan, and after the occupation of the region, took no extraordinary steps to construct defenses on the seacoast. Two factors possibly influenced his thinking in this matter. In the first place, the coast of Glamorgan was vulnerable to sea-raiders at too many points to make effective fortifications feasible. While such raids could have been irritating, the raiders could have threatened Fitz-Hamon seriously only if they possessed a mainland base. The Normans could reasonably expect to be able to control any base which such raiders might attempt to establish. Secondly, in all probability there existed a relatively large Scandinavian agricultural and trading community in the vale of Glamorgan.[94] It seems likely that Fitz-Hamon expected amicable relations with the countrymen of his new tenants.

The sources are silent concerning the Scandinavian settlement, which may have aided him in his conquest of the region. In any event it is clear that the existence of this colony influenced the disposition which Fitz-Hamon made of the newly won area. The area of Scandinavian settlement, which corresponded roughly to the vale of Glamorgan proper, became the core of his lordship, and was retained under his direct control as the body of the shire.[95] This region, comprising the only lands of any appreciable agricultural worth in the county, was apparently devoid of Welsh, and Celtic place-names are nonexistent in the area. The northern frontier of this region was formed by the old Roman road, and Fitz-Hamon took care to retain personal control of Cardiff, Cowbridge, and Kenfig, all centers lying along this northern border and linked by the Via Juliana. At Cardiff and Kenfig he maintained fortresses which not only protected the northern borders of the body of the shire, but were also able to act as

[93] D. T. Williams, "Gower: A Study in Linguistic Movements and Historical Geography," *Archaeologia Cambrensis*, LXXXIX (1934), 312.

[94] See B. G. Charles, *Old Norse Relations with Wales*. The possibility and extent of Norse settlement in Wales have been much inflated. Charles rejects these claims in every area except Glamorgan, where the evidence indicates that a permanent agricultural settlement was made.

[95] Place-name studies have roughly defined the area of Scandinavian settlement. See D. R. Paterson, "The Scandinavian Settlement of Cardiff," *Archaeologia Cambrensis*, Series VII, Vol. LXXVI (1921), pp. 53–83; "Scandinavian Influences in the Place-Names and Early Personal Names of Glamorgan," *Archaeologia Cambrensis*, Series VI, Vol. XX (1920), pp. 31–89.

ports for a coastal fleet.[96] Fitz-Hamon thus retained direct control of
the most fertile areas of the old kingdom of Morgannwg, together
with a relatively large settlement of non-Welsh people from which he
could draw manpower in case of need. The care which was taken to
organize and defend this area makes it clear that the vale of Glamorgan and its Scandinavian settlement was regarded by Fitz-Hamon as
forming the core of his holdings and providing the firmest base for
his power.

To a greater or lesser extent, Welshmen and Celtic influences were
present throughout Glamorgan outside of the vale proper. The general rule seems to have been that Welsh population and culture was
concentrated in the uplands, while the river valleys were largely devoid of such influences. This entire region was organized into member lordships, perhaps corresponding to earlier Welsh commotes,
each of which was accorded special treatment based upon particular
local conditions. From the Norman point of view, the most valuable
lands were those in which Celtic influences were least, both because
this allowed the importation of a more subservient population and because such lands were of a higher agricultural potential than those
favored by the Welsh. With these considerations in mind, we need
not be surprised to see that the lordships of Meisgyn and Glyn
Rhondda, comprised of the valleys of the Taff and Rhondda respectively, were kept under the direct control of the earl himself. To these
two must be added the somewhat mountainous, but strategic district
known as Tir yr Iarll (Earl's Land), lying between the Avon and
Ogmore rivers. Four districts, Coety, Llanblethian, Neath, and Tala-
van were placed in the hands of Fitz-Hamon's vassals. Each of these
constituted a separate member lordship, but their organization was
somewhat similar. Norman power in each was concentrated in the
fertile and arable lowland area. The mountainous portion of the district, however, constituted a "welshery," in which Welsh laws and
customs were allowed to continue with a minimum of Norman interference. The Norman lords apparently endeavored to maintain a dual
position with respect to the Welsh and non-Welsh tenants, for in
Neath and Coety, at least, there is some indication that the ruling
families of Grenville and Turbeville married Welsh heiresses.[97]

[96] At least these places were *able* to provide ports. There is no evidence that
any such fleet existed.
[97] For the family of Turbeville, see G. T. Clark, "Coyty Castle and Lordship,"
Archaeologia Cambrensis, Series IV, Vol. VIII (1877), pp. 1–21; "The Manor-

Finally, three mountainous districts were allowed to remain under the direct control of Welsh chieftains. One of these, Senghenydd, was granted to Eneon, the "Eneon Fradwr" of the Elizabethan narrative. Welsh life and customs remained undisturbed in this region for many years. The Welsh lords of the region were little affected by Normanization, and maintained a fierce independence for many centuries.

To the west the situation was quite different. The lordships of Ruthyn and Avon were granted to two sons of Jestyn ap Gwrgant. These Welsh lords of Avon especially showed the effects of Normanization. Under Caradog ap Jestyn (*ca.* 1078–1148), Avon was transformed into a Norman lordship. A castle was constructed on the bank of the Avon River, and a Welsh borough established at Aberafon. Intermarriage brought the ruling family closer to conformity with the ideals of Anglo-Norman aristocracy. The lords of Avon thus became benefactors of Margam and Neath, dropped the Welsh system of patronymics, and adopted the family name of Avene. By the fourteenth century, Avon was, to all intents and purposes, an English district, and its lords members of the English aristocracy.[98]

The processes by which Glamorgan was conquered are obscure, but the general outlines of its settlement are clear. The governing philosophy of the conquerors is evident in the details of the post-conquest political organization of the region: to reduce friction and reach an early *modus vivendi* through decentralization and recognition of the local problems of each of the separate districts which composed the lordship. There appears to have been no single rule which governed the organization and administration of Glamorgan. This is, in itself, most significant.

Brecknock and Glamorgan were only two of a number of Norman lordships established in Wales in the closing years of the eleventh century. In the course of time, the Normans succeeded in extending at least nominal authority throughout all South Wales, and organizing the region into the distinctive political entities which we know as the marcher lordships. Cemais, Pembroke, Kidwelly, Laugharne, Gower, and others, not to mention such inland districts as Buellt and

---

ial Particulars of the County of Glamorgan," *Archaeologia Cambrensis*, Series IV, Vol. VIII (1877), pp. 249–269; Vol. IX (1878), pp. 1–21 and 114–134. For the Grenvilles, see J. H. Round, *Family Origins and Other Studies* . . ., p. 138.

[98] For the lords of Avon, see G. T. Clark, "The Lords of Avan, of the Blood of Jestyn," *Archaeologia Cambrensis*, Series III, Vol. XIII (1867), pp. 1–44; "The Manorial Particulars of the County of Glamorgan."

Elfael, are all worthy of study. The character of each of these lordships was unique, representing, as it did, a particular response to
unique local conditions and problems. The differences between the
marcher lordships were sometimes striking. Cemais, situated on the
very edge of the border, faced constant danger of being swamped by
the overwhelming numbers of native Welsh who surrounded the
lordship on all sides. Lacking a firm agricultural base to attract immigration, Cemais gradually absorbed Celtic influences and population, until it became decidedly pro-Welsh in outlook. In return, Cemais became an area of acculturation, through which Norman influences percolated into Welsh Wales.[99] Only a few miles to the south,
the lordship of Pembroke presented a strikingly different aspect. This
lordship consisted of a relatively extensive and fertile plain, the limits
of which were sharply defined. The Norman conquerors of the region
imported English and Flemish settlers into this fertile area to defend
it against all Welsh encroachments. Welsh-English relations along
the borders of Pembroke were marked by the most unrelenting hostil-
ity and uncompromising distrust. As a result, Pembroke took little
part in the development of distinctive Cambro-Norman institutions,
and was content to remain an imperiled outpost of almost purely
English society—a "Little England Beyond Wales."[100]

The Norman response to the frontier in South Wales was marked
by variety. Each lordship was, in large measure, independent, and
each strove to establish the *modus vivendi* best suited to the particular local circumstances. Glamorgan represents a miniature example of
the processes of conquest and settlement in South Wales as a whole.
There were, however, characteristics common to Norman frontier experience throughout Wales. For this reason, the marcher lordships,
although exhibiting extreme variety in many aspects of their development, show great similarity in others.

In the first place, there was a certain newness and freedom surrounding the establishment of these lordships. In Wales, the conquerors were able to construct new societies, and, in the absence of a
restrictive central authority, were able to model their new states after

[99] For Cemais, see E. Laws, *The History of Little England beyond Wales and
the Non-Kymric Colony Settled in Pembrokeshire*, and G. Owen, *Prooffes Out of
Auntient Recordes, Writings and Other Matters That the Lordship of Kemes is
a Lordshippe Marcher, Baronia de Kemeys, from the Original Documents at
Bronwydd*.
[100] For Pembroke, see footnote 99 above.

their hearts' desires. Throughout the conquered regions, the barons sought to institutionalize and formalize their independence of a reguation which royal authority had been unable to enforce on the turbulent border.

Secondly, the marcher lords faced the necessity of establishing and maintaining peace within their holdings. To do this, they attempted to avoid unnecessary disturbance. Finding that Welsh population tended to concentrate in upland regions of little or no agricultural potential, the marcher lords expended no effort in dispossessing the natives of these lands. They found that immigrants tended to prefer agricultural land and the Welsh preferred pastoral land. They attempted to maintain this division and to rule each people in accordance with that people's custom. Intercultural contacts were kept at a minimum in the interests of peace.

Lastly, there was the necessity of defending these small lordships against the attacks of the turbulent and still-unconquered Welsh. The task of conquest had been slight compared to the problems of defense. The problems grew greater as time passed. Faced with a common enemy, the Welsh people responded by developing a degree of common identity and a cultural vigor which made them an ever more formidable adversary.

vi. The Welsh Reaction

THE YEAR 1093 marked the opening of a flood tide of Norman conquest which, within the year, had submerged all but the most mountainous and barren regions of South Wales. Bernard of Neufmarché held Brecknock, Fitz-Hamon held Glamorgan, the Montgomerys were in possession of Deheubarth, and Fitz-Baldwin had constructed a royal castle dominating the vale of Towy. By the end of the same year of 1093, the earl of Chester had succeeded in establishing Norman outposts along the northern coast of Wales, and his garrisons controlled the fertile island of Anglesey. Organized Welsh resistance had completely disintegrated, and it appeared that the ancient traditions of Welsh independence had come to an end.

Such was not to be the case. In 1093 and 1094 a number of events conspired to weaken the Norman cause considerably and to make possible a popular Welsh uprising which altered the situation drastically. In the first place, Roger of Montgomery, the earl of Shrewsbury, died, and was succeeded by Hugh, his second son.[1] Roger had been the most powerful lord on the Welsh marches, and he had been, perhaps more than any other single man, responsible for the massive conquest which was still underway. His armies had recently occupied Deheubarth, but the honor of settling the conquest which he had begun was denied him. The removal of his strong and directing hand at this critical time represented a serious loss to the Norman cause.

---

[1] For the date of Earl Roger's death, see J. E. Lloyd, *A History of Wales from the Earliest Times to the Edwardian Conquest,* II, 403, n. 18.

Leadership of the marcher lords would have fallen to the doughty earl of Chester, had this earl not chosen this time to return to the continent to attend to his affairs there.[2] The Norman conquerors were also denied royal leadership and support, since the king chose the critical year of 1094 to wage war against his brother, Robert Curthose.[3] The cause of Norman conquest in Wales had lost the leadership which might have been expected to give it proper direction. Norman power in Wales appeared everywhere to be at its height, but direction and reserve strength were lost. Behind their appearance of power, the Norman invaders were critically weak.

This need not have been disastrous, had it not been for the fact that in the same year in which the Normans lost their leadership, the Welsh regained theirs. A daring plot succeeded in freeing Gruffydd ap Cynan, hereditary ruler of Gwynedd, from the Chester prison in which he had languished for twelve years.[4] Allied with his energetic brother, Cadwgan, Gruffydd gathered some forces, attacked the Norman fortresses on Anglesey and speedily freed the island of its invaders. The uprising spread rapidly, and great expanses of territory were returned to Welsh control. The great castle of Montgomery itself was taken by a sudden Welsh attack. Once again Welsh raiders were able to range freely, and they struck across the border to bring devastation deep into the heart of Shropshire.[5]

The situation along the border deteriorated so rapidly that it soon became apparent that royal intervention was necessary to stabilize affairs. It was not until the fall of 1095, however, that Rufus was either willing or able to attempt to restore Norman ascendancy in Wales.[6] He realized that the core of Welsh resistance lay in the resurgent kingdom of Gwynedd and accordingly directed his efforts toward that region. The Welsh replied by employing tactics which had frustrated the effort of many previous expeditions of a similar character. Falling back before the royal force, they transferred their families and chattels to the mountain wilderness of Snowdonia. As

---

[2] *The Anglo-Saxon Chronicle, According to the Several Original Authorities,* ed. and trans. B. Thorpe, Part I, p. 361, s.a. 1093.

[3] *Brut y Tywysogion: or The Chronicle of the Princes of Wales,* ed. J. Williams ab Ithel, s.a. 1092 [sic], p. 57. One might note that there exists a confusion in the *Brut* concerning the purpose of William's trip to the continent.

[4] The complete story of this romantic figure may be found in *The History of Gruffydd ap Cynan. The Welsh Text with Translation, Introduction and Notes,* ed. and trans. A. Jones.

[5] *Annales de Margan,* ed. H. R. Luard, p. 6.

[6] *The Anglo-Saxon Chronicle,* s.a. 1096, Part I, pp. 362–363.

the campaigning season drew to a close, Rufus was faced with the prospect of leading his force into a region in which supply would be difficult and the danger of ambush great. He had failed in his purpose of drawing the Welsh into an open combat in which he could crush their power. Frustrated, he withdrew to Chester and brought the campaign to an end.

He had done little harm to the cause of Welsh resistance. On the contrary, his failure appears to have encouraged the Welsh insurgents. The men of Deheubarth joined in what soon became a general revolt. By the end of the year virtually all of the Montgomerys' conquests had been erased. The tide of revolt then rolled inland to Brecknock and Gwent. Only Glamorgan appears to have been untouched, though our reason for saying so lies mainly in our lack of information concerning it. The open countryside lay at the mercy of the Welsh, and the Normans were restricted to those castles which they had constructed during the previous few years and which were relatively proof against the assaults of Welsh raiders.

It was not until the spring of 1097 that Rufus could again gather forces to lead against the Welsh.[7] Once more he failed to force the Welsh into open battle and to defeat them. Despite these repeated failures, large parts of Wales were gradually brought back under Norman control in the next few years. This success was accomplished by Norman pursuit of a new strategy, one based upon a vastly expanded program of castle building. In the light of this fact it seems possible that the major purpose of the royal expedition of 1097 was not to defeat the Welsh in open combat, but to provide a screen for the construction of additional castles in rebellious regions.[8] Rufus' failure in 1095 seems to have led the Normans to develop a castle-building strategy which was to make of Wales a land dominated by fortresses.[9]

To appreciate the effectiveness of this new strategy, it is necessary to understand the two types of military organization which opposed each other during the conquest of Wales. One was the Norman military machine, basically a product of the plains of northern France and of the agrarian society which flourished there. It was, like all

---

[7] Lloyd, *A History of Wales*, II, 408, n. 3.

[8] *The Anglo-Saxon Chronicle*, s.a. 1087, Part I, p. 355; also see E. A. Freeman, *The Reign of William Rufus and the Accession of Henry I*, II, 69–71.

[9] See J. H. Beeler, "Castles and Strategy in Norman and Early Angevin England," *Speculum*, XXXI (1956), 581–601.

military organizations, designed to seize and hold the bases of power. In this case, the bases of power consisted of arable land which produced the wealth of this society, which in turn supported the professional soldiers who composed its armies. The Norman military machine was, therefore, composed of specialized, full-time, mounted men admirably adapted to fighting in that type of terrain which it had been designed to control. The military organization of the Welsh was very different. It had been produced in a mountainous region by a nonagricultural society. The bases of power of this society consisted of tribal and clan rights over grazing lands, and the cattle upon which the society subsisted. The Welsh military machine was, accordingly, a loosely organized, part-time, infantry force primarily designed to pursue feuds, and to engage in cattle raiding and looting expeditions.

By placing their primary emphasis upon castles, the Normans changed the way warfare was carried on in Wales. Hitherto they had aimed at complete conquest by devastation and the destruction of enemy field forces. This had proven to be ineffective, since Welsh society neither produced nor possessed much wealth which could be devastated or destroyed by the tactics available to the Normans, and because the Welsh army was not the sort of organized field force which could be crushed in regular campaigns. The tactics and organization of the Normans, on the other hand, were not such as to allow them to carry on the desultory and irregular warfare which was necessary to meet the Welsh on their own terms.

It is important, however, to note that when the Normans began to emphasize defensive works, they changed their military objectives from success in open combat to success in positional warfare. The Welsh were both militarily and socially incapable at this time of competing with the Normans in any such struggle. Their economy and customs were those of a pastoral people, and it was extremely difficult for them to maintain continuous occupation and control of any given area. The practice of transhumance, for instance, made it necessary for the normal Welsh community to relinquish control of its lowland meadows each summer and to migrate to the uplands. In their temporary absence, the Normans could quickly construct a castle which could then dominate the area and deny it to its previous owners.

Furthermore, the Norman castles which began to dot the Welsh countryside struck at yet another weakness in the Welsh social and military organization. Contemporary Welsh sources make it clear that the primary objective of their military activity lay in the acquisition of booty. The *Brut y Tywysogion*, in describing the failure of the royal expedition of 1095, states: ". . . and William returned home empty, without having gained anything."[10] The phrase "empty, without having gained anything," appears again applied to an unsuccessful Norman expedition of 1096. This characterization of failure must be compared with the manner in which the *Brut* describes the successful expedition of the Welsh against Pembroke in the same year of 1096. The words of the *Brut* are that they "despoiled it of all its cattle, ravaged the whole country, and with an immense booty returned home."[11] This emphasis upon the success of a military operation being reflected primarily in the plunder gained is reiterated in entries for 1095, 1100, 1102, and succeeding years. The *Brut* thus makes it clear that Welsh military efforts were primarily directed at the seizure of booty. Other instances illustrate that when any Welsh leader failed in this aim, his following quickly dispersed to less dangerous and more profitable pursuits.

The Norman strategy of castle building played upon this peculiarity of Welsh military tradition. In the first place, the castle not only provided a refuge for men, but also a place for the safekeeping of chattels. In any case other than a surprise attack, all movable wealth could be placed within the castle. In order to obtain any appreciable amount of plunder, the Welsh would have to carry at least the outer works of the castle. Since they lacked the organization and technology for effective siege operations, this was anything but an easy task. The expansion of castle building slowly brought to an end the possibility of quick and profitable raids on the part of the Welsh.

The castles which the Normans constructed also acted as a defense for the rich lands to their rear. The way in which they performed this task is not apparent at first glance. In terms of guarding the exits from the Welsh uplands, the castles were relatively weak and ineffective. Welsh raiders who cared to strike into the comparatively unfortified heartland of Norman holdings no doubt found it an easy task to bypass the Norman fortresses by stealth, celerity, or a simple diversion of route. On the return trip, however, such raiders found that the castles also guarded the *entrances* to the hills. Burdened with captives, cattle, and other booty, the raiders were now denied evasive

[10] *Brut y Tywysogion*, pp. 56–59.
[11] *Ibid.*, pp. 56–59.

action. In order to gain the safety of the uplands, they had to move slowly along a practicable route. This was a course which inevitably brought them under the walls of a Norman fortress. This fact meant that the choice of battle, which had hitherto lain with Welsh raiders, now belonged to Norman garrisons. This was an advantage which quickly brought a much greater measure of security to the lowlands of Wales.

In the long run, the Norman policy of castle building succeeded in consolidating most of the conquests which the invaders had made. At the same time, however, it set a limit on that conquest, for in adopting it the Normans admitted their incapability of meeting and defeating the Welsh in the upland plateaus where they made their home. This first successful Welsh revolt presented the embryonic Cambro-Norman society with a real challenge. It challenged the Normans to produce a military machine capable of waging successful mountain warfare, and to develop social and economic institutions able to settle and exploit the wilderness which lay above the six hundred foot contour line. The Normans failed to meet this challenge. At this crucial point, they gave up the initiative which had been so brilliantly seized by William Fitz-Osbern and his immediate successors. This Norman failure set the pattern for the next century and a half of Welsh history.

By 1100, then, Norman occupation of the fertile valleys and rolling plains of southern Wales was essentially complete. The tide of Norman conquest had washed up to the six hundred foot contour line, and had come to a halt. The history of the area for the next 150 years was to be one of transient political hegemonies established across this line by one side or the other. It was also to be the story of the complete failure of Anglo-Norman society to establish itself in the highland moors. A society which was based on the mounted knight and the manor was incapable of adjusting to an environment where the horse brought no power, and the manor brought no profits.

As the eleventh century drew to a close, an era of opportunity and high hopes came to an end for the Normans along the Welsh frontier. We have already remarked that the last decade of the century saw the end of the dynamic flexibility of the Normans in this region. Contact and interchange was to continue, but largely on Welsh terms. In the years to come, it was the backward Welsh society of the uplands which was to derive the greater benefit from the stimulation of the frontier environment. The Welsh were to develop a culture not only

capable of maintaining itself, but even of expanding in the face of
Anglo-Norman influences. The Cambro-Norman culture which developed in the lowlands tended to isolate itself from Welsh influences
and, except for a few exceptions, remained relatively passive and
derivative. Cultural initiative had clearly passed into the hands of the
Welsh. Norman loss of cultural initiative was coupled with a loss of
political initiative which, in the early years of the twelfth century, set
a seal upon the failure of Norman hopes of conquest and expansion
into all of Wales. This was in part the result of the revolt of Robert
of Bellême; an uprising that called forth a revised royal frontier policy
which radically altered the situation along the border.

It happened in the following way. In the summer of 1098, during
the Welsh rebellion we have been discussing, Earl Hugh of Chester
and Hugh, second earl of Shrewsbury, had joined forces in driving
the Welsh from the fertile isle of Anglesey. At the height of their
success, however, their forces were attacked by the fleet of Magnus
Barefoot of Norway, who happened to be cruising in the area. A
battle ensued in which Hugh of Shrewsbury was killed, and the Normans were forced to retreat in disorder. Magnus made no attempt to
hold the island, and departed, leaving Anglesey to be reclaimed by
Gruffydd ap Cynan.[12]

With Hugh of Montgomery dead, the earldom of Shrewsbury now
fell to his eldest brother, Robert of Bellême, by all accounts the most
vicious and ambitious man the Welsh marches had yet seen. By this
inheritance, his earlier acquisitions, and an advantageous marriage,
a great amount of wealth and power were concentrated in his hands.
Shropshire, with its great castle of Shrewsbury, was his, as were extensive tracts in Sussex, together with the great castle of Arundel in
that shire. His possessions in Normandy included the lordships of
Montgomery and Alençon, the *vicecomtes* of Argentan and Falaise,
and the wardship of a number of castles along the Norman border.
Finally, through his marriage into the house of Talvas, he held the
entire county of Ponthieu. Thanks to these holdings, Robert was
something more than a vassal of the king; he was the equal of many
of the princes of Europe.

His power did not end with his personal holdings since his brother
Arnulf was lord of the newly acquired region of Pembrokeshire and
of the strong fortress which had been constructed there. The latter

[12] *Brut y Tywysogion*, pp. 60–63.

was also allied with King Murtagh of Ireland, whose daughter he had married.[13] He also had a second brother, Roger of Poitou, holder of great estates in the region of Lancashire. In addition to these family ties. Robert sought to increase his power yet further by reaching a *modus vivendi* with his Welsh neighbors. He granted Powys and Ceredigion to a rebel, Cadwgan ap Bleddyn; in exchange for this grant the sons of Bleddyn—Cadwgan, Maredudd, and Iorwerth—became his vassals.[14] He allowed Gruffydd ap Cynan peaceable possession of Gwynedd, probably as part of a general armistice. It seems clear then that in a very short time after 1098 Robert was able to restore order along the Welsh border, and, if not to reoccupy the Montgomery conquests, at least to maintain a nominal sovereignty over them.

His ambition was not such as to be satiated with the power and wealth which were already his, and he soon found a possible means of increasing them. On the second of August in 1100, William Rufus died of an arrow wound received while hunting in the New Forest. The king's younger brother, Henry, quickly seized upon the confusion, took control of the treasury at Winchester, and, only three days after Rufus' death, was crowned king at Westminster. Henry's succession did not go unchallenged, however, for a large number of the Norman nobility would have preferred to see Robert Curthose, duke of Normandy, take the throne. It may be that these dissidents saw in Robert a weakness and permissiveness which might have allowed them to gain the same unbridled liberty in England which they had come to exercise in their Norman possessions. At any rate, Robert of Bellême was prominent among those who pledged their support of Robert's claim to the English crown.[15]

So when in July of 1102 Robert invaded England with a sizable force of Norman adherents, he was soon joined by many of the nobles of England. He quickly proved, however, to be an ineffectual leader. A personal confrontation of the two brothers was arranged, which led to a compromise and eventually a treaty between the two.[16] Duke Robert returned to Normandy, and Robert of Bellême and his friends found themselves without a cause.

[13] Orderic Vitalis, "Historiae Ecclesiasticae libri XIII in partes tres divisi," in *Patrologia Latina*, ed. J. P. Migne, Vol. CLXXXVIII, cols. 794–795.

[14] *Brut y Tywysogion*, pp. 66–69.

[15] Orderic Vitalis, col. 787.

[16] *Ibid.*, col. 788.

The terms of the treaty which had been concluded seem to have guaranteed that no retaliation would be visited upon Duke Robert's adherents for their espousal of his cause. It soon became evident, however, that Henry intended to circumvent this agreement if at all possible and to destroy the power and fortunes of those who had opposed him. In the next few months the lesser members of the dissident party were haled into court on trivial or trumped-up charges, and saddled with ruinous fines and forfeitures. A group of royal spies meanwhile haunted the footsteps of Robert of Bellême, compiling reports on his activities. By Easter of 1103, Henry had gathered enough evidence to summon Robert to the Easter assembly to answer to a series of no less than forty-five separate charges.[17] Robert was probably fully aware that the outcome of his trial was predetermined. Rather than answering the royal summons, he attempted to stall for time, and meanwhile made preparations for war. His castles and those of his brother Arnulf were repaired and strengthened. Mercenaries were hired, and the two brothers' vassals were called on for service. A special reliance was placed upon those Welsh with whom Robert had allied himself.[18] Most of the earl's movable wealth was delivered into the hands of the Welsh for safekeeping and was transported by them into the mountain fastnesses of central Wales. Cadwgan, Maredudd, and Iorwerth gathered large war bands and, led by the earl, raided deep into the heart of Staffordshire. Once again the dilemma of border defense had been raised. A border lord strong enough to ensure peace and stability to the frontier had also proven strong enough to use the enemy for his personal ends. The alliance of a fierce enemy and an equally fierce border captain was a formidable combination.

Henry's strategy was twofold; first, to reduce Robert's strongholds piecemeal, and, second, to dislodge the Welsh from their alliance with the earl. Both programs were eminently successful. Arundel was speedily invested and soon surrendered to royal authority. Tickhill, in Yorkshire, quickly followed, and Henry marched upon Robert's newly constructed castle of Bridgenorth, in Shropshire. The menace of the Welsh allies of Robert who were roving in this region seriously interfered with Henry's siege of Bridgenorth. He quickly sent William Pantulph, a holder of extensive lands in Shropshire, to arrange an audience between the king and Iorwerth, one of the rebellious

[17] *Ibid.*, col. 791.
[18] *Brut y Tywysogion*, pp. 66–69.

Welsh chieftains.[19] He offered Iorwerth dominion over all of South
and Central Wales, with the exception of the marcher lordships of
Brecknockshire, Gwent, Glamorgan, and part of Pembrokeshire,
and the offer was quickly accepted. Iorwerth took command of the
Welsh bands and began to harry Earl Robert's lands. This defection
broke Robert's resistance. Bridgenorth soon surrendered, and Robert
forestalled a royal siege of Shrewsbury only by his prompt submission to the king. The rebel was deported to Normandy, and the power
of the house of Montgomery came to an end in England.

With the end of Robert of Bellême's power the Norman political
system along the border took on a vastly different aspect. The great
semi-independent earldoms which had hitherto dominated the border, and had provided the primary direction and power for the conquest of Wales, had come to an end. Hugh of Chester, one of the
great warriors of marcher tradition, was dead; Hereford and Shrewsbury were escheated to the crown; and Gloucester lay in the hands
of Robert Fitz-Hamon, a man increasingly involved in the continental
struggles between King Henry and Duke Robert.[20] No power existed
along the frontier sufficient to challenge the authority of the king.
Henceforth, expansion and conquest were to be directed from the
royal court, and freedom of opportunity was to be strictly limited in
the royal interest. The great earls and the border barons who had
achieved the successes of the previous century, had proved incapable
of consolidating and holding what they had won, and, what is more,
had proven extremely dangerous to the peace of the realm of England. Under Henry, these freebooters disappeared, and, with them,
much of the dynamic character of Norman society. The strength of
the Anglo-Normans was still so overwhelming that expansion continued, but it was vastly different in character.

King Henry's regard for organization and stability was too great,
however, to allow the marches of Wales to remain in a leaderless state
for long. In the years that followed, a new leadership developed
along the border as Henry introduced a new personnel into the region
and established and regularized their position there.

The death of the Welsh chieftain, Hywel ap Gronw, in 1106, offered Henry his first opportunity to make basic readjustments in the
situation in South Wales. In the general settlement which had followed the fall of Robert of Bellême, Hywel had been granted do-

---

[19] Orderic Vitalis, col. 793; *Brut y Tywysogion*, pp. 70–71.
[20] See Chapter V above.

minion over the vale of Towy, Kidwelly, and Gower, and his death released these areas for reassignment. Kidwelly was now granted to Roger, bishop of Salisbury and justiciar of England. A castle was soon constructed and a borough sprung up under the castle's walls. The old commote soon became a regular marcher lordship. Much the same fate awaited Gower, which was granted to the powerful Henry, earl of Warwick. Warwick began the pacification of the area from the great castle which he built at Swansea.[21]

Consolidation and expansion now continued in other regions. By 1108, Norman control was re-established in Pembrokeshire, and a colony of Flemish weavers and mercenaries was established in the region by royal order.[22] A new and increased royal interest was shown to the lower vale of Towy. By 1109 a new castle had been constructed at Carmarthen which replaced the old fortress of Rhydygors. The area was governed by Walter, sheriff of Gloucester, in the royal interest.[23] In 1110, the king awarded the plains of Ceredigion to Gilbert Fitz-Richard of Clare, a member of a noble family that had firmly supported Henry in his first steps to the throne. Gilbert brought a group of followers with him into the region, and divided the area into a series of dependent lordships, much upon the model of Glamorgan. Two great Clare castles arose at Cardigan and Aberystwyth, while smaller castles in each of the dependent lordships provided local protection.[24] By 1119, the lordship of lower Gwent, which had escheated to the crown as a result of the rebellion of Roger of Breteuil in 1075, was revived and was granted to Walter Fitz-Richard of Clare, brother of the lord of Ceredigion.[25] The lesser lordships of Abergavenny and Monmouth were strengthened by being placed in the hands of active supporters of the king.

Perhaps the most important element in Henry's work of reorganization, though, lay in the marriages which he arranged. The earldom of Gloucester, which lay in royal hands after the death of Fitz-Hamon in 1107, finally passed to Henry's illegitimate son, the able Robert of

[21] For the Anglo-Norman settlement of Gower, an interesting commentary is provided by D. T. Williams, "Gower: A Study in Linguistic Movements and Historical Geography," *Archaeologia Cambrensis,* LXXXIX (1934), 302–327.

[22] See H. Owen, "The Flemings in Pembrokeshire," *Archaeologia Cambrensis,* Series V, Vol. XII (1895), pp. 96–106.

[23] For an excellent history of the Norman settlement of Carmarthenshire, see J. E. Lloyd, *A History of Carmarthenshire.*

[24] See J. E. Lloyd, *The Story of Ceredigion (400–1282).*

[25] See J. H. Round, "The Family of Clare," *The Archaeological Journal,* LVI (1899) Series II, Vol. VI, 221–231.

Caen, by his marriage to Fitz-Hamon's heiress, Mabel. The honor of
Gloucester was reconstituted an earldom, and Robert emerged as the
paramount leader of the marcher lords of South Wales. Bernard of
Neufmarché, the first of the original conquerors of Wales, was perhaps the last to leave the scene, dying sometime around 1125. His
place was taken by Miles, son of Walter, the sheriff of Gloucester.
Miles had been married to Bernard's daughter, Sybil, in the spring of
1121, and the succession had been assured to him at that time.[26]

The remainder of Henry's reign saw the slow, but steady, consolidation of Norman power in South Wales. The overall pattern of
settlement in the region was relatively uniform, and seems almost
consciously based upon the organization of Glamorgan, the only
lordship to endure the rebellions of the close of the eleventh century
with any degree of stability. It seems strange that such advances
could have been made under the direction of an authority which was,
as we have said, more interested in stability than in conquest. The
reason for this peculiarity lies partly in the character of the settlement, and partly in the political situation of the times. The Normans
took, held, and settled only those areas which were capable of supporting the agrarian society necessary to maintain a feudal structure.
Everywhere the pattern was similar to that observable in Glamorgan; the Normans were content to exercise only a vague suzerainty
over such lands as were not capable of sustaining intensive agriculture. Since it was exactly these relatively barren regions which the
Welsh valued most highly, the friction between Welsh natives and
Norman settlers was minimized. Secondly, throughout this period
the Welsh were politically paralyzed by disastrous feuds between
the ruling families.[27] They could present no united front against the
invaders, and time and again the Normans were able to use jealousies
and rivalries to prevent the growth of unity and able leadership
among their enemies.

The history of South Wales during the reign of Henry I then is one
of apparent Norman success. Under the directing authority of the
great king, the second generation of conquerors achieved much of
what the first generation had sought. Two major elements were miss-
ing, however. In the first place, the original attacks had aimed at the
political conquest and eventual absorption or complete subjugation

[26] *Calendar of Documents Preserved in France, Illustrative of the History of
Great Britain and Ireland*, ed. J. H. Round, pp. 8–9.
[27] Lloyd, *A History of Wales*, II, 417 ff.

of the Welsh. The new program had more limited objectives. It was in the royal interest that certain Welsh communities and political groups be maintained intact to act as a counterbalance to the marcher lords. This was a program which had most serious consequences. In such areas as were protected by royal authority, Welsh society was allowed to develop unhindered, to the point where it was capable of supporting a sense of national identity which was to make the ultimate conquest of Wales extremely difficult. In the second place, the initial conquest had brought power and a large measure of independence to those nobles who had led the advance. This aspect of the process of conquest had changed greatly. The precedents established in the earlier period were not discarded, but, under Henry, the trend was not allowed to continue. The security and success which royal leadership brought to the marcher lords had been purchased by a distinct limitation in the opportunities which the Welsh frontier afforded.

Henry's ascendancy in Wales established an era of relative peace which was unparalleled in the history of the region. In the long run, however, the royal policy which secured this peace worked against the interests of the Norman invaders. Peace brought an increase of wealth and population to the Welsh people; and peaceable contact with the Normans brought them knowledge of new techniques in military and political affairs. Peace also afforded them an opportunity to absorb these new techniques at their leisure and to integrate them into the native culture.[28] Throughout this period Welsh society grew more dynamic and developed a greater sense of nationality.

This process occurred in many spheres of Welsh life, but a single example may suffice for the many trends which can be observed. Nowhere was cultural borrowing more dramatically illustrated than in the Welsh adoption of the typically Norman process of castle building. A total of 123 castles were constructed in Wales prior to 1189, and of these no less than 14 were built by the native Welsh princes.[29] Of these, 8 are mentioned in contemporary sources, and, for this reason, something is known concerning their foundation. The earliest known, Cymmer in Merioneth, was constructed in 1115 by Uchtred ab Edwin, a man whose name suggests strong English connections. In the 1140's, the castles of Cynfael and Llanrhystud were built at the

---

[28] Giraldus Cambrensis, *Opera*, eds. J. S. Brewer *et al.*, Part VI (*Itinerarium Kambriae*), pp. 217–218.
[29] See Beeler, "Castles and Strategy in Norman and Early Angevin England."

command of Cadwaladr ap Gruffydd ap Cynan, who had, for some time, been an ally and protégé of the Normans.[30] The remainder of the list includes Aberdovey (1155), Caernion (1155), Walwen (before 1163), Abereinion (1169), and Rhaidrgwy (1177).[31] This list is assuredly incomplete. Many castles were probably constructed by the Welsh the existence of which is unrecorded in the sources. At the same time, the list is restricted to those castles whose original foundations were Welsh, and thus omits many castles rebuilt and occupied by the Welsh princes. On the other hand, the list does indicate that the Welsh castles were constructed mostly by chieftains who were subject to unusually heavy Anglo-Norman influences. Secondly, the remains of these native Welsh works show that the original construction was of the typically Norman motte-and-bailey type. Taken together, these facts provide sufficient indication that such castles represent a technology which the Welsh were borrowing directly from the Normans, and turning to their own advantage.

At the same time a continuous influence of Anglo-Norman legal and political techniques is observable in the development of Welsh institutions.[32] The Welsh quickly borrowed many of the institutions of the typical feudal state of the times. This development was not of such a magnitude as to allow the Welsh to compete with the other states of western Europe in terms of organization, but it did become possible for the Welsh to unify and coordinate their activities with a degree of efficiency hitherto impossible.

One can see the immediate results of this when the strong hand of Henry was removed from Wales. Shortly after Henry's death, when Stephen, his successor, had been crowned, the Welsh of Western Brycheiniog rose in revolt. They raided into Gower and inflicted a stunning defeat upon the Anglo-Norman forces defending the region.[33] Old names soon rose to haunt the Normans as Gruffydd ap Rhys ap Tewdwr appealed to Owain ap Gruffydd ap Cynan to join in a general revolt. The uprising received another stimulus when Iorwerth ab Owain ap Caradog ap Gruffydd managed to ambush Richard Fitz-Gilbert of Clare, and to kill this powerful lord of Ce-

---

[30] Lloyd, *A History of Wales*, II, 491, n. 18.

[31] E. S. Armitage, *The Early Norman Castles of the British Isles*, pp. 299–301.

[32] For details of this process, see T. Jones-Pierce, "The Age of Princes," *The Historical Basis of Welsh Nationalism*, pp. 42–59; T. P. Ellis, *Welsh Tribal Law and Custom in the Middle Ages*, I, 11.

[33] *Gesta Stephani*, ed. and trans. K. R. Potter, p. 10.

redigion. Soon again the countryside was at the mercy of the Welsh.
Faced by this danger, King Stephen took vigorous measures to meet
the challenge. Large sums were expended upon two expeditions sent
into Wales but both attempts to subdue the rebellious Welsh failed.
After these two fiascos, the *Gesta Stephani* states,

> It seemed to the king that he was striving in vain, in vain pouring out his
> vast treasure to reduce them to peace; and so, advised by more judicious
> counsel, he preferred to endure their insolent rebellion for a time, in order
> that, with fighting at a standstill and disagreement setting them all at vari-
> ance, they might either suffer a famine or turn on each other and be ex-
> terminated by mutual slaughter.[34]

What Stephen's apologist is trying to say, of course, is that the king
had abdicated royal leadership in Wales, and left the marcher lords
to their own devices.

This loss need not have been so disastrous to the Norman settlers
in Wales had it not been for the political conflict that arose concerning King Stephen's right to the English throne. The only son of
Henry I had preceded his father in death, leaving only a daughter,
Matilda, as heir to that king. Henry's intention appears to have been
that the crown should pass through Matilda to his infant grandson,
Henry of Anjou. In accordance with this desire, Henry had had most
of his nobles swear fealty to Matilda before his death. Stephen, however, had acted swiftly when Henry died, renounced his oath, and,
with the aid of a number of other nobles, seized the throne. A rival
party soon developed among the Normans, however, which saw advantages in supporting the rival claims of Matilda. A lengthy civil
war was the result, which almost completely absorbed the energies
of the nobility and devastated large areas of England. The paramount leader of the dissident party was Robert, earl of Gloucester,
and virtually all of the marcher lords joined him. This had the result
of protecting the marches and South Wales from the full effects of
the anarchy which the civil war caused. At the same time, by divert-
ing their energies eastward, this solidarity of allegiance among the
border barons left South Wales almost defenseless against the encroachments of the Welsh.

Thus the disorders of Stephen's reign meant that the English,
Flemish, and Norman settlers were left to provide their own defense
against the resurgent Welsh. This was a time of trouble and fear for

[34] *Ibid.*, p. 13.

the settlers, and during this period many of them abandoned their homes and returned to more secure estates.[35] The Welsh of Cantref Mawr, organized under Gruffydd ap Rhys and his sons, began extending their control in every direction and soon dominated all of southwest Wales. They gained control of the lower vale of Towy in 1137 by capturing the royal fortress of Carmarthen. Some years later Llanstephan fell, and the Welsh were able to move into Pembrokeshire. In 1153, Gower fell before their attack; and shortly after, they were able to press an attack on the western border of Glamorgan. Other Welsh chieftains were similarly successful. Hywel ap Maredudd ap Rhydderch managed to expel the Clifford family from Cantref Bychan, while Morgan ab Owain, grandson of Caradog ap Gruffydd, was able to take the castle of Usk and to erect a lordship centered on Caerleon, in the heart of Norman Wales.[36] The political events in Wales during the reign of Stephen are complex and confusing, but one fact stands out clearly—the Welsh were everywhere on the offensive. Under Henry, the limits of Norman settlement had been greatly extended, and Norman political power had embraced all of South Wales. The resurgence of Welsh power caused the frontier of Norman authority to shrink rapidly, until it coincided exactly

[35] Very few documents remain to attest to the problems these early settlers faced, and, for this reason, the one extensive document which does remain is worth quoting in full.

Frater G. Gilbert Foliot Gloucestriae dictus abbas, dilecto filio suo Osberno, 'non trepidare ubi non est timor (Psal. LII)'.

Moneo te, fili charissime, aedificare et plantare, et terram tuam eo vomere quo tu scis exercere et diligenter excolere. Satis hactenus spinas et tribulos germinavit (Gen. III), sed, sicut bene coepisti, si labori bono et exercitio instanter incubueris, scio, scio quod fructu bono non fraudabit te Dominus. Volo vera vasa omnia domus tuae salva et munda custodias, et ipsam domum tuam qua poteris supellectile munda et honesta munias et exornes. Laudo etiam te seras portarum tuarum confortare, domum tuam vallo bono et muro inexpugnabile circumdare, ne scilicet gens illa quae, sicut tu dicis, hirsuta fronte et torvis oculis respicit, irrumpat in eam et omnes labores tuos et sudores impetu uno diripiat. Nolo vasa transmigrationis sint apud te, nec quod in aliquo praetendas transmigrationis habitum, sed stabilitatis in terra vestra quam dedit vobis Dominus Deus et mansionis diuturnae propositum. Dices vero amicis nostris Wallensibus vos de hoc quod audierunt nihil penitus illis inconsultis acturos. Videmus vero gentem vestram timorem Domini et reverentiam sactuarii parvipendere, et illos audimus Deum et loca sancta at personas consecratas Domino diligenter honorare. Propter haec omnia durum est nobis illis qui fere non curant vos magnis inseri et ab his qui vos venerantus avelli. Vale et noveris nos malle stationarum vel progressionarum te esse quam retrogradum." (Gilbert Foliot, "Epistola XXIX," in "Gilbertus Foliot, ex abbate Gloucestriae episcopus primum Herefordensis . . .," *Patrologia Latina*, ed. J. P. Migne, vol. CXC, cols. 766–767.)

[36] Lloyd, *A History of Wales*, II, 478–479.

with the frontier of actual Norman settlement. Furthermore, under the pressure of continuous Welsh attack, both frontiers were moving backward.

As soon as strong government replaced anarchy in England, these Welsh successes came to an end. Henry II dedicated himself to the task of restoring the stable rule which had characterized his grandfather's reign. He quickly took active measures against the Welsh. By 1158 he succeeded in overawing Rhys ap Gruffydd, the paramount prince of Deheubarth, and in restoring royal authority in South Wales. The Norman barons returned to their possessions and attempted to repair the damages of the previous twenty years. Rhys proved to be irrepressible, however, and broke the king's peace time and time again. Operating from the wilderness of Cantref Mawr, his bands kept southwest Wales in a continual state of apprehension. But as long as royal power remained strong, Rhys could achieve little lasting success. Henry's growing controversy with the archbishop of Canterbury, however, soon caused his authority to wane. Rhys sensed this weakness and seized on the opportunity to conclude a firm alliance with Owain Gwynedd, the leader of North Wales. Lesser chieftains quickly joined this coalition, and a Welsh alliance of unprecedented proportions marked the end of the peace which the king had enforced in Wales.

Even in the midst of his difficulties Henry realized the danger which these Welsh developments presented. Great and expensive preparations were made for a large-scale invasion of the rebellious areas of Wales.[37] This Anglo-Norman expedition entered Wales in the summer of 1165 and pursued approximately the same course as had that of William Rufus, striking directly toward the heart of Welsh resistance in Gwynedd. Again the entire campaign proved a fiasco. Welsh ambushes made movement difficult, and an unseasonably wet summer finally made further progress impossible. Henry was forced into an ignominious retreat without having struck a single blow against the insurgents. Welsh tactics and the topography of their homeland had once again proven more than a match for the feudal levies of England.

By defeating this royal expedition, the Welsh gained what proved to be more than a temporary respite. There is every indication that Henry regarded this expensive and ill-fated expedition as the final

[37] This is especially apparent in a perusal of Pipe Roll 11 Henry II, particularly membrane 31.

blow to his unprofitable attempts to maintain royal supremacy over all Wales.[38] He seems to have determined not to try to conquer the Welsh princes again in such a manner. On the other hand, he was not willing to relinquish royal control over his Anglo-Norman border barons. What Henry did in effect was to return to the policy which William the Conqueror had established to maintain an equilibrium along the border. Time had shown that the Welsh could be conquered only through a long and profitless war. At the same time, Henry recognized that the border barons presented a far greater danger to the peace of the realm than the Welsh. He jealously maintained his ascendancy over the barons by limiting their power and opportunities, often with the aid of the Welsh princes, whose favor and support he actively sought.

The events of the reigns of Stephen and Henry II thus clearly indicate how the Norman frontier—in a Turnerian sense—came to an end in Wales. Opportunities for wealth, power, and independence had lured the early invaders to their conquests. In the face of determined resistance, however, the first generation of conquerors had lacked the cohesiveness and organization to hold what they had gained. The second generation of conquerors—those established under Henry I—had such cohesiveness and organization, but it had been purchased at a price. They had accepted immediate royal direction in frontier affairs and had given up the hope of independent power which Wales offered them. Under Henry, however, this loss was more than balanced by the success which the Norman magnates enjoyed in those limited areas in which the king allowed them to act. The events of the reigns of Stephen and Henry II showed the weakness of this arrangement. Royal direction of frontier affairs was only effective when the king was strong and willing to take an active personal role. The paralysis of royal authority which had attended Stephen's reign inaugurated a period of Norman weakness in Wales which proved almost disastrous. During this period the Welsh developed a capacity for resistance which made the task of the next king even greater. Even so, the energetic measures taken by Henry II in the early years of his reign showed some signs of effectiveness. As Henry's power and authority diminished, however, Norman supremacy was once again threatened. The final blow to the hopes of the Normans came with Henry's abandonment of aspirations toward

[38] Lloyd, *A History of Wales*, II, 518.

royal supremacy in Wales. The border barons still found themselves subject, in large measure, to the restrictions of royal overlordship but without enjoying any of the benefits of royal leadership. The forward progress of the Normans in South Wales and the frontier conditions which attended this progress were completely arrested by the curious combination of a suspicious and troubled English monarch and a resurgent and dynamic Welsh people.

vii. The Cambro-Norman Reaction
The Invasion of Ireland

WE HAVE SEEN that frontier conditions came to an end for the Cambro-Norman society which had developed in South Wales. Opportunities for conquest, and for increased power and independence, diminished and in time disappeared. This society, based ultimately upon expansion and conquest, faced a future in which its primary function would be that of garrison duty. It was a future in which there was little hope of rewards which would be commensurate with the heavy task to be performed. By and large, the society accepted its future and performed its specialized function until such time as it, and the Welsh society it faced, began to be absorbed into the main stream of life in Tudor Britain.

A society, however, is made up of individuals, and, for this reason, one should not expect any society to react monolithically. In the Cambro-Norman society of the mid-twelfth century, there were varied reactions to the relatively ordered and humdrum way of life that was slowly replacing the turbulent days of old. The old virtues and talents had no place in this new order of things. The ambitious barons and reckless knights who would have been, a half-century earlier, in the forefront of conquest and glory, were now failures, misfits, and troublemakers. A peaceful and regulated society had no room for such men. Many, no doubt, accepted their lot and lived out their days as relatively useless anachronisms; but some refused to adapt, and cast about for new frontiers. They found one close at hand.

In effect, the Cambro-Norman invasion of Ireland represents the last gasp of the Norman frontier in Wales. The closing of this frontier squeezed out those men who found it impossible to relinquish the ideals and attitudes which had made the frontier what it was. They carried their way of life to a new area of conquest, and, for a time, the Welsh frontier was reborn in the fens of Ireland. We are fortunate that two relatively full accounts of this period have survived. One, *The Song of Dermot and the Earl*, is a *chanson de geste*, composed in the mid-thirteenth century but partially based upon oral tradition and on an earlier poem of similar character.[1] The other prime source is provided by Giraldus Cambrensis' *Expugnatio Hibernica*, probably based, at least in part, upon personal interviews with some of the principals, to whom Giraldus was closely related.[2] Both accounts are relatively full, but their accuracy is often doubtful. What is important is that, because of the sources upon which they ultimately rest, the *Song* and the *Expugnatio* present this frontier experience somewhat as the participants saw it. Although the first generation of Cambro-Norman conquerors is silent, the last generation does speak, and what they have to say is well worth hearing.

The occasion for the Cambro-Norman invasion of Ireland stemmed from the conflict between two Irish chieftains, Dermot MacMurrough and Tiernan O'Rourke. Dermot had been successful in extending the power of his small tribe to the point where he was recognized as paramount king of all Leinster. This expansion had brought him to the borders of Meath, where friction developed between him and Tiernan, the prince of Breifne. Antagonism between the two deepened when, in 1152, Dermot took advantage of Tiernan's temporary absence to abduct his wife. Although the lady was returned the following year, the event sealed a bitter enmity between the two chieftains. Tiernan's opportunity for full revenge came in 1166, when he was able to conclude an alliance with the king of Connaught, who was, at that time, high king of Ireland. The two allies attacked Dermot, and, in the face of such powerful enemies, he was forced to flee Ireland. On August 1, 1166, he sailed from an Irish port and directed his voyage to Bristol. This rising city had long enjoyed cordial relations with the Dansk cities of Ireland's eastern shore, and Dermot

---

[1] *The Song of Dermot and the Earl: an Old French Poem from the Carew Manuscript No. 596 in the Archiepiscopal Library at Lambeth Palace*, ed. and trans. G. H. Orpen. Also see J. F. O'Doherty, "Historical Criticism of the Song of Dermot and the Earl," *Irish Historical Studies*, I (1938–1939), 4–20.

[2] Giraldus Cambrensis, *Opera*, eds. J. S. Brewer *et al.*, Part V (*Expugnatio Hibernica*).

no doubt established contacts with some of the merchants of Bristol. The end of his voyage found him hospitably received by Robert Fitz-Harding, the reeve of the city and a close friend of Henry II.

After a short stay in the city, Dermot departed for the continent to seek aid from King Henry. His motives for this action seem somewhat obscure. A more natural course would appear to have been for him to have sought support from amongst the Welsh as so many dethroned Welshmen had done in Ireland. It may have been that he had learned of Henry's contemplated extension of English power to Ireland, and had been advised by Fitz-Harding that the king might not be adverse to espousing his cause as an excuse for intruding into Irish affairs.[3] If this were the case, Dermot was disappointed. The Irish chieftain visited Henry's court on the continent in the winter of 1166–1167 and made his plea for support. Whatever Henry's intention had been earlier, his ardor for an invasion of Ireland had by now cooled. Problems in France, and those arising from his conflict with Becket, had involved him too deeply. He listened to Dermot's case and, in exchange for his act of homage, simply provided him with a letter authorizing him to recruit allies from among the king's subjects. With this poor prize, Dermot returned to Fitz-Harding's hospitality in Bristol.

He remained in this city for some time, attempting to arouse interest in his proposed venture, but apparently with little success. Finally, however, he established contact with Richard Fitz-Gilbert of Clare, earl of Strigoil, and today better known as Strongbow. Strongbow was only too ready to listen to Dermot's offer, since such a desperate plan seemed the only way to repair the lost fortunes of the Clares.

Richard's father, Gilbert, had been one of the greatest lords of England. He had held large tracts of ancestral lands in Kent and Sussex, and had greatly extended his power under Stephen. In 1138, he had been made earl of Pembroke by Stephen, and in the same year acquired the earldom of Strigoil through the death of his uncle. Gilbert had broken with King Stephen in 1147, but his son apparently continued his allegiance to that monarch and succeeded to his fa-

[3] G. H. Orpen, *Ireland under the Normans, 1169–1216,* I, 79–84. Henry had contemplated an Irish conquest as early as 1155, and Pope Adrian IV had been persuaded to give official approval to the scheme. A considerable body of literature has grown up concerning the bull *Laudabiliter* which purports to embody this approval. A good résumé of this material may be found in H. W. C. Davis, *England under the Normans and Angevins, 1066–1272,* pp. 532–533.

ther's estates upon the latter's death in the succeeding year. Little is
known of Richard's activities between this date and his conference
with Dermot in 1167, but it is clear that in the intervening twenty
years his fortunes had declined considerably.[4] It is difficult to per-
ceive the course of the decline of the Clare fortunes, but it is probable that a number of factors contributed. During the period of
Welsh resurgence, the great Clare estates of Wales had slipped from
his hands. Ceredigion was lost as early as 1136, Carmarthen and
Llanstephen fell in 1146, Tenby in Pembrokeshire was taken by the
sons of Gruffydd ap Rhys in 1153, and the years following 1159 saw
the steady increase in the power of the Lord Rhys. By 1166, all of
Ceredigion, Ystrad Tywy and a large part of Dyfed lay in his hands,
and Clare fortunes in southwest Wales were at low ebb.

This was not the only source of Richard's troubles, however. He
had been ill advised in his continued support of Stephen and, after
the accession of Henry II, he began to experience the consequences
of his error. It is probable that his title to the earldom of Pembrokeshire was extinguished soon after the latter's accession, along with
the other earldoms of Stephen's making.[5] More than that, that normally suspicious monarch was exceptionally watchful and unfriendly
toward Richard, who was forced to act with the greatest circum-
spection in order to avoid incurring any more active an indication of
royal disfavor. He was ill suited to be a courtier, and his warlike
proclivities were thwarted by the powerful figures of the Lord Rhys
and the suspicious King Henry. Neither England nor Wales held any
opportunity for him, and he was quite ready to try his fortunes in
another, less restricted, environment.[6]

Despite the attractiveness of the proposed venture, Richard hesi-
tated. Fearing that Henry would take advantage of any unauthorized

[4] Giraldus Cambrensis, *Opera*, Part V (*Expugnatio Hibernica*), p. 247.
[5] See J. H. Round, "Richard de Clare, or Richard Strongbow," in *The Dictionary of National Biography*, X, 390. Round disagrees with this view, stating,
"It appears that he was allowed to retain his title even after the accession of
Henry II, when so many of Stephen's earldoms were abolished." No record
exists of his possession of the title after Henry's accession, and he certainly did
not hold it in 1167. The only mention of Richard in the intervening years is his
witness of a royal charter of January 1156. He appears on this document simply
as Richard Fitz-Gilbert. Considering the disfavor in which he found himself, it
is unlikely that the loss of his title was delayed much after Henry's succession.
[6] William of Newburgh, *Historia Rerum Anglicarum*, ed. H. C. Hamilton,
Book II, Ch. vi. William says of Richard "exhausto fere patrimonio, creditoribus
erat supra modum obnoxius; atque ideo proclivius ad majora invitantibus
acquievit."

action to confiscate his few remaining estates, he stipulated that any arrangements on his part would be conditional upon the acquisition of proper license from the king.[7] With this stipulation understood, Richard proceeded to drive a hard bargain with Dermot. The Irish chief was forced to promise Richard the hand of his daughter in marriage and the eventual succession of the throne of Leinster.[8] In exchange, Richard gave Dermot his conditional promise to gather his forces and to come to Leinster the coming spring.

The tentative nature of these arrangements apparently left Dermot unsatisfied, for he next directed his steps to St. David's. Here he no doubt hoped to find more immediate support, either from some of the triumphant followers of the Lord Rhys or from the hemmed-in marcher barons of Pembrokeshire.[9] He was successful in this endeavor, finding some advantage in a rather peculiar dilemma which faced one of these barons, Robert Fitz-Stephen.

Robert was the son of the Norman castellan of Cilgerran and of the famous Nest, daughter of Rhys ap Tewdwr. He had followed his father as castellan of Cilgerran until it fell before the attack of the Lord Rhys, Robert's cousin by virtue of their common grandfather, Rhys ap Tewdwr. Robert was captured and placed in Rhys' prison, where he remained for three years. The price of his release was his promise to aid Rhys in the latter's struggle against King Henry. This promise placed Robert in an intolerable position. To honor his agreement would have meant betrayal of his Norman heritage and betrayal of his King, and would have ultimately led him into war against the barons of Pembrokeshire, many of whom were his half-brothers, by virtue of their common mother, Nest. Not to honor his agreement, on the other hand, would have meant betrayal of his Welsh heritage and of his kinsman who championed that heritage, and would have eventually led him back into a Welsh dungeon. The simple fact of the matter is that Robert was a half-breed, and had now to face the problem of divided loyalties which have so often plagued such men.[10]

Dermot's arrival offered Robert an escape from his dilemma. Lord

[7] *The Song of Dermot and the Earl,* ll. 353–361.

[8] The value of this promise is somewhat dubious, since, in theory at least, Irish monarchies were elective.

[9] It must be remembered that Strongbow was well-acquainted with this area and had many supporters there. It is quite possible that Dermot's actions were done at Richard's request.

[10] Giraldus Cambrensis, *Opera,* Part V (*Expugnatio Hibernica*), p. 229.

Rhys was not adverse to the suggestion that his cousin be released from his promise and be allowed to accompany Dermot. In the first place, Rhys had less need of Robert now, since the danger which had faced the Welsh in 1166 had disappeared with Henry's growing involvement in the controversy with Becket. Secondly, Rhys foresaw that such an expedition would attract the attention of many of the more adventurous of Robert's Norman kinsmen, and Pembroke would be weakened by the loss of its best warriors. Under license from the Lord Rhys a bargain was quickly struck between Dermot and Robert. Robert was joined by his half-brother Maurice Fitz-Gerald in his decision to escape the confining atmosphere in Wales and to seek his fortune in a land where the strength of the enemy was the only limitation upon success. Their resolve earned them the promise of the city of Wexford and the two *cantrefs* adjoining it.[11] Robert and Maurice began their preparations to embark for Ireland in the coming spring.

Thus, by the summer of 1167, Dermot had achieved the promise of substantial aid. Evidently, however, the prospect of waiting a year for the recovery of his position was too much for the Irish chieftain. After concluding his agreement with Robert Fitz-Stephen, he immediately contacted Richard Fitz-Godebert, a Fleming from near Haverford who apparently commanded a small body of mercenaries. At any rate, Dermot and Fitz-Godebert and his small body of troops sailed from St. David's in August, and landed in Leinster. Dermot and his allies were attacked by a large army under the leadership of O'Conor of Connaught and Tiernan O'Rourke. Dermot's force was overwhelmed in the skirmish that followed, but the victors were generous. Dermot was allowed to retain the chieftainship of his own small tribe, and retired to Ferns. The small mercenary band returned to Wales,[12] where they no doubt spread the word of Dermot's defeat and the terms of the peace he had accepted.

The spring of 1168 came and went, and none of the Cambro-Normans who had prepared to sail made a move to leave. Dermot remained in Ferns, licking his wounds and making no effort to re-

[11] As in his agreement with Strongbow, Dermot granted what was not his to give. Wexford, like the other Dansk towns, was independent. Surely Robert and Maurice knew this.

[12] *The Song of Dermot and the Earl*, ll. 414–415. Here it is stated that this force did not remain in Ireland long. The most reasonable time for their departure was *after* Dermot's defeat, since such a mercenary force, however small, would have been of some value to Dermot in battle.

assure his foreign allies. Apparently his grandiose plans had been abandoned. With the coming of winter, however, his energy and ambition returned. Dispatching Morice Regan, his personal interpreter to Wales, Dermot had him circulate an appeal to mercenaries, and to the poor and land-hungry of that country.

> Que tere vodra u deners,
> Chevals, harnes, u destres,
> Or e argent, lur frai doner
> Liuereson asez plener;
> Que tere u herbe voidra aver,
> Richement lus frai feffer
> asez lur durra ensement
> Estore riche feffement[13]

In response to this appeal, Robert Fitz-Stephen began organizing an expedition which was to embark in the following spring, 1169. The make-up of this small force deserves considerable attention in that it illustrates the character of the other Cambro-Norman contingents which were to follow. Also, Fitz-Stephen's group represents in miniature the type of military machine which the marchers had developed to meet the rather stringent requirements which a century of frontier life had laid upon them. Fitz-Stephen's force, like the smaller group of Fitz-Godebert before him, was tripartite in character. According to *The Song of Dermot*, the contingent was composed of "*Chevalers, archers, e serianz.*"[14] Giraldus Cambrensis states that the group consisted of *milites, arcarii* or *sagitarii*, and *loricati*.[15] The identity of these men is clear, but some further discussion of the terms is desirable.

The *milites*, it must be understood, were not "knights" in the more restricted sense of the term. Their very number on this small expedition makes this obvious. Fitz-Stephen numbered thirty such *milites* in his contingent, drawn mainly from his kinsmen and their retainers. These men were not necessarily members of the nobility, but were rather the fully armored horsemen who performed the "knight-service" which formed the basic obligation of feudal land-tenure. One commentator states that "this class of military men represented what we should now call the landed gentry of the country; a class

---

[13] *Ibid.*, ll. 431–438.

[14] *Ibid.*, l. 412.

[15] Giraldus Cambrensis, *Opera*, Part V (*Expugnatio Hibernica*), pp. 230–231.

below barons and knights but of sufficient substance to provide themselves with a war horse and complete armour."[16] The *milites* formed a company of heavy cavalry which represented the core of Fitz-Stephen's organization. Included within this group were three of Fitz-Stephen's nephews, all members of the Geraldine clan: Miles Menevensis, Meiler Fitz-Henry, and Robert of Barri.[17]

The *milites* each possessed two or three retainers, mounted but more lightly armed, who formed a supporting light cavalry corps.[18] These were the *loricati*, of whom Fitz-Stephen was able to field sixty. The nature of their armor is difficult to establish. One commentator suggests that the *loricati* were "half-armoured,"[19] but this term seems scarcely definitive. It must suffice to say that the *loricati* represented a light cavalry force, usually about double the number of the heavy cavalry group with which it operated.

The remaining group, the *sagitarii*, constituted perhaps the most distinctive feature of the marcher contingents. Certainly the attachment of a body of archers to a basically cavalry force was no innovation in Norman warfare.[20] The innovation lay rather in the character of the force, its skill, and the close coordination with which it was employed. The body of *sagitarii* which accompanied Fitz-Stephen numbered three hundred, a number in accordance with the normal Cambro-Norman ratio of ten archers for each *miles*. The most surprising thing about Fitz-Stephen's archer force is that they were Welsh. Giraldus describes the group as *"de electa Gualliae juventutae."*[21] This says much for their skill. The bow had long been the national weapon of the men of South Wales, and they had developed their equipment and techniques through over a century of frontier skirmishes and ambushes. The arrows of the Welsh could penetrate three-inch oak slabs and could inflict mortal wounds through the

[16] Giraldus Cambrensis, *The Historical Works of Giraldus Cambrensis . . .*, eds. and trans. T. Forester and T. Wright, pp. 202–203, n. 1.

[17] Miles was the son of David Fitz-Gerald, bishop of St. David's. Robert of Barri was the brother of Giraldus Cambrensis. Meiler Fitz-Henry was not, properly speaking, a member of the Geraldine clan, but was the illegitimate son of Nesta by Henry I.

[18] These men were possibly similar to the *servientes francigenae* often encountered in *Domesday Book*.

[19] Giraldus Cambrensis, *The Historical Works of Giraldus Cambrensis*, p. 203.

[20] This is amply illustrated by *The Bayeux Tapestry*. Also see R. Glover, "English Warfare in 1066," *The English Historical Review*, LXVII (1952), 1–18.

[21] Giraldus Cambrensis, *Opera*, Part V (*Expugnatio Hibernica*), p. 230.

armor of the heavily armored cavalryman.[22] It is only natural that the Norman marcher lords adapted this peculiarly effective weapon to their own purposes. It is most probable that this process of assimilation began quite early, and that the seal of Earl Gilbert of Clare (d. 1148), which depicts him holding an exaggerated arrow, was intended as a tribute to his proficiency with the national arm of South Wales. Indeed, considering the invaluable role which this weapon played in the endemic strife of the Welsh frontier, it is likely that Welsh "friendlies" were employed at a date much earlier than the redoubtable earl. At any rate, by 1170, Welsh archers appear to have been thoroughly integrated into the Cambro-Norman military organization, and their longbows were recognized as an essential element for military success.

These archers provided the key to the impressive victories which the Cambro-Normans achieved in the difficult terrain which was characteristic of Leinster. The rational use of flexible contingents of cavalry and archers in combination uniformly proved too powerful even for Irish levies of overwhelmingly superior numbers. The Irish were foot soldiers, disdaining armor, and employing spears, javelins, and the battle-axe which they had borrowed from the Dansk warriors of the coastal towns. Only when hard pressed would they employ slingers as missile troops. Although their impetuous tactics, characteristic and obligatory for lightly armed troops, served them well in broken country, they were no match for cavalry in open terrain. Hence, when possible, the Irish would choose broken and forested terrain in which to fight their battles. In their chosen terrain, however, the Irish now had to face the undoubted superiority of the Welsh archers. Throughout the Cambro-Norman campaigns in Ireland, archers and cavalry were combined, and with devastating results.[23]

The core of the invading force, however, was still the heavy cavalry so basic to the typical Norman plan of battle. Here, too, the Cambro-Normans had developed special characteristics which better enabled them to wage successfully the type of warfare with which they were faced. Giraldus contrasted the Anglo-Norman and Cambro-Norman *milites* at great length. His analysis was clouded in some measure by his desire to exalt the role which his kinsmen had played, and in the future could resume, in the subjugation of the Irish. In some

---

[22] Both instances may be found in Giraldus Cambrensis, *Opera*, eds. J. S. Brewer *et al.* Part VI (*Itinerarium Kambriae*), p. 54.

[23] Giraldus Cambrensis, *Opera*, Part V (*Expugnatio Hibernica*), p. 397.

measure, too, his comments no doubt reflected the natural antagonism which the Cambro-Norman "pioneers" must have felt toward the recently arrived Anglo-Norman royal "regulars." The essence of Giraldus' remarks is worthy of consideration, however. He pointed out that the conditions of warfare in France, and in Wales and Ireland, were vastly different, and that each set of conditions had developed its own type of warrior.

Warfare in France consisted of massive battles fought in open country between closely marshalled bodies of heavily armored horsemen. In such battles, the best warrior was the one who was the most heavily armored, had the firmest seat, and was the most skilled in close fighting. The equipment and training of the Anglo-Norman knights were designed to secure exactly these qualities. On the marches of Wales, however, warfare consisted of sudden attacks launched or suffered under a variety of conditions, interspersed with long periods of uneasy quiet. The primary virtue of the marcher warrior, therefore, lay in his flexibility. As conditions warranted, he must needs be a mounted knight, an archer, or a light infantryman. These stringent requirements were reflected in his lighter armor and his peculiar saddle.[24]

These differences in equipment and tactics were paralleled by an equally great difference in psychology. Warfare in France was normally restricted to a definite season; campaigns proceeded along previously determined lines; there was little element of surprise; and the troops were usually well supplied. Between campaigns, there was generally the security and luxury of the winter months. The Anglo-Norman troops in Ireland preferred to be stationed near administrative and supply centers, not only where they could enjoy plenty and hope of advancement, but where there was some measure of collective security and camaraderie.[25] The marchers, on the other hand, were well accustomed to the decentralized and desultory nature of frontier warfare. They were prepared to undergo the privations and boredom which attended frontier service, because this was their way of life. In effect, the Cambro-Norman warriors were willing to face the hard, dull, and brutal facts of frontier warfare in a way the Anglo-Normans could not. There was little honor, less glory, and no sportsmanship here; fighting was neither a profession nor a mystique on

[24] *Ibid.*, p. 386. Giraldus notes that this enabled him to mount and dismount unaided and more quickly.
[25] *Ibid.*, pp. 394–395.

the Welsh frontier—it was a necessity made into a way of life.[26]

Such was the character of the small force which Robert Fitz-Stephen landed on the coast of Ireland near the town of Wexford in May of 1169. The next day the 400 Cambro-Normans were joined by two additional contingents. One, led by Maurice of Prendergast, consisted of a body of about 150 Flemings from Wales, probably mercenaries with whom Dermot had reached a special arrangement.[27] It was maintained as a separate corps, and *The Song of Dermot and the Earl* generally accords Maurice equal dignity with Fitz-Stephen. To these forces, were added 500 native Irish who arrived under Dermot himself. The allied force, numbering less than 1,100 men, marched immediately upon the town of Wexford.

The Cambro-Norman assault upon Wexford reflected little credit upon their ability, for they were quickly beaten off. The Dansk of Wexford, however, were sufficiently impressed to avoid a second attack, and came to terms with Dermot. The Irish chief immediately fulfilled his promise to Fitz-Stephen by granting him the town. At the same time, he granted two nearby *cantrefs* to Hervey of Montmorency, a knight who had accompanied Fitz-Stephen. Montmorency's role in the expedition is difficult to ascertain, but the size of the grant indicates that Dermot considered him of some importance. Since he was an uncle of Richard Fitz-Gilbert, and since Giraldus terms him an *"explorator,"* and states that he acted *"ex parte Ricardi comitis,"*[28] it seems likely that he was Strongbow's official representative. In any event, Hervey was, like most of the others, a failure at home—*"vir quoque fugitivus facie fortunae, inermis et inops . . ."*[29]

With the capture of Wexford, the Cambro-Normans had secured a port which assured them a safe haven for reinforcements and supplies, and a possible route of escape if misfortune befell them. Their numbers were swelled by the Dansk axemen of the town and by the growing number of Irish who chose to support a successful cause. Under Dermot's direction, they expanded their range of operations, especially inland, into the kingdom of Ossory, ruled by an old foe of

---

[26] *Ibid.*, p. 396.

[27] This assumes that Maurice's force was similar in make-up to that of Fitz-Stephen. Maurice commanded ten *milites*. This would mean twenty *loricati* and one hundred archers.

[28] Giraldus Cambrensis, *Opera*, Part V (*Expugnatio Hibernica*), p. 230.

[29] *Ibid.*, p. 230.

Dermot. A massive raid was organized which spread wide destruction in the heart of the little kingdom. As the Cambro-Normans returned through the heavily forested highlands lying above the river Barrow, they were set upon by the armies of MacGillipatrick, king of Ossory. Here the Irish first experienced the devastating effects which the Cambro-Normans could achieve through the coordinated use of cavalry and archers. Hard-pressed by the Irish, Maurice of Prendergast posted his small force of archers in the cover lying along the pass leading into the uplands and then ordered a feigned retreat by the cavalry down into the valley floor.[30] The Irish were completely deceived and pursued in disorder. They found themselves completely unable to cope with the regrouped cavalry on the valley floor and equally unable to regain the uplands in the face of the sharp-eyed archers. Caught between the two forces, the army of Ossory broke, and the Dansk and Irish axemen finished the bloody work. That evening, over two hundred heads were piled before an exultant Dermot.

Flushed with this success, Dermot began directing his army in similar raids which extended throughout Leinster, apparently with uniform success.[31] Soon, however, the Cambro-Normans were faced with a more formidable opponent than the local levies of the small kingdoms of Leinster. The men of Connaught under the high king, Rori O'Conor, joined with the armies of Tiernan O'Rourke and Dermot O'Melaghlin, and with the Dansk of Dublin, and marched into northern Leinster. This was the same combination of enemies that had toppled Dermot in 1166, and now, as then, his supporters rapidly began to fall away from him. Numbered among these deserters was Maurice of Prendergast and his Fleming contingent.

For some time now Dermot had been pursuing a program based upon raids directed against the primitive kingdoms of the Irish inland. Such a policy could not have been very popular with the mercenary troops whom Maurice led. These areas held little promise of plunder commensurate with the dangers and difficulties which such operations entailed. To their dissatisfaction was now added the news of the approach of an immense host bent upon their destruction. About two hundred men, or one-third of the Cambro-Norman force, left for Wexford, where they intended to embark for Wales. Dermot,

---

[30] For Maurice's tactical dispositions, see *The Song of Dermot and the Earl*, ll. 664–703.

[31] For details of these raids, see *ibid.*, ll. 864–1055.

with whom Maurice had parted on bad terms,[32] sent word to Wexford that Maurice was not to be allowed passage. Maurice quickly reacted by offering to sell his services to MacGillipatrick, king of Ossory. Having had ample demonstration of the worth of these Cambro-Norman troops, MacGillipatrick quickly accepted, and Maurice began the march inland to join his forces to those of Dermot's enemies. Dermot was forced to deplete his own forces yet further by dispatching five hundred men to obstruct Maurice's passage into Ossory, an attempt which completely failed.

The Cambro-Normans under Robert Fitz-Stephen now found themselves in desperate straits. The armies of their Irish ally were sadly depleted by defections and by the ill-fated expedition against Maurice, and their own forces had been reduced greatly by the withdrawal of the Flemings. Advancing on them from the north was a vast host led by O'Conor, and to the west lay the men of Ossory, now strengthened by the addition of a dangerous Cambro-Norman force under a skilled leader. Fitz-Stephen and Dermot withdrew to a position of some natural defensive strength near Ferns, and, under the former's direction, the Cambro-Normans constructed additional defenses while they awaited the advent of O'Conor's host.

The events that followed were exhaustively described by Giraldus Cambrensis.[33] His handling of the events, however, is rather confusing, for his Cambro-Norman bias led him to misjudge completely the significance of what was occurring. And yet, his account is not without a peculiar worth. His materials and prejudices were drawn mainly from the actual participants, no doubt including his uncle, Robert Fitz-Stephen himself. He received uncritically, and perhaps embellished a little, the memories which these old warriors proudly treasured of the critical time of the conquest. What Giraldus wrote in these passages was not history; it was the earliest stages of a frontier epic, a legend in the making.

He described a time when the small group of original settlers waited in their rough fortifications as an entire nation in arms marched against them. Though they were few, the far-sighted O'Conor, high king of Ireland, had seen that they were but the advance guard of the whole Cambro-Norman race. If they were to be stopped, it must be

---

[32] *Ibid.*, ll. 1092–1093.

[33] Giraldus Cambrensis, *Opera*, Part V (*Expugnatio Hibernica*), pp. 236–243.

then. O'Conor first made an attempt to separate the settlers from their barbarous but loyal ally. A message sent to Fitz-Stephen offering rewards and safe-conduct if he were to abandon Dermot, was curtly refused. A second message was sent to the latter, offering him the kingdom of Leinster if he were to abandon his allies, and help exterminate these dangerous foreigners. True to his faith, Dermot refused, even with defeat and death confronting him. O'Conor realized that only battle would solve the issue, and so called his troops together, and called upon them to embark on a national crusade, saying, in part:

"Wherefore, defending our country and liberty, and acquiring for ourselves eternal reknown, let us by a resolute attack and the extermination of our enemies, though they are but few in number, strike terror into many, and by their fate forever deter foreign nations from such nefarious attempts."[34]

On the other side, Fitz-Stephen also made a speech to his Cambro-Norman troops. His words, as reported by Giraldus, probe deeply into the mentality of these early conquerors, the "old warriers," then in their youth. He made it clear that the Cambro-Normans considered themselves a special, and superior, breed of men, when he said:

"We derive our descent, originally, in part from the blood of the Trojans, and partly we are of the French race. From the one we have our native courage, from the other the use of armour. Since, then, inheriting such generous blood on both sides, we are not only brave, but well armed . . ."[35]

It is clear from these words that the archers and men-at-arms of this Cambro-Norman expedition had developed a sense of nationality, an amalgam of Norman and Welsh traditions created in the peculiar conditions on the frontier in South Wales. But the frontier was gone, and their talents no longer found any scope there. These were men for whom conditions in Wales had grown too restrictive; they were losers at home. Fitz-Stephen made this clear, not only in his own life, but when he stated, "we have left behind in our native land ample patrimonies which we lost through domestic frauds and intestine mischief."[36] But it was not adversity at home that had caused

---

[34] *Ibid.*, p. 240; translation from *The Historical Works of Giraldus Cambrensis*, p. 199.

[35] Giraldus Cambrensis, *Opera*, Part V (*Expugnatio Hibernica*), p. 242; translation from *The Historical Works of Giraldus Cambrensis*, p. 200.

[36] Giraldus Cambrensis, *Opera*, Part V (*Expugnatio Hibernica*), p. 242; translation from *The Historical Works of Giraldus Cambrensis*, p. 200.

them to leave South Wales. They had come out voluntarily, seeking
a land where, with bravery and determination, a man could carve out
new patrimonies and find new opportunities. "Wherefore, we are
come hither not for the sake of pay or plunder, but induced by the
promise of towns and lands, to be granted to us and our heirs forever."[37] They had found their new land of scope and opportunity.
They were planting a new race in a country in which the sky was the
limit. Their sons might rule the land, and the prophecies of their own
ancestors might be fulfilled.[38] This was a land of promise, but they
were also aware that it was a land of danger. They might fail in their
endeavor, but that was a matter of little consequence—they would
die with honor in a good clean fight, and fighting was their business.
"One must die, since this is unavoidable and common to all. And yet,
if you avoid dishonor, either glory will illuminate your life or the
memory of praise will follow your death."[39]

Despite the speech-making, the fight never occurred. When
O'Conor found himself facing the steadfast Cambro-Normans, he
began to have second thoughts about the advisability of an attack.
Instead, he entered into secret negotiations with Dermot offering him
the possibility of an honorable peace. The latter agreed, gave his son
to O'Conor as a hostage, and recognized O'Conor's position as high
king. In return, O'Conor confirmed him as king of Leinster, and
promised him his daughter in marriage. In pursuance of his primary
objective, O'Conor extracted a secret promise from him that he would
send the Cambro-Normans back to Wales at the earliest possible opportunity. Having achieved this compromise, O'Conor and his force
withdrew, and the danger was past. Never again would the Cambro-
Normans be so weak. They had faced an entire nation in arms bent
upon their destruction, and, by steadfastness and courage, had forced
their enemies to falter, temporize, and lose their opportunity. The
moment of crisis had come and had passed.

Such at least was the legend which Giraldus Cambrensis preserved for us. These are memories, aided by the passage of two decades, and embellished by the rhetoric of a masterful romanticist.
What was the historical actuality? Our other Norman source, *The
Song of Dermot and the Earl*, is of little help, for it chooses to ignore

---

[37] Giraldus Cambrensis, *Opera*, Part V (*Expugnatio Hibernica*), p. 242;
translation from *The Historical Works of Giraldus Cambrensis*, p. 200.

[38] Giraldus Cambrensis, *Opera*, Part V (*Expugnatio Hibernica*), pp. 242–243.

[39] *Ibid.*, p. 243. Author's translation.

the entire series of events. This in itself, however, is indicative that
Giraldus' account may be somewhat distorted. There can be only two
explanations for the *Song's* omission of this episode. Either it represents an attempt to suppress an affair which was a defeat for Dermot,
the hero of the account, or else the entire series of events was of little
real significance. Although the former interpretation appears the
more likely, either is in poor accordance with the heroic account contained in Giraldus.

The Irish *Annals of the Four Masters* contains an account of the
encounter near Ferns, but with a far different emphasis. Here was no
nation in arms bent upon the destruction of the hated foreigners, but
only one of a series of expeditions which O'Conor led into various
parts of Ireland in that year. At the end of a long passage describing
the events of the year 1169, the annalist summarized the Leinster
affair as follows:

The King of Ireland . . . O'Conor . . . afterwards proceeded into Leinster,
and . . . [with] Tiernan O'Rourke and Dermot O'Meaglaughlin, king of
Teamhair . . . and the foreigners of Atha Cliath Dublin, went to meet the
men of Munster, Leinster, and Osraigh; and they set nothing by the Flemings; and . . . Dermot MacMurrough . . . gave his son as hostage to . . .
O'Conor.[40]

The brevity with which the annalist records the event gives some indication of the true significance of the expedition into Leinster and
of Dermot's subsequent capitulation. Viewed as part of the broad
sweep of Irish events, the expedition against Leinster was but a single
episode in O'Conor's governmental policy. In G. H. Orpen's opinion,
O'Conor's

object, primarily at least, was not to get rid of the handful of foreigners,
in his eyes almost a negligible quantity, still less was it to expell Dermot,
but to obtain his submission, exact more important hostages, and regularize
his position in Leinster. These objects he for the moment obtained.[41]

In some measure, however, the legend contains more truth than
the historical actuality. This *was* a critical episode, not only for the

----

[40] *Annals of the Kingdom of Ireland, by the Four Masters, from the Earliest
Period to the Year 1616 . . .*, ed. and trans. J. O'Donovan, II, 1172–1173.
[41] Orpen, *Ireland under the Normans*, I, 173.

beleaguered Cambro-Normans, but for the Irish themselves. At this moment, O'Conor could have expelled or exterminated the handful of intruders and indefinitely postponed the massive invasions which were to follow. Against the broad background of Irish politics, however, it was difficult for the Irish king to gauge the true significance of the presence of this small group. If he had been able to do so, he would no doubt have bent every effort to exterminate them. The Cambro-Normans were saved, but not by their strength and determination; rather they were protected by their weakness. Giraldus and the Cambro-Normans erred in crediting O'Conor with a great deal more insight than he in fact possessed.

With danger from O'Conor past, at least for the moment, Fitz-Stephen and Dermot turned to the threat posed by the alliance between MacGillipatrick and Maurice of Prendergast. By the fall of the year they were successful in this area: the men of Ossory had been thoroughly cowed and Prendergast and his Flemings had returned to Pembrokeshire. Thus, by the close of the year 1169, Dermot had achieved all those aims which had originally impelled him to seek foreign aid. He had been confirmed as king of Leinster, and all major areas of this kingdom had been pacified. The time had now come when, according to his agreement with O'Conor, he was to send his Cambro-Norman allies home. Dermot's ambitions had increased, however, as he became better aware of the power with which the possession of these foreign troops had endowed him. He now resolved to increase the size of his Cambro-Norman contingent as much as possible and, through them, to seize Connaught and the monarchy of all Ireland.[42]

To do this, he soon saw, he must persuade Richard Fitz-Gilbert to end his procrastination, and to take an active part in the expedition. According to Giraldus, he sent a letter to Strongbow, which stated, in part, "if you come in time with a strong force, the other four parts of the kingdom will be easily united to the fifth . . ."[43] Needless to say, this new proposal was extremely attractive to the earl. Dermot had promised that he should be heir to the kingdom of Leinster; he now offered all of Ireland. The offer also presented the earl some diffi-

---

[42] Giraldus Cambrensis, *Opera*, Part V (*Expugnatio Hibernica*), p. 246.
[43] *Ibid.*, pp. 246–247; translation from *The Historical Works of Giraldus Cambrensis*, p. 205.

culties, however. The original letter of patent which Henry had
granted Dermot had stipulated:

> Wherefore, whosoever within the bounds of our territories shall be will-
> ing to give him [Dermot] aid, as our vassal and liegeman, in recovering his
> territories, let him be assured of our favor on that behalf.[44]

Dermot's new proposal went far beyond the terms of Henry's original
grant. Far from merely recovering his own territories, he now contemplated the conquest of all Ireland. The prospect was alluring, but
it became doubly necessary for Strongbow to receive specific permission from his monarch. It also was necessary that he hide from Henry
how favorable his prospects were. He went to the court, assuming the
role of a man driven to desperation, and petitioned the king either to
grant him those lands which were his by right of inheritance, or to
give him permission to depart the country and seek his fortune in
other realms. Apparently Henry refused to give a direct reply, but
Strongbow seized upon a chance remark the king made and in-
terpreted it as the permission he had sought.[45] He departed the court
and made preparations for an expedition to Ireland.

About the middle of August in 1170, Strongbow began to move
along the old coast road, heading for Milford and gathering recruits
along the way. In Pembrokeshire the addition of Maurice of Prendergast's force brought his total strength to about two hundred *milites*
and a thousand infantry. It must be noted that the symmetry of the
earlier Cambro-Norman contingents here breaks down. This was a
more cosmopolitan group, numbering among its members groups of
javelin men and of English infantry. Meanwhile, Henry had been re-
considering his rather hasty words, and, even as this force was prepared to embark, a message came from the king forbidding the expedition.[46] It was too late for Strongbow to yield, and, on August 23,
1170, he landed his force near Waterford. On the 25th, they moved

---

[44] Giraldus Cambrensis, *Opera*, Part V (*Expugnatio Hibernica*), pp. 227–228;
translation from *The Historical Works of Giraldus Cambrensis*, p. 186.

[45] Giraldus Cambrensis, *Opera*, Part V (*Expugnatio Hibernica*), p. 248.
Giraldus states that Richard "*accepta igitur quasi licentia, ironica namque magis
quam vera. . . .*" Also see Gervase of Canterbury, *The Historical Works of Gervase of Canterbury, edited from the Manuscripts*, ed. W. Stubbs, Part I, p. 234.
Gervase states clearly, "*. . . unde praedictus comes tristis effectus licentiam
abeundi petiit et abtinuit. . . .*"

[46] Giraldus Cambrensis, *Opera*, Part V (*Expugnatio Hibernica*), p. 259.

against the town and, after having been twice repulsed, effected a breach in the walls. The troops entered, and a general slaughter took place.

A few days later, Dermot arrived and, under the watchful eyes of the Cambro-Norman garrison, consummated his alliance with Richard Fitz-Gilbert by wedding his daughter, Eva, to the Cambro-Norman leader. This wedding marks the high point of Cambro-Norman hopes in Ireland. Their recognized leader was now heir to the entire kingdom of Leinster, and was ready to lead them to the conquest of the rest of Ireland. Great accomplishments lay behind them, and vast opportunities lay ahead.

Even at that very time, however, their period of high hopes was drawing to an end. Their Irish frontier was to be denied to them, much as had been Wales. King Henry, hearing of the Cambro-Norman successes, began to fear the effects of an independent or even semi-independent kingdom in the hands of these turbulent and untamed warriors. He took immediate steps to halt their progress and to bring them to heel. An edict was issued ordering the adventurers to return home upon pain of confiscation, and, at the same time, Irish ports were closed to all English shipping. The Cambro-Normans were thus cut off from their sources of supply and reinforcement. Strongbow took the only course open to him, and dispatched a lieutenant to the royal court, humbly offering Henry immediate overlordship of all lands which had been won.[47]

On the 18th of October, 1171, King Henry landed at Waterford, and commenced the task of regulating and ordering the realm which he had so easily won. The details of this process are irrelevant; the Cambro-Normans were robbed of their frontier, and the repressive and restrictive royal authority which they had sought to escape had followed them across the sea. Courtiers, sycophants, politicians, and other johnnie-come-latelys followed in the wake of the king, and it was by these people that Ireland was carved up and divided. The frontiersmen were forced to step aside, and see a new order of things instituted; an order in which they had no part. Giraldus is bitter in his denunciation of this injustice:

. . . therefore we treated the old soldiers of the land, through whose attack we gained entry into this island, as if they were suspect, as if they were

[47] *Ibid.*, p. 259.

repudiated. Taking counsel only with newcomers, having faith only in newcomers, we considered only newcomers worthy of honor.[48]

There was no place further for the old warriors to go, and so they settled down to the thankless task of garrison duty along a frontier which no longer meant opportunity, but toil. Their frontier had come to an end. As these men passed away, so, too, did the last generation of the Cambro-Norman conquerors.

[48] *Ibid.*, p. 395 (Author's translation).

viii. The Cambro-Norman Society of South Wales

WE HAVE SEEN that the Norman frontier in South Wales came to an end only a century after its inception. Viewed against the broad sweep of British history, a century is a rather short time, and South Wales but a small corner of the island. It is well to remember, however, that this century was a long enough period for three generations to pass through the experience of frontier life, and that three generations of men are quite sufficient to leave a deep impression upon the society of the region in which they live. This was especially true in South Wales, where the three frontier generations established a set of traditions and a way of life which were both distinctive and enduring and which even today have set South Wales apart from the rest of Britain.[1]

Neither the duchy of Normandy nor the monarchy of England had ever devised a governmental policy which enabled them to stabilize and regularize the marcher regions which lay along their borders. Generally speaking, the marches lay beyond the power of central authority, and beyond the pale of society dominated by that authority. Social and political institutions are basically designed to promote stability in the society which adopts them. They are maintained, however, at the price of personal liberties, and, historically speaking, the social institutions which have promoted social stability have also acted to limit social mobility. Such at least appears to have been the

---

[1] A number of uniquely Welsh characteristics are noted by C. Hughes, *Royal Wales: The Land and Its People.*

case in medieval England. These restrictive social and political institutions extended into the marches of Wales only in the most attenu-
ated form, and, for this reason, the frontier was a land of opportunity.
Slowly at first the settlers began to move into the area. Not only Normans and English, but a variety of peoples came—French, Flemish,
Breton, Angevin, and others. Each of these peoples brought with
them their own peculiar ideas of how things were to be done, and
they brought them into an area where generally accepted modes of
behavior were at a minimum. Far more than in the firmly established
societies of Europe, the men of the Welsh frontier were at liberty to
develop their own institutions and to work out their own destiny.

The various regulating institutions of early England—the king,
the Church, and others—set limits upon the lengths to which the in-
novators might go. By and large, however, the settlers of South Wales
seem to have been allowed to draw upon their cosmopolitan background, and to devise a way of life by which they could adapt to the
peculiar conditions which characterized the Welsh frontier. The frontier society of South Wales was subjected to a number of unusual
stresses: the cultural diversity of its members, a chronic lack of manpower, the necessity of accommodating large numbers of native
Welsh within the social order, the constant threat of encroachments
by unconquered Welsh tribesmen, the desire not to stray too far from
the mainstream of life of Anglo-Norman society, the desire to prevent
royal and ecclesiastical domination, the goal of exploiting the frontier
through further conquests—the list could be endless. These and other
pressures reshaped the traditions and institutions which the early
settlers brought with them, and gave them new emphases. A society
emerged with certain peculiarities which set it apart from the rest
of Anglo-Norman society. In the present chapter we will discuss four
aspects of the Cambro-Normans' way of life, in an attempt to show
that these peculiarities simply reflect the special stresses to which
their frontier experience had subjected them.

(a) The Marcher Lords

Perhaps the most distinctive of the institutions of Cambro-Norman
society was its peculiar political and judicial system. Throughout
England, the Middle Ages saw the slow extension of royal authority
in virtually every area of life, and the parallel standardization of
usages and elimination of localism. In the marches of Wales, however,
these processes were completely arrested and, in some instances,

even reversed. The political structure of the Welsh frontier was anything but monolithic. Norman holdings were composed of a series of semi-independent lordships, each dominated by its marcher lord. The marcher lord was a semiregal figure, supreme within his own realm. The king's writ did not run in the marcher lordships of the Welsh frontier, and each lordship was like a petty kingdom, possessing its own parliament and system of justice.

The marcher lords claimed the right to their own personal chancery, and it is apparent that many of them exercised this right. One would expect to find that the records of these chanceries would provide reasonably full accounts of the legislation and administration of the Cambro-Norman lordships. Such is not the case, however, for the records which these chanceries must have compiled have been completely lost though some individual charters which they issued have survived. It is difficult to discover the cause of this loss, but the answer may lie in the destruction attending the English Civil War. When the marcher lordships were abolished under the Tudors, the center of administration for Wales was established at Ludlow in Shropshire. It may well have been that the records of the chanceries of the marcher lordships were removed to Ludlow at this time to be placed in a central repository. The city was almost completely destroyed in the course of the Civil War, and it may be that the records were lost at that time.[2]

Whatever the possible cause of their disappearance, most of the records are no longer available, and we must gain our information largely from other sources. Royal records provide the most important of these sources: pleas to the crown, *inquisitiones post mortem*, feudal services owed to the crown, and records of escheats, especially when royal officials administered a lordship for a reasonably lengthy period. The fact that we must depend mainly upon royal records creates great difficulties in evaluating the political life of the marcher lordships. We have seen that the most distinctive characteristic of these lordships was their extensive independence from royal authority. And yet, our major data concerning the lords and their lordships comes most often from those instances in which they come into direct contact with agencies of the crown. We know when the marcher lords quarrel and appeal to the king, or when local government breaks down and royal authority steps in to administer an area. We

[2] G. T. Clark, *The Land of Morgan: Being a Contribution towards the History of the Lordship of Glamorgan*, pp. 26–27.

know but little of the orderly and regular workings of the Cambro-Normans' legal and political system, and of the cooperation which must have been characteristic of the invaders' way of life. In short, the data which we do possess is such that the student must infer the rule from his knowledge of the exceptions.

We do, however, possess an appreciable amount of information concerning the powers and privileges of the marcher lord himself, the focus of the Cambro-Norman political system. In the course of time, the processes of standardization and of extension of royal authority reached the Welsh frontier, and attempts were made to strip the marcher lords of their traditional, but anomalous, rights. The border barons vociferously protested such attempts, and, in so doing, threw some light upon the nature and extent of the privileges they were defending.

The marcher lords recognized the fact that they were feudal nobles. They held their land by right of their and their fathers' conquests, and, as Gilbert, earl of Gloucester, stated, "*sicut regale.*"[3] They were tenants *in capite*, each holding directly from the king. They occupied a special status, however. Their holdings did not form part of the realm of England, and within them, they enjoyed an almost complete immunity from royal interference. The royal legalists recognized the peculiar status of these lordships "in the marches, where the King's writ does not run."[4] In addition, despite the fact that they were feudal vassals of the kings, the marcher lords denied the necessity of referring their quarrels to the king's court. On the contrary, they claimed the right of settling their disputes among themselves, according to their own customary law, the Law of the March, or even *viribus armatis et vexillis explicatis.*[5] Their immunity from royal authority was not absolute, of course, but the conditions under which the king could interfere were extremely limited:

A lordship escheated to the Crown if there were no heir of age at the death of the lord, if the lord rebelled or was convicted of felony or treason,

---

[3] British Museum, MS Cotton Vitellius, CX, folio 172b. This MS has been edited and published by G. T. Clark, "The Appeal of Richard Siward to the Curia Regis from a Decision in the Curia Comitatus in Glamorgan, 1248," *Archaeologia Cambrensis*, Series IV, Vol. IX (1878), pp. 241–263.

[4] *Statutes of the Realm*, I, 226.

[5] Clark, "The Appeal of Richard Siward," pp. 249–250. Also see *The Welsh Assize Roll, 1277–1284*, ed. J. C. Davies, pp. 309 and 315.

if the lord deserted his lordship in time of war, or if the lordship were in dispute.[6]

Even in these cases, the lordship was not absorbed into the realm of England, but, like an honor, it was maintained intact until again granted as a marcher lordship with all of the rights and privileges that were attached to this status.

This almost complete freedom from royal interference allowed the marcher lords to exercise within their lordships many powers which were elsewhere in England the sole prerogatives of the crown. They acted as kings in their own right, appointing their own sheriffs, possessing their own chanceries and their personal great seals. They had jurisdiction over all cases, high and low, civil and criminal, with the exception of crimes of high treason. They established their own courts to try these offenses, executed sentences, and amerced fines. They possessed all of the royal perquisites—salvage, treasure-trove, plunder, and royal fish. They could establish forests and forest laws, declare and wage war, establish boroughs, and grant extensive charters of liberties. They could confiscate the estates of traitors and felons, and regrant these at will. They could establish and preside over their own petty parliaments and county courts. Finally, they could claim any and every feudal due, aid, grant, and relief. The list of the powers, incomplete as it is, is still very impressive. Petty frontier barons exercised in their little lordships powers and privileges which were far beyond the aspirations of the greatest lords of England.[7] They were the embodiment of sovereignty within their lordships.

Within the lordship itself, the inhabitants exercised a more powerful and immediate limitation on the powers of the lord. As we have said before, the frontier suffered from a chronic shortage of manpower. Each individual man was important to the security and prosperity of the lordship, be he a trader, an artisan, a man-at-arms, or a simple farmer. The threat of emigration was an effective and immediate method of coercion by which the people could maintain a direct voice in the manner in which the marcher lord exercised the powers at his discretion. At the same time, the lordships were small,

---

[6] W. Rees, *South Wales and the March, 1284–1415: A Social and Agrarian Study*, p. 44, n. 2.

[7] Clark, *The Land of Morgan*, pp. 24–25.

yielded little profit, and lay in constant danger of Welsh attack. The threat of civil strife or disobedience was proportionately more distasteful to the lord.[8] The extensive immunities and powers which the marcher lords enjoyed were of distinct benefit to the inhabitants of the Welsh frontier, since the situation gave them an immediate and relatively responsive ruler, rather than the distant and all-powerful monarch to whom the rest of England looked.

The symbol of the marcher lord's power, and of his position in his community, was his castle, and virtually every marcher lord possessed one. He could build his castles when and where he pleased, a right apparently denied to the lords of England.[9] The castle represented more, however, than just a symbol of the lord's power; it was the focus of Cambro-Norman life. It was not only their refuge in time of war, but the center of their political life in time of peace.

Each lordship had its castle. We are apt to think of a castle merely as a military fortification. But the castle was something more than a place of defence . . . The Court of the Castle Gate, as it was called, embodied the courthouse of the old Welsh kings, though not its spirit. Amid hostile surroundings the courthouse had now to be fortified . . .[10]

The castle was the center of the legal and legislative activities of the Cambro-Normans. There remains no record of how the conquerors ordered these affairs. In Glamorgan, however, the Court of the Castle Gate endured into the sixteenth century. An Elizabethan author who was familiar with the later practices attempted to describe what the original might have been. The survival may indicate some flavor of the original proceedings:

He [Robert Fitz-Hamon] dwelt himselfe in the said castell or towne of Cardyff, being a faire haven towne. And bicause he would have the aforesaid twelve Knights and their heires give attendance vpon him euerie Countie daie, (which was alwaies kept by the Sherife in the vtter ward of the said castle on the Mondaie Monethlie as is before said) he gave everie one of them a lodging within the vtter ward, the which their heires, or those that purchased the same of their heires, doo enioie at this daie.

Also the morow after the countie daie, being the tuesdaie, the Lord his Chancellor sate alwaies in the Chancerie there, for the determining of mat-

---

[8] Rees, *South Wales and the March*, pp. 51–52.

[9] F. Lieberman, *Die Gesetze der Angelsachesen*, I, 556 and 558. Also see C. H. Haskins, *Norman Institutions*, p. 282.

[10] W. Rees, "Medieval Gwent," *The Journal of the British Archaeological Society*, XXXIV (1928), 202.

ters of conscience in strife, happening as well in the said Sherfee as in the members; the which daie also, the said Knights vsed to give attendance vpon the Lord; and the Wednesdaie everie man drew homeward, and then began the courts of the members to be kept in order, one after another.[11]

Whether or not this is an accurate portrayal of twelfth-century usage, a general picture can be derived from other scattered data. The knights and landowners who gathered at the castle gate formed both a parliament and a court, a legislative and judicial assembly. Led by the lord, or by his representative, these bodies helped to formulate and apply the laws by which the emergent Cambro-Norman society coordinated its activities. Thus the lordships were independent, not only of royal authority, but of each other. Each was allowed to develop its own local usages, and to treat with its lord as to how and to what extent he would exercise the massive powers vested in him. Thus it is erroneous to speak of a Cambro-Norman legal system; rather there existed a number of such systems, flexible and developing independently. The nature of these various systems was lost with the chancery records of which we spoke earlier. A single fact stands out clearly, however. The laws of the Cambro-Normans stood untouched by the impetus for uniformity and consistency which elsewhere in twelfth-century Britain was producing the basis for the final supremacy of English common law.

The Cambro-Norman courts of the Welsh frontier did not recognize any great need for standardization. Both Welsh and Norman usages were recognized as valid, and archaic practices were steadfastly retained. Cases involving Welsh tenure and Norman feudal tenure were handled indiscriminately by the same court.[12] Other lordships maintained both Welsh and English courts, each administering its special brand of justice.[13] Insofar as Cambro-Norman legal arrangements did achieve some sort of consistency they represented

a partial fusion of such customary law as was known to the first conquerors, c. 1100, and Welsh customary law. . . . the system which thus began developed independently of that development of the common law in England which rendered the customs of c. 1100 archaic. No such develop-

[11] D. Powel, *The Historie of Cambria Now Called Wales* . . ., pp. 95–96.
[12] G. Owen, *Prooffes Out of Auntient Recordes, Writings and Other Matters That the Lordshipp of Kemes is a Lordshippe Marcher, Baronia de Kemeys,* from the Original Documents at Bronwydd, pp. 72–74.
[13] *Cartae et alia munimenta quae ad Dominium de Glamorgancia pertinent,* ed. G. T. Clark, III, 831, and VI, 2277–2278.

ment would have been possible in even the greatest of English or Anglo-Irish franchises, for the writ of error which ran in all of them meant that the lord must be careful to see that the common law was applied in his court if the writ was not to be used against him, but in Wales this check did not operate, and local usage could prevail unhampered.[14]

This much is clear; the legal systems of the Welsh frontier were peculiar. They became so and remained so because the immunities which the marcher lords enjoyed protected the frontier, in large measure, from the forces which elsewhere were producing uniformity and centralization. It is impossible to say whether or not the laws of the marcher lordships were repressive or liberal. One can only point out that the people of the frontier were free to develop their own laws in cooperation with a ruler who was close to them and dependent upon their support. It would be surprising if they developed a legal system which they did not find congenial.

It should be evident by now that the political system of the Welsh frontier was unique, in terms of British constitutional development. It is also clear that most of those features which made it distinctive stemmed from a single factor—the extensive and anachronistic immunities and powers which the kings of England allowed the marcher lords to enjoy. The question remains as to why these minor barons were allowed to acquire and exercise rights which were jealously denied to even the greatest and most loyal magnates of England. This is not a simple question to answer. The traditional explanation has been that the rights and powers were granted partially as a reward for undertaking the arduous task of conquering the turbulent Welsh, and partially to enable them to accomplish this task more easily. This explanation is, on the face of it, inadequate. It is difficult to explain how the right to wage private war on one's Norman neighbors or to have first claim on the royal sturgeon could have aided the border baron in subduing his Welsh opponents. It is necessary to look elsewhere for the source of these anomalous privileges.

Sir Goronwy Edwards has considered this problem at some length, and has arrived at the not too surprising conclusion that the marcher lords derived their powers directly from the Welsh chieftains whom

[14] A. J. Otway-Ruthven, "The Constitutional Position of the Great Lordships of South Wales," *The Transactions of the Royal Historical Society,* Series V, Vol. VIII (1958), p. 12.

they replaced.[15] This explanation removes many difficulties. It can easily be seen that the powers that the marcher lords claimed, and the manner in which they exercised them, were quite similar to powers and activities of the lords of the commotes they had conquered. Such a process places the powers of the marcher lords in their proper perspective as an unusual, but integral, part of the process of British constitutional development. The initial principle which had governed the development of Anglo-Norman society had been that enunciated by the Conqueror himself—that the Anglo-Saxon system was to remain, and that the Norman conquerors were simply replacing Anglo-Saxon tenants. Finally, the grants he made to his followers carried with them every privilege and obligation which they had entailed under the English kings.[16] It can be clearly seen that the Normans carried this principle with them into Wales. Edwards comments:

In Wales, as well as in England, they planted their feet firmly into the shoes of their *antecessores*. But in Wales, of course, their *antecessores* happened not to be Englishmen. And that is the historical explanation of the contrast between Norman handiwork in the March of Wales and Norman handiwork in England.[17]

As the border barons moved into Wales, they assumed a dual role— that of feudal lord and vassal of the king in the eyes of their Norman followers, and of *tywysog* for the conquered Cambrians. As Cambro-Norman society emerged, the two roles became one, and the functions merged. The formative period came during the reigns of kings who were either incapable or uninterested in arresting the process.

Thus it is seen that the almost pure feudalism of the Welsh frontier came about, not as a result of English or Norman development, but as the amalgamation of the intensely flexible institutions of the early invaders and of the relatively inflexible institutions of the conquered tribesmen. The peculiar political structure of the marches of Wales was determined in large measure by the peculiar political system of preinvasion Wales. In the end result, however, this amalgamation would not have occurred if it had not worked to the advantage of

---

[15] J. G. Edwards, "The Normans and the Welsh March," *The Proceedings of the British Academy*, XLII (1956), 155–177.

[16] F. M. Stenton, *Anglo-Saxon England*, p. 618.

[17] Edwards, "The Normans and the Welsh March," pp. 174–175.

those concerned. The possibility of acquiring the semiregal status of marcher lords drew turbulent and adventurous settlers to the frontier, and, in some measure, hope may have made up for the toil, frustration, and failure which was often their lot. The development of the marcher lord's power also created a governmental institution which both invaders and invaded could understand, and through which they might eventually be integrated. The wide range of powers in the hands of the border barons allowed them to develop organizations capable of facing and adapting to the rapidly changing fortunes of frontier life. Finally, the concentration of power in the hands of the marcher lord, and his independence of royal authority, provided the frontiersmen an immediate and responsive government, and the possibility of individual freedom and power which such a government brought.

(b) The Church on the Frontier

In the last analysis, Cambro-Norman society faced two great challenges: to develop institutions which could utilize not only the lowland environment of Wales but also the uplands which lay above the 600-foot contour line, and to develop institutions which could be shared by both the typically lowland culture of the Anglo-Normans and the typically upland culture of the Welsh tribesmen. We have seen how the Anglo-Norman conquerors of the eleventh century failed to meet these challenges, and attempted to insulate their lowland environment and their lowland culture through the erection of a line of fortresses. In the course of time, however, a distinctive Cambro-Norman society emerged in the area which, in some aspects of life at least, managed to make a start toward bridging the gaps between the two cultures. This appears to have been true of the political system which emerged along the frontier. Let us now turn to the role played by the Church along the Welsh frontier.

One would think that their common faith would have provided a meeting ground for the invaders and the Welsh tribesmen. Both peoples considered themselves as integral parts of the Universal Church which dominated western Europe. Within this faith, however, there existed a great range and diversity of practices, and the Welsh and the Normans found themselves at opposite ends of this range. Their cultural differences were perhaps more apparent in their religious practices than anywhere else.

As we have said before, Welsh religious practice was of the

Celtic variety, and was dominated by the *clas*, a monastic organization firmly based upon Welsh tribal structure. Organization was extremely decentralized, and the enforcement of discipline was virtually nonexistent. This led to a wide variety of practices, ranging
from the excessive asceticism of the holy hermits to the secularism
and corruption of monks scarcely distinguishable from the tribesmen
about them. This is not to say that the Church in Wales did not
serve the Welsh people effectively. The important fact is that the
organization of the Welsh Church was extremely decentralized, and
closely integrated into the tribal structure of Welsh life. It could not
help but be a part of its society and a rallying point for Welsh
nationalism.[18]

The Church in Normandy exhibited characteristics almost dia-
metrically opposed to the Welsh Church. It observed Roman usage,
and was already one of the most highly organized representatives of
this type. It exhibited fully the internal division between secular and
regular clergy which the Welsh Church completely lacked. The
secular clergy was firmly organized into a diocesan structure based
upon territorial divisions of the duchy. The Church possessed immense wealth and engaged in a great number of activities, both
spiritual and secular, on the local level. These activities were regulated by a chain of command running directly through the bishops
to the local clergy. The final power, however, ultimately lay in the
hands of the duke of Normandy. Thus the Norman Church was
organized, centralized, and, in large measure, a tool of the central
government. The regular clergy, on the other hand, were more closely
connected with the feudal barons than with the central authority of
Normandy. The Normans had taken monasticism to their hearts,
and the monastic establishments of Normandy were perhaps the best
regulated and most dynamic of Europe. The great families of the
duchy vied with each other in founding and richly endowing monasteries on their estates. In exchange for these grants, the monasteries
provided their patrons with chaplains, clerks, preferments for
younger sons, and final resting places.[19]

This was the pattern of religious organization which the Normans
brought with them into England, and later imported into Wales. The

---

[18] G. W. S. Barrow, *Feudal Britain: The Completion of the Medieval Kingdoms, 1066–1314,* p. 220. Also see J. W. W. Bund, *The Celtic Church of Wales.*
[19] The evidence of numerous charters attests to the services which the monasteries provided their benefactors.

Church in Wales was quickly Normanized by the early conquerors, and used as a means of enhancing the authority of the king. The *clas* system was replaced by an episcopal structure which was soon staffed with Norman prelates. This had the double effect of destroying one of the dynamic elements of Welsh tribal life, and of placing the Church in Wales under direct royal domination. The Norman bishops of Wales were responsible to the archbishop of Canterbury, who was, in turn, responsive to the needs and desires of the king. Thus the Church in Wales became closely bound to the interests of the conquerors.[20] So close was this identification that in some areas the distinction disappeared between the Norman cleric and the Norman conqueror. The bishop of St. David's, for instance, was himself a lord marcher, maintained a military force at his disposal, and exercised the right to erect fortifications within his diocese.[21] Indeed, the church architecture of South Wales even today bears witness to this early fusion of spiritual and military functions. The parish churches of this region are distinguished by their defensible sites, their thick walls, and, above all, their massive square towers which resemble keeps far more than campaniles. They are, in effect, small fortresses.

This manipulation of the Church in Wales to aid Norman interests and to weaken Welsh resistance may have been of immediate benefit to the early conquerors, but it worked to the eventual disadvantage of the emergent Cambro-Norman society. In the first place, the pro-Norman bias of the new ecclesiastical organization alienated the Welsh. The tool of domination could never become a means of reconciliation. Secondly, the episcopal structure of the Church in Wales was such that it was less responsive to the needs of the marcher lords and of Welsh society in general than could have been wished. In its secular aspects, Cambro-Norman society was able to develop in response to its frontier environment because of its relative immunity from royal authority. The Church in Wales did not enjoy such immunity, and hence found it impossible to adapt freely to its immediate environment. This is not to say that it made no attempts to do so. During the anarchy of Stephen's reign, Cambro-Norman prelates gained control of the bishoprics of Llandaff and St. David's.[22] They immediately began a campaign to have St. David's recognized as the

[20] T. P. Ellis, *Welsh Tribal Law and Custom in the Middle Ages,* I, 11–12.
[21] M. Davies, *Wales in Maps,* p. 43.
[22] *Handbook of British Chronology,* eds. F. M. Powicke *et al.,* pp. 198–199 and 204.

metropolitan church of Wales. This would have substantially diminished the power of Canterbury, and hence of the king, to dominate Welsh ecclesiastical affairs. This attempt, and others that followed, failed, and the Church in Wales remained the captive of authorities whose interests were far removed from the problems of the frontier.[23]

Much the same is true of the role which the regular clergy played in the conquest of Wales. The monks were even more closely tied to the interests of the invaders than was the ecclesiastical structure which was established. As the Normans moved into Wales, they enriched their Norman abbeys with the fruits of their conquests. These great abbeys—Fècamp, St. Vincent, and their English sisters such as Battle and St. Peter's—established priories in their new possessions. The monks of these priories, mostly Benedictine, performed a number of functions. They exploited the lands and sent the profits back to the mother abbeys; they furnished the frontier garrisons with chaplains and the new lordships with clerks; and they attempted to supplant the influence of the native Welsh clergy on the local scene. They succeeded fairly well in all of these roles but the last. The very location of these early priories—Chepstow, Monmouth, Abergavenny, Brecon, Ewyas Harold, and others—gives some indication of the causes of this failure.[24] The early priories were erected in the shadow of the invader's castles, and drew their sustenance from land which had been but lately acquired from the Welsh.[25] These Benedictine monks were too closely connected with recent injustices and too firmly allied with the interests of the conquerors to inspire the trust and devotion of the Welsh. The monastic orders which the early Norman invaders had imported into Wales uniformly failed to adjust to the frontier environment and to form a bridge over which the two peoples might communicate. The Benedictine monk and the Norman knight were equally out of place on the windswept and barren moors in which the Welsh made their home. This should not be too surprising. These monastic orders, like the Welsh episcopates, were not free to adapt to their environment. The priories were, after all, merely a device by which the distant and uninterested Norman

[23] J. E. Lloyd, A History of Wales from the Earliest Times to the Edwardian Conquest, I, 480 and 559.

[24] See A. H. Williams, An Introduction to the History of Wales, Vol. II, Part I, p. 25, table 1, for a more complete list.

[25] See Davies, Wales in Maps, p. 43. For a description of a few of these priories, see R. Graham, "Four Alien Priories in Monmouthshire," The Journal of the British Archaeological Society, new series, XXXIV (1928), 102–121.

and English abbeys attempted to draw profit from their Welsh holdings. They, and the abbeys which were founded in South Wales in
the early days, were instruments more of exploitation than of
evangelism.

It was not until near the end of the frontier in South Wales that
the Church introduced a monastic order which was capable of span-
ning the gap which existed between the native Welsh and the emergent Cambro-Norman society, and of bringing about some sort of
communication between the two. This was, of course, the Cistercians,
whose industry finally succeeded in developing the sheep-raising
which gave the Welsh highlands a viable economy and allowed them
to gain entry into the mainstream of European life. The success of
the Cistercians in Wales was rapid. A small community was established in southwest Wales by Bernard, the Cambro-Norman bishop
of St. David's, and eventually took up residence at Whitland, a place
hallowed by the memory of Hywel Dda. In 1147, the Cistercians
absorbed the order of Savigny, and, at a single stroke, became the
possessor of the greatest abbeys of South Wales: Tintern, Margan,
and Neath. The Cistercians seemed an order almost designed to
fulfill a dynamic role along the frontier, since the creed of their order
compelled them to seek out and to develop the wasteland and wilderness. It was not long before this compulsion led them to do what no
lowland institution had been able to do—to cross the 600-foot contour line and establish themselves firmly in the barren Welsh uplands. In 1164, Robert Fitz-Stephen granted an extensive tract to
Whitland for the establishment of a cell in the uplands of Cardigan.
A cell of monks was sent out and established the community which
soon became known as Strata Florida.[26] The austerity and rural attitudes of the Cistercians struck a responsive chord in the Welsh among
whom they settled. At the same time, the new arrivals shared none
of the odium of having been the running dogs of the conquerors.
The Welsh enthusiastically joined in support of the Cistercians, and
the Lord Rhys became the patron of Strata Florida. From this center, high in the plateaus of central Wales, daughter abbeys were established throughout the Welsh peninsula. The Cistercian order became the first institution fully shared between the Cambro-Normans
and the native Welsh. Its final victory, however, lay after the frontier
era had come to an end, and it was the product not of the Norman

[26] For the history of the Cistercian establishment in Wales, the best single
source is L. Janauscheck, *Originum Cisterciencium tomus 1....*

frontier in Wales, but of the internal frontier which lay within the lowland environment of Europe itself.

In the last analysis, the Normans in South Wales failed to adapt their religious institutions fully to the frontier environment in which they lived and to use these institutions as a means of establishing a stable and integrated culture which could unite the upland and lowland environments of Wales. They failed for two reasons. In the first place, the early invaders used their religion as a means of conquest and of domination. The native Welsh rejected an institution which was patently but another instrument of the invaders' power. Secondly, and perhaps more important, the pattern of religious organization was such that control of the Church's activities along the frontier was placed in the hands of authorities who were more interested in profit and power than in creating an organization capable of adapting to the peculiar conditions existing along the Welsh frontier. It was only as the Norman frontier in Wales drew to a close that a religious institution appeared that was something more than merely a means to an end.[27]

(c) The Growth of Towns along the Frontier

The societies of the native Welsh and of the Norman invaders were far different. We have discussed many of the distinctive Norman institutions, such as the castle, the mounted knight, the manor and the royally dominated episcopates; and we have attempted to explain the role which each played in the Norman frontier experience in Wales. One last institution remains to be treated—the towns and cities which sprang up in the wake of the conquerors. These were as alien an intrusion into the land as the castles which were erected by the invaders. The small boroughs were hated by the native Welsh, who attacked them repeatedly. Plunder was, of course, a primary motivation, but looting was invariably followed by the most complete devastation possible.[28] The Welsh saw that these settlements were a vulnerable, but necessary, part of the Normans' program for the subjugation and settlement of Wales.

[27] Others were to follow. The friars became popular among the Cambro-Normans and, in some cases, among the Welsh. See R. C. Easterling, "The Friars in Wales," *Archaeologia Cambrensis*, Series VI, Vol. XIV (1914), pp. 323–356. See also R. P. Conway, "The Black Friars of Wales: Recent Excavations and Discoveries," *Archaeologia Cambrensis*, Series V, Vol. VI (1889), pp. 97–105.

[28] For instances of such attacks, see *Annales Cambriae*, ed. J. Williams ab Ithel, pp. 36–71 *passim*.

Town life was essentially foreign to Welsh society. The Welsh were a pastoral people, and moved their residences frequently. As a consequence, there was little in the way of fixed habitations anywhere in Wales outside of the *clas* communities. As a matter of preference, and as a result of the necessity of possessing adequate grazing land, the Welsh avoided concentrating in any one location. Their normal unit of settlement was the isolated family homestead, or, at most, the rude hamlets which sometimes huddled around the courts of local chieftains. Family groups tended to be largely self-sufficient, and there existed little trade to stimulate the growth of market centers. The very bases of urbanization were nonexistent in Wales, and urbanism tended to be repugnant to the sensibilities of the free tribesmen.

Such was not the case in Normandy. The people there were primarily agrarian, and their method of tillage demanded a large measure of cooperation amongst a substantial number of people. The result was that the agricultural population of Normandy tended to concentrate in small village communities and to operate on a communal basis. The isolated farmstead was a rarity there, and the people tended to favor community living.

Beginning in the early part of the eleventh century, a number of factors began to operate which concentrated numbers of these people in towns, or *bourgs*, and made this new urban settlement an essential feature of Norman life. In the first place, the economic life of Europe as a whole began to quicken, and everywhere, Normandy included, favorably situated agricultural villages, cathedral towns, and crossroads began to blossom out as marketing centers. It was not lost on the nobles that control of such centers could bring wealth and power. Where it was possible, the nobles simply extended their authority over the centers which had grown up, and demanded tolls and dues. For many feudal lords, however, this was impossible, since no marketing centers had grown up within their jurisdiction. As a result, many nobles were led to establish such *bourgs* by fiat and to concentrate all trading in their lands in these centers, where tolls and duties could be regularly collected.

The success of such ventures led to a craze for borough-founding throughout northern Europe. It was soon found that the combination of a castle and a borough formed an economic unit of unprecedented vitality. The castle attracted merchants with its promise of protection and its guarantee of a local monopoly of trade. At the same time, the garrison of the castle provided the merchants and artisans of the borough with at least a minimal market. The borough provided for the material needs of the castle, and brought the lord a substantial revenue. Finally, the burghers frequently produced enough agricultural goods to provide an adequate food supply for the entire community, and constituted an additional force of defenders in time of attack. The castle plus the borough possessed a strength and unity which the old combination of castle and manor had never exhibited.

Thus the second motive for borough-founding emerged. It was soon seen that the borough, and its attendant fortification, formed an admirable unit for the settlement of uninhabited areas. It was but a small step to the realization that such communities were the most effective method of attracting settlers to occupy and control newly conquered or disputed areas. The details of this process are particularly clear in Languedoc, where T. F. Tout notes that:

> The origin of the *bastides* of Languedoc is to be found in the days before the northern conquest when monasteries, possessing large tracts of land and no tenants to till them, attracted settlers to their estates by setting up little fortresses for them to live in and investing the inhabitants with modest immunities.[29]

A regular and clearly defined process of *bourg* establishment grew up in the area, a process which was turned against the inhabitants of the region when their northern conquerors used the same methods to relocate numbers of their adherents in the heart of the conquered land. The *bastides* and *villeneuves* finished a process of conquest only begun by the mounted knights.

Thus we can see the advantages which the Normans saw in the establishment of *bourgs*—they provided revenue, a means of settling waste lands, and an admirable adjunct to border fortresses. The feudal nobility of Normandy entered enthusiastically into the new process of artificially stimulated urbanization. The years immediately preceding the Conquest of England saw the establishment of boroughs in all parts of the duchy, and the growing integration of such communities into the Norman way of life.[30]

By the time the Normans appeared on the Welsh frontier, they had had over a generation's experience in using boroughs as a means of

---

[29] T. F. Tout, *Medieval Town Planning: A Lecture,* pp. 10–11.
[30] Haskins, *Norman Institutions,* pp. 48–49.

pacifying and controlling marcher areas. It was only natural that they should embark on a similar course along their new frontier. The process was begun quite quickly.

When William I directed Fitzosbern to build castles . . . he sanctioned borough-making on a large scale, and only in a few cases is royal confirmation spoken of. The makers of boroughs who are not themselves tenants in chief get the consent of their overlord, but the king was a lord who was not likely to refuse, and, within their earldoms the earls Hereford, Shrewsbury, and Chester had regalian rights that made royal consent unnecessary. As the "Leges Willelmi" say, castles and boroughs and cities were founded and built to be places for buying and selling under control . . . so Fitzosbern and Roger Montgomery and Hugh Lupus, at the Conqueror's desire, civilized the border.[31]

The first step in this process lay in the establishment of Norman appendages or suburbs, to the English boroughs which the conquerors found already established along the border. Thus small colonies of French and Normans were located near the English communities of Hereford, Bristol, Shrewsbury, and others. These new communities differed from their English neighbors in two important respects. In the first place, the English boroughs were fundamentally agrarian in character, and trade was a purely secondary pursuit. The new Norman burghers were granted such small and barren tracts of land that they were obviously intended to devote their time primarily to trade and industry.[32] The second major distinction between the English and Norman settlements lay in the fact that each possessed a separate charter of liberties. The English continued to operate under the grants and immunities they had received under the Anglo-Saxon kings, while the Norman settlers enjoyed liberties derived from the charters granted to towns in Normandy.

It must be remembered that the borough charters of Normandy varied widely in their terms. The particular needs of the settlers, the generosity of the lord, and the prevailing standards of the time all had a role in determining the particular form and content of a given charter. Along the Welsh frontier, however, one set of customs derived from a particular Norman *bourg* achieved such popularity that it set the pattern for urban organization in South Wales for the next

[31] M. Bateson, "The Laws of Breteuil," *The English Historical Review*, XVI (1901), 335–336.
[32] *Ibid.*, pp. 335–336 and 339–340.

century, and was exported to Ireland by the early conquerors' grand-
sons. We refer, of course, to the famous laws of Breteuil.[33]

Breteuil, a small *bourg* located near the border of Maine and Blois,
lay in a Norman marcher territory in the hands of William Fitz-
Osbern. The land was not good, but the town was firmly established
and more than held its own in the face of repeated devastation of the
area. It was perhaps only natural that Fitz-Osbern should turn to
Breteuil as a model for the urban settlement of his new lands on the
marches of Wales. The specific conditions embodied in the laws of
Breteuil are difficult to reconstruct, but enough can be discerned to
determine that they were distinguished by their liberality. The burgesses were allotted specific building sites within the *bourg* and were
allowed small amounts of agricultural land outside the walls. They
were allowed to sublet or to rent parts of their lots and to engage in
trade within the town. For all of these privileges, they were charged
a maximum of twelve pence, and their annual rent was not allowed
to exceed this same figure of twelve pence. The burgesses were free
to give up their positions and to leave their burgages at will, without
penalty. If the lord were forced to borrow money from one of the
burgesses, a maximum limit was set upon the time for which the lord
could enjoy the loan. The burgesses were especially well protected
against abuses of the law. They could not be forced to serve or stand
trial in any court other than that of the *bourg*. Within the *bourg*, they
could not be amerced a fine of more than twelve pence (except in
certain royal offenses), and, if imprisoned, were allowed to meet their
own bail.[34] All in all, the laws of Breteuil provided the burgesses with
a considerable amount of freedom of action, and immunity from the
possible abuse of his power by the founding lord, and all for a quite
modest sum.

It was, in all probability, this very liberality which made the laws
of Breteuil so successful in providing the model charter for new
boroughs established on the Welsh frontier. Life on the Welsh frontier was not such as to encourage artisans and merchants to forsake
the secure and fertile fields of England and Normandy to re-establish
themselves in the raw wilderness which the early frontier must have

[33] Miss Bateson's famous article on "The Laws of Breteuil" was carried in a
series of issues of *The English Historical Review*, XV (1900), 73–78, 302–318,
496–523, 754–757; XVI (1901), 92–110, 332–345. For a dissenting opinion, see
M. deW. Hemmeon, *Burgage Tenure in Medieval England*.

[34] See M. Bateson, "The Laws of Breteuil," and J. H. Round, *Studies in Peerage and Family History*, pp. 183–184.

been. And yet we know that such men did immigrate into this region and did set up such boroughs. We also know that most of these boroughs had a single feature in common—they were organized under the laws of Breteuil. This similarity is too frequent to be a mere coincidence. It is far easier to believe that the early conquerors had simply found that liberties and immunities which had drawn men to the isolated and beleaguered *bourg* of Breteuil were also capable of inducing them to undertake the immense task of establishing cities in the Welsh wilderness.

The settlers often succeeded, and the modern cities of Hereford, Cardiff, Builth, Brecon, Carmarthen, and others bear eloquent testimony to this success.[35] Far too frequently, however, they failed. The boroughs which must once have lain under the walls of Clifford's Castle, Wigmore, Ewyas Harold, Skenfrith, and the other castles which the conquerors constructed, have disappeared, and, at the most, quiet villages remain, existing as farm residences and as centers for the slight tourist trade which comes to view the nearby ruins. It must never be forgotten that for the most part the *bourgs* of the Welsh frontier were an artificial growth, stimulated by the needs of a garrison society.[36] The *bourgs* and *bourg* life of the frontier were merely extensions of the castles near which they were built. There existed no organic economic basis for their existence until the growth of the sheep-raising industry of the Welsh interior provided the region with an exportable commodity other than a few hides, horses, and slaves.[37] Only then did a true urban development take place in South Wales.

This is not to say that the original establishments failed in their purpose, but merely that the purposes of these frontier towns were more limited than one might recognize at first glance. They monopolized trade within their various localities and thus made it possible for the marcher lords to control this important activity. They ministered to the material needs of the frontier garrisons, and, to some extent, brought a touch of civilization to an otherwise lonely and isolated region. Through trade they slowly introduced the Welsh tribesmen to luxuries which, in time, lessened the isolation and fierce

[35] M. Bateson, "The Laws of Breteuil," XV (1900), 516.

[36] *Ibid.*, XVI (1901), 345.

[37] See E. A. Lewis, "The Development of Industry and Commerce in Wales during the Middle Ages," *The Transactions of the Royal Historical Society*, new series, XVII (1903), 121–173.

independence of their enemies and rendered them more susceptible to other civilizing influences which were to follow. Above all, however, these small communities offered a security in numbers, and the laws of Breteuil offered liberties and immunities which drew badly needed men to the frontier and integrated them into a social organism which existed there. Neither the Norman castle nor the Norman borough in South Wales can be considered as separate entities. The basic organization in the Norman conquest of South Wales was a combination, or better still, an amalgamation of the two.

(d) Literature

Up to the present, our discussions have been mainly confined to those social institutions which were characteristic of Norman society along the Welsh frontier. Although such analyses are important, they do little to illuminate the personal attitudes of the people who made up this society. We are fortunate that the Welsh frontier in the twelfth century produced two men of letters who were able, in some measure, to speak for a population otherwise rather silent and impersonal. It is not our purpose to speak of the literary merits of the works of these men, nor to discuss their roles in the history of literature, but to attempt to see in them some personal reactions to the peculiar environment of frontier life.

The first of these literary figures in point of time was Geoffrey of Monmouth (d. 1155), renowned as the author who introduced the Arthurian romances into European literature. It seems most probable that Geoffrey was neither Welsh, English, nor Norman, but Breton in extraction. He may have been the son of a settler in, or himself an immigrant to, the Breton colony established at Monmouth by Wihenoc, who took over the area after the fall of Roger of Breteuil. At any rate, Geoffrey probably knew the Breton language and was thus able to communicate with the Welsh inhabitants of the region where he spent his youth. His writings make it obvious that he was well acquainted with this lovely area, the locale of many of the folk tales which the Welsh and Bretons held in common. The greater part of his life, however, was not spent in this frontier region, but in Oxford. He first appears as a witness to an Oxford charter in 1129, and it seems likely that he spent most of the remainder of his life there.[38]

---

[38] See Lloyd, *A History of Wales*, II, 524 ff., for a short discussion of the details of Geoffrey's career.

In 1136 his great work, the *Historia Regum Britanniae*, appeared, and it is probable that much of the work was done at Oxford. The subject matter of the work, however, returns to the traditions and region of his youth. In form, the *Historia* purports to be a history of the kings of Britain from the earliest times to the death of Cadwaladr. In essence, however, the book is a vehicle for the presentation of the Celtic romances surrounding Arthur, a messianic hero who would someday return to free the Celts of their oppressors. The scene of action ranges over the entire island of Britain, but tends to concentrate in South Wales, and especially the region of Monmouthshire, where the Celtic golden age reached its height under Arthur. The book glorifies the Celts, but Geoffrey takes pains throughout to impress upon the reader that he means to glorify the Breton Celts, and not the Welsh, who were but the remnants of the once-mighty race.[39]

The millennial element dominates the close of the book, which ends with the Saxons in complete control, and the Celts awaiting the time appointed by God when they should again gain control of Britain. Geoffrey emphasizes, however, that the restoration was not to come from Wales, but from Britanny. Is there a general point to this entire account? Geoffrey is nowhere explicit, but it seems as if he is pointing out in the *Historia* that the long-awaited day of liberation had already arrived; the Bretons, and their Norman friends and allies, had returned to "Ynys Prydain," and had overthrown the Saxon oppressors. If this is true, then the *Historia Regum Britanniae* represents a Breton's attempt to justify his people's status along the Welsh frontier as a fulfillment of the messianic legends to which both Bretons and Welsh paid homage. Inherent in this is the plea for the Welsh to recognize this fact, to embrace their Breton brothers, and rebuild the golden age in Monmouthshire.

The *Historia* was written in the flush of success that attended the effective frontier policies of Henry I. The native Welsh were controlled, if not conquered, and the work of settlement and building in the frontier proceeded in security. It was quite possible, in these years, for Geoffrey to see in the new order of things the beginning of the long-awaited golden age. In the years that followed, however,

---

[39] Geoffrey of Monmouth, *The Historia Regum Britannia of Geoffrey of Monmouth*, ed. A. Griscom, especially pp. 532–535. For an excellent discussion of the Arthurian romance and its relation to Irish and Welsh folklore, see R. S. Loomis, *Wales and the Arthurian Legend*.

Geoffrey's faith must have been severely shaken. The anarchy attending the reign of Stephen followed quickly on the heels of the appearance of the *Historia,* and the entire frontier was plunged into chaos. The work of the preceding generation vanished overnight, and all hopes of brotherhood and peace vanished in the settlers' grim struggle for survival. This was a period of disillusionment for the settlers along the Welsh frontier, and also for Geoffrey.

Little of this would be known were it not for the fact that, in his old age, Geoffrey published a second and relatively little-known work, the *Vita Merlini.*[40] It first appeared in about 1151,[41] after twenty-five years of anarchy in English affairs. The *Vita* is an incredibly involved Latin poem of over 1,500 hexameter lines purporting to present the life and prophecies of the famous Celtic seer, Merlin. It was inevitable that much more of Geoffrey than of Merlin went into the complicated and obscure poetic prophecies which dominate the work. Although most of these are almost incomprehensible, some few stand out with startling clarity. These few indicate that a great change had come over Geoffrey's attitude toward life along the frontier, and over his millennial hopes.

In the course of his account, Geoffrey puts the following prophecy in the mouth of a raving Merlin:

Then the Normans, sailing over the water in their wooden ships, bearing their faces in front and in back, shall fiercely attack the Angles with their iron tunics and their sharp swords, and shall destroy them and possess the field. They shall subjugate many realms to themselves and shall rule foreign peoples for a time until the Fury, flying all about, shall scatter her poison over them. Then peace and faith and all virtue shall depart, and on all sides throughout the country the citizens shall engage in battles. Man shall betray man and no one shall be found a friend. The husband, despising his wife, shall draw near to harlots, and the wife, despising her husband, shall marry whom she desires. There shall be no honor kept for the church and the order shall perish. Then shall bishops bear arms, and armed camps shall be built. Men shall build towers and walls in holy ground, and they shall give to the soldiers what should belong to the needy. Carried away by riches they shall run along the path of worldly things and shall take from God what the holy bishop shall forbid.[42]

This impassioned speech can only be a description of the anarchy

[40] Geoffrey of Monmouth, *The Vita Merlini,* ed. and trans. J. J. Parry.
[41] *Ibid.,* pp. 9–15.
[42] *Ibid.,* pp. 70–71 (J. J. Parry's translation).

existing in Britain under the reign of Stephen. It is especially applicable to conditions along the border at this time. The phrase, "Then shall bishops bear arms . . . Men shall build towers and walls in holy ground . . ." seems especially indicative, since we have only recently pointed out that such activities were especially characteristic of the Church in Wales. If it is true that Geoffrey earlier pictured the Norman Conquest of England and the settlement of the frontier as the fulfillment of God's ancient promise to the Celtic people, then it is equally true that the *Vita Merlini* is witness to his terrible disillusionment. Earlier he had envisaged the settlement of South Wales as a cooperative venture between the natural heirs, the Bretons, their faithful friends and allies the Normans, and the native Welsh. The Normans had betrayed this noble venture, and it was now evident that the time had not yet arrived for the golden age to begin. Faced with this fact, and troubled by the calamities which were being visited upon the Welsh frontier where he spent his youth, Geoffrey took his stand firmly on the side of his Celtic heritage—both Breton and Welsh—when he spoke through the mouth of Merlin's sister, Ganieda, saying:

Normans depart and cease to bear weapons through our native realm with your cruel soldiery. There is nothing left with which to feed your greed for you have consumed everything that creative nature has produced in her happy fertility. Christ, aid thy people! restrain the lions and give to the country quiet peace and the cessation of wars.[43]

Ganieda speaks not only for the Welsh, but for the entire people of England. Whether intentionally or not, Geoffrey has her speak especially for the settlers along the Welsh frontier. The reign of Stephen and the anarchy which attended it was a period of disillusionment for the settlers, and nowhere does this disillusionment appear more clearly than in the writings of Geoffrey of Monmouth. In 1136, he awaited the imminent arrival of the golden age of ancient prophecy; in 1151, he longs only for peace.

In the course of time, peace, after a fashion, did return to the frontier. In the intervening period, however, the character of the settlers had changed, and the bases had been laid for a distinctive Cambro-Norman society. This society was little prone to chiliastic dreams of peace. Nurtured on war, they viewed the world about them with a realism that would have been abhorrent to Geoffrey. This new

[43] *Ibid.*, pp. 116–117 (J. J. Parry's translation).

society accepted their Norman and Welsh traditions with pride, and confronted their frontier environment with aplomb.

It was not until the Norman frontier in South Wales was drawing to a close that this Cambro-Norman society found a spokesman. The character of this man, Giraldus Cambrensis, made the wait worthwhile. Like his fellow Cambro-Normans, he was proud, turbulent, and realistic. He was, moreover, one of the most prolific authors of his age.[44] Enough has been written about him, both by himself and by others, to make any extended analysis of his work superfluous. At the same time it is unnecessary to say much about his observations and attitudes regarding life on the Welsh frontier, for they have formed one of the major bases for the present work.[45] One observation may not be out of place, however, for, as Geoffrey of Monmouth represents the first disillusionment of the early settlers' hopes, Giraldus illustrates the final disappearance of the frontier—in the Turnerian sense—from the Cambro-Norman mentality.

In the *Descriptio Kambriae* Giraldus, in typical fashion, undertakes to advise the world as to the proper way to go about the conquest and final subjugation of Wales. His final solution (omitted in later editions) was couched in the following words:

Further, I would not know how to hold a land so wild and so impenetrable, and inhabitants so untameable. There are some who think that it would be far safer and more advised for a prudent prince to leave it altogether as a desert to the wild beasts and to make a forest of it.[46]

There is a sad note of defeatism in these words. The mentality of the frontier is one that sees opportunity and progress lying over the horizon. Giraldus feels none of this. He instead suggests that the complete elimination of the frontier, and its transformation into a desert fit only for wild beasts, would represent a final victory for the Cambro-Normans. It is a long way from the golden age of Geoffrey to the desert of Giraldus.

---

[44] Giraldus Cambrensis, *Opera*, eds. J. S. Brewer *et al.*

[45] See especially chapter VII above.

[46] Giraldus Cambrensis, *Opera*, eds. J. S. Brewer *et al.* Part VI (*Itinerarium Kambriae*), pp. xxx-xxxi, and 225, n. 4.

ix. Conclusions

IN THE PRECEDING PAGES we have often used the term, "the Welsh frontier." In many respects, this is a misnomer; South Wales represented not one, but many frontiers; and in each of its aspects it profoundly affected the attitudes and activities of those who came in contact with it.

For the central administration of England, the Welsh frontier revolved about the pressing, but apparently insoluble, problem of border defense. From time immemorial, marchers have been both necessary and dangerous to the development of centralized states. In the third century after Christ, generals in Pannonia made an emperor of Rome; in the twentieth century, generals in Algeria made a president of France. The situation was not much different in twelfth-century Britain. The rich heartland of England required security from Welsh attacks, and the central administration of England was unable to provide this except by the creation of a marcher class, a permanent, resident, and relatively independent border guard. The kings of England were aware of the dangers which this expedient created—if their central administration could not directly control the Welsh border, neither could it directly control the powerful noble who had been established in the area. The crown's only recourse was to attempt to develop devices for maintaining an indirect control.

The Norman kings of England succeeded in developing only two such devices. The first method was to establish personal bonds of loyalty and solidarity of interest between the marcher lords and the crown. The second method was the establishment and maintenance of a balance of power between the marchers and the native Welsh. Both were attempts to avoid and defer, rather than to solve, the problem, and both were failures. The former method failed because it was based upon personal relationships which were disrupted with every change of personnel either at court or on the marches: hence the marcher revolts in 1075, 1088, 1100, and other years. The native Welsh played upon this Norman weakness, rising in rebellion at the death of every monarch and finding their opponents momentarily paralyzed by the mutual distrust of the new king and the old frontier nobility. The latter method failed because maintenance of a balance of power depended upon the action of a strong central authority. Under a weak or preoccupied king the delicate balance always broke down. Under William Rufus, the balance was upset in favor of the Normans; under Stephen, in favor of the Welsh. In both cases, however, the marchers gained power and influence in England itself. Each crisis that passed found the independence of the marcher lords increased, and the power of the crown in the marcher lordships correspondingly diminished. Royal frontier policy based on these two methods of indirect control proved to be incapable of controlling either the Welsh or the marchers, and yet the twelfth-century kings of England could apparently devise no better one. Royal policy regarding the Welsh frontier during this period was nothing more than a series of variations wrung from these two essential themes.

For the native Welsh, both chieftains and free tribesman, the frontier represented the ultimate challenge; one in which the very bases of the traditional Welsh way of life were threatened with extinction. The Norman frontier in Wales was a gateway through which new influences were belligerently forcing their way.

The political aspects of this intrusion are the more readily seen. Entering into Wales, the Norman marcher lords moved with a vengeance into the traditional Welsh political system of internecine strife and dynastic struggles. The *tywysogion* were now confronted with opponents of such efficiency and organization as to make resistance almost hopeless. Welsh political organization came very close to complete collapse under the first shock of this attack. The tactical inability of the Normans to meet the Welsh in mountain warfare, however, coupled with ineffectual Norman frontier policies, gained the natives a brief respite. During this period, the Welsh absorbed enough elements of Norman organization to allow them to establish some relatively large and stable political units, notable among them being the kingdoms of Gwynedd and Deheubarth. These were to form effective bases for resisting further Norman advances into Wales until the close of the thirteenth century.

A more silent battle was fought at the same time between the cultures of the Anglo-Normans and the Welsh. The invaders brought with them new patterns of speech, dress, agriculture, architecture, worship, and all of the other things that go to make up a way of life. These new standards competed with Welsh traditions for supremacy. Many, such as the lords of Avon, chose the ways of the invaders and were, in time, absorbed into Anglo-Norman society. For the great majority of the Welsh, however, the competition simply provided a stimulus to expand, develop, and refine their native institutions. During this period, Welsh culture was solidified into a way of life which has maintained its essential integrity down to the present day.

It can be clearly seen that the frontier experience of the Welsh provided them with a powerful stimulus to political and cultural unity. Norman pressure led the Welsh to emphasize those common elements which distinguished them from their enemies. The greater the Norman political and cultural pressure, the greater was the impetus to Welsh unity. We have seen the disorganized and fratricidal character of Welsh society before the advent of the Normans. After a century of frontier experience, however, a Welshman was able to tell Henry II,

This nation, O king, may now, as in former times, be harassed, and in a great measure weakened and destroyed by your and other powers, and it will often prevail by its laudable exertions; but it can never be totally subdued through the wrath of man, unless the wrath of God shall concur. Nor do I think, that any other nation than this of Wales, or any other language, whatever may hereafter come to pass, shall, in the day of severe examination before the Supreme Judge, answer for this corner of the earth.[1]

There is a spirit of nationalism in these words which was new in Welsh history. It is a spirit which was born on the frontier.

Our primary concern, however, has been with neither the Welsh nor the crown, but with those people who settled the frontier and eventually formed the bases for the development of Cambro-Norman

[1] Giraldus Cambrensis, *Opera*, eds. J. S. Brewer *et al.*, Part VI (*Itinerarium Kambriae*), p. 227.

society. What aspect did the frontier present to them? This is not an easy question to answer; as we have often emphasized, the frontier was not a location, but a process, and the character of this process changed with the passage of time.

The Welsh frontier of the year 1070 lay along Offa's Dyke, the traditional western limit of Anglo-Saxon settlement. By this year, however, it was a political concept rather than an actuality, for the lands lying immediately behind the frontier lay ravaged and depopulated. Fifteen years of Welsh incursions coupled with the disorders attending the Norman Conquest of England, had succeeded in driving the limits of English settlement and effective political control a good distance eastwards. Villages lay everywhere deserted, and oaks were springing up in what were once well-tilled fields. There lay no barrier between the unpacified Welsh chieftains and the rich heartland of England.

William the Conqueror determined that the security of England required a strong western border defense and the re-establishment of the traditional western political frontier. For such a policy to be effective, it was necessary that the English lands lying immediately along the frontier be repopulated and redeveloped, and so settlers were imported. These immigrants were not moving into a new land to seek a new way of life, but rather were being imported into an old land to perform the specific function of border guard.

Despite this fact, the Welsh frontier offered its settlers great opportunities. In order to counterbalance the insecurity and the onerous duties attending such frontier life, the crown and other developers of the region found it necessary to offer extensive grants of liberty to immigrants. By 1081, William I had succeeded in establishing a rapport with the Welsh chieftains, and the period of extreme insecurity along the Welsh border came to an end. By the time of *Domesday*, redevelopment was progressing rapidly, and the region gave every sign of increasing prosperity. Admittedly, the Welsh frontier of the reign of William the Conqueror was an artificially induced process; this did not affect the result. The hallmark of the Welsh frontier of *Domesday* lay in the relative freedom of its inhabitants and the potential riches it offered settlers.

The nature of the frontier process was drastically altered in the closing decade of the eleventh century, when, under William Rufus, the royal policy of maintaining a balance of power to insure peace

along the border was allowed to collapse. The frontiers of Norman
political control and of Norman settlement now moved into regions
formerly occupied by the independent Welsh buffer states. The frontier of political control moved far more rapidly than the line of actual
Norman settlement, but the events of the Welsh rebellion showed
clearly enough that this was a dangerous policy. Under the pressure
of violent Welsh resistance, the limit of Norman political power was
made to coincide more closely with the frontier of actual settlement.
Under Henry I, the frontier was again stabilized, and a measure of
peace brought to those areas now occupied by the Normans.

The frontier now lay in what was essentially a new land, beyond
the traditional limits of English society. No longer were the settlers
attempting to reinforce the traditional claims of the English kings, or
guaranteeing the heartland of England some degree of security from
Welsh attack. The settlers were moving out on their own, creating
new social units—manors, lordships, abbeys, *bourgs*—where none
had existed before, and they were creating them in a region which
lay beyond the power of the traditional institutions of social control.
The settlers of the Welsh frontier of the early twelfth century were
uniquely free to work out their own way of life, and to determine
their own destinies.

The results of this short period of freedom of action are dis-
appointing; the general effect was not progressive, but highly reactionary. The social order generated by the Welsh frontier represented a reversion to a pure and archaic feudal prototype. Perhaps
nowhere in Europe could a more classic example of feudalism be
found than in the marcher lordships of Brecknock and Glamorgan
established during this period. We see no growth of a yeoman farmer
class; the settlers instead imported manorialism in its purest form.
The *bourgs* which were established simply followed the model of
Breteuil, a prototype already a half-century old. A more perfect example of social and cultural continuity could scarcely be found; the
most highly Normanized society to be found anywhere, including
Normandy, was on the marches of Wales.

Perhaps the influence of the frontier would in time have produced
a more egalitarian way of life. The settlers were not allowed this
time. With the anarchy of Stephen, the balance of power was once
more upset, and this time in favor of the resurgent and dynamic
Welsh. The Welsh frontier once more assumed the character of a
garrison society and became a beleaguered and insecure outpost.

Social experimentation and individual freedom were luxuries which these people could not afford. Their feudalized way of life offered them a responsive and effective organization with which to meet the daily threat of Welsh attack and was thus retained.

Under Henry II, peace was once again restored to the border, although it was more or less upon Welsh terms. The possibility of marcher political expansion had come to an end, but so too had the ever-present Welsh menace. As the arable lowland zone of Wales was slowly filled up and brought under cultivation, the Welsh frontier presented yet another aspect to settlers. It now lay somewhere around the 600-foot contour line, at the hither edge of the Welsh uplands. These areas now challenged the settlers to cross the line and take up the task of developing untilled moors and slopes. Crossing of this frontier demanded the development of new social techniques. The earlier Welsh frontiers had been conquered by the traditional feudal-manorial social organization but this was no longer sufficient, for the Welsh uplands could support neither manor nor mounted knight. It could, on the other hand, have supported a substantial population of Cambro-Norman yeoman farmers and pastoralists, organized in a frontier militia.

The Welsh frontier of the mid-twelfth century challenged the settlers to abandon their traditional corporate institutions, and to develop a system based upon the individualism which might allow them to cross the frontier and begin the exploitation of the uplands. They failed to respond to this challenge; instead they clung to an institutionalized way of life which effectively restricted them to those lowland areas of Wales which could support such an organization. With their failure, the Welsh frontier drew to an end.

In view of its complexity, it is difficult to define the frontier process in South Wales in terms of any single characteristic. It is, on the other hand, possible to discern the operation of certain basic forces which helped to determine the course which this process would take. The forces derived from the very nature of the land where the process took place and from the basic tools with which the settlers dealt with their environment. This entire account of the Norman frontier in South Wales has been more or less simply a study in human ecology, but such a study is of some value in testing some traditional concepts regarding the nature of the frontier process.

In the words of Frederick Jackson Turner, the founder of American frontier study, the frontier was defined by the fact "that it lies at the hither edge of free land."[2] The Welsh frontier illustrated the inadequacy of this simple definition when the limits of Cambro-Norman society came to a rest firmly and finally at the 600-foot contour line. The world did not end at this line; a few feet further up the slope lay great tracts of free land, waiting for the cultivation of clover, barley, alfalfa, oats, broccoli, beets, and a host of other crops. Land sufficient for a thousand farms and a hundred ranches lay within easy reach of the Cambro-Normans, and yet the Welsh frontier came to a halt and to an end at this "hither edge of free land." The question is, why?

The answer is simple. Although the Welsh slopes and uplands were suitable for the cultivation of a number of crops, they were not suitable for the cultivation of wheat, and wheat was the basis of Anglo-Norman society. The Anglo-Norman manor could not sustain itself without a yearly crop of wheat, and hence the Cambro-Norman manors of South Wales were restricted to those limited areas which could support the growth of wheat.[3] This was an important factor, because Anglo- or Cambro-Norman society was simply a complex superstructure reared upon the basis of manorial agriculture. Only in very special circumstances could either castle or *bourg* flourish in the absence of nearby manors to sustain them. At the same time, Cambro-Norman agronomy was not such as to allow them to improve the capacity of the land to any great extent. Fertilization and crop rotation were quite rudimentary, while drainage and deep-ploughing were virtually unknown. Land which could not support both extensive and intensive wheat cultivation, and do so without artificial improvement, was not, in terms of twelfth-century English society, "free land." It was, as Giraldus Cambrensis suggested, "a desert," and unsuited for human habitation.

But what of the effects of the frontier? Turner's answer was that "the most important effect of the frontier has been in the promotion of democracy . . . the frontier is productive of individualism. Complex society is precipitated by the wilderness into a kind of primitive organization based on the family."[4] This was certainly not true of the Welsh frontier. The early settlers *were* lured to the border by the promise of liberty, but it is important to note that the forms this

---

[2] F. J. Turner, "The Significance of the Frontier in American History," *The Turner Thesis*, ed. G. R. Taylor, p. 14.

[3] W. Rees, *An Historical Atlas of Wales from Early to Modern Times*, plate 47.

[4] Turner, "The Significance of the Frontier," p. 14.

liberty took were dictated by the peculiar characteristics of the "complex society" of medieval England. Unattached men-at-arms were guaranteed a limitation of fines, burghers were given the liberal laws of Breteuil, *hospites* were allowed assarts, *bovarii* were granted the legal forms of freedom, and, finally, the lords themselves obtained extensive immunities. The liberty of the Welsh frontier was not a freedom *from* social control, but freedom *within* an accepted social framework. Society did *not* break down in the wilderness of the Welsh frontier, although it did undergo certain modifications.

Nowhere, however, do we see the development of "a kind of primitive organization based on the family." On the contrary, the palmiest days of the conquest of South Wales instead saw the accelerated growth of the manor, feudal lordship, *bourg*, and priory as the primary social institutions of the frontier. Except for the accidental resemblance between feudalism and local sovereignty, the Welsh frontier nowhere exhibited the slightest tendency to promote individualism or to develop a social structure based upon the family unit. In this aspect, the Welsh frontier was quite unlike the American.

The reasons behind this divergence are not difficult to discover. Turner erred when he characterized the frontier emphasis upon the family unit simply as a reversion to a primitive social and economic organization. The basic institution of twelfth-century England had been the cooperative village manor. Even as early as the thirteenth century, however, this agrarian organization had begun to break down in a process which was accelerated by the Black Death of the fourteenth century and the emergence of capitalistic agriculture beginning in the fifteenth century. By the seventeenth century, the manor had been replaced by the family as the basic unit of agricultural exploitation in England. The other, corporate, institutions which characterized English society of this period were of a secondary nature, and were ultimately based upon the activities of the yeoman and tenant farmers. Thus the emphasis upon the family unit along the American frontier represented no reversion, but precisely the sort of agrarian structure we should expect to see seventeenth-century Englishmen establish on virgin ground.

The social organization of a people is one of the most powerful tools with which they seek to control and exploit their environment, and there is a tendency for them to accentuate and emphasize the development of successful institutions. The basic unit for the exploitation of land among the English of the seventeenth century was the family, and its success along the American frontier led to an accentuation of its importance, and an attending growth of individualism. The basic unit of the Anglo-Normans of the twelfth century, on the other hand, was the manor, and its success in South Wales led to the development of a heightened form of feudalism. Thus the difference between the two frontiers. The effect of the frontier experience was in neither case drastic, nor did it produce basic changes in the social order; it simply accentuated and emphasized tendencies which were already present. The new societies were but caricatures of the old.

A SELECTED BIBLIOGRAPHY

I. PRIMARY SOURCES
   A. Documents, Statutes, and Other Official Records
      1. *Manuscripts*
      2. *Printed Materials*
   B. Narrative Sources

II. SELECTED BIBLIOGRAPHIC AIDS

III. SECONDARY SOURCES
   A. Books and Manuscripts
   B. Articles

I. Primary Sources

A. Documents, Statutes, and Other Official Records

1. Manuscripts

British Museum, MS Cotton Vespasian B. XXIV.
British Museum, MS Cotton Vitellius CX, folio 172b.
British Museum, MS Harleian 3,763.

2. Printed Materials

Ancient Charters, Royal and Private Prior to A.D. *1200.* Ed. J. H. Round. Pipe Roll Society Publications, Vol. X. London: Pipe Roll Society, 1888.

Ancient Laws and Institutes of England: Comprising Laws Enacted under the Anglo-Saxon Kings from Aethelbirht to Cnut, with an English Translation of the Saxon; The Laws called Edward the Confessor's; The Laws of William the Conqueror, and Those Ascribed to Henry I; Also Monumenta Ecclesiastica Anglicana, from the Seventh to the Tenth Century; and the Ancient Latin Version of the Anglo-Saxon Laws, with a Compendious Glossary, etc. Two vols. London: Record Commissioners, 1840.

Ancient Laws and Institutes of Wales; Comprising Laws Supposed to be Enacted by Howel the Good, Modified by Subsequent Regulations under the Native Princes Prior to the Conquest by Edward the First; and Anomalous Laws, Consisting Principally of Institutions Which by the Statute of Ruddlan Were Admitted to Continue in Force; with an English Translation of the Welsh Text, to Which Are Added a Few Latin Transcripts, Containing Digests of the Welsh Laws, Principally of the Dimetian Code, with Indexes and Glossary. Ed. A. Owen. London: Record Commissioners, 1841.

"The Bayeux Inquest," otherwise called "Scripta de Feodis ad Regem spectantibus et de Militibus ad exercitus vocandis, E Philippi Augusti Regesta Excerpta," in *Receuil des Historiens des Gaules et de la France.* Eds. M. Bouquet *et al.* Vol. XXIII. Paris: Académie des Inscriptions et Belles-Lettres, 1903. Pp. 605–723.

Cartae et alia munimenta quae ad Dominium de Glamorgancia pertinent. Ed. G. T. Clark. Six vols. Cardiff: William Lewis, 1910.

Chartes Anciennes de Prieuré de Monmouth en Angleterre au Diocèse d'Hereford, Membre de l'Abbaye Benedictine de Saint-Florent près Saumur. Ed. P. Marchegay. Les Roches-Baritaud: published by the editor, 1879.

"Chartes normandes de l'abbaye de Saint-Florent près Saumur, de 710 à

1200," ed. P. Marchegay, in *Mémoires de la Société des Antiquaires de Normandie*, XXX (1880), 663–711.

Codex Diplomaticus Aevi Saxonici. Ed. J. M. Kemble. Six vols. London: English Historical Society, 1839–1848.

Councils and Ecclesiastical Documents Relating to Great Britain and Ireland. Eds. W. Stubbs and A. W. Haddan. Three vols. Oxford: Clarendon Press, 1869–1871.

Domesday Book: or The Great Survey of England by William the Conqueror A.D. *MLXXXVI.* Southampton: Ordnance Survey, 1862.

Foedera, Conventiones, Litterae, et cujuscunque Generis Acta Publica, inter Reges Angliae et Alios Quosvis Imperatores, Reges, Pontifices, Principes, vel Communitates; ab ingressu Gulielmi I in Angliam A.D. *1066 ad Nostra Usque Tempora Habita Aut Tractata Ex Autographis, Infra Secretiores, Archivorum Regiorum Thesaurarias, Asservatis; Aliisque Summae Vetustatis Instrumentis, Ad Historiam Anglicanam Spectatibus, Fideliter Exscripta.* Ed. T. Rymer. Three vols. in eight. London: Record Commissioners, 1816.

Herefordshire Domesday, circa, 1160–1170, Reproduced by Collotype from Facsimile Photographs of Balliol College Manuscript 350. Eds. V. H. Galbraith and J. Tait. Pipe Roll Society Publications, Vol. LXIII. London: Pipe Roll Society, 1950.

Itinerarium Antonini Augusti et Hierosolymitanum ex libris manuscriptis ediderunt. Eds. G. Parthey and M. Pinder. Berlin: n.p., 1848.

The Liber Landavensis, Llyfr Teilo, or the Ancient Register of the Cathedral Church of Llandaff: from MSS in the Libraries of Hengwrt, and of Jesus College, Oxford. Ed. and trans. W. J. Rees. Llandovery: Welsh MSS Society, 1840.

Monasticon Anglicanum: A History of the Abbies and of Other Monasteries, Hospitals, Frieries, and Cathedral and Collegiate Churches, with Their Dependencies in England and Wales; Also of All Such Scotch, Irish and French Monasteries, as Were in Any Manner Connected with Religious Houses in England; Together with a Particular Account of Their Respective Foundations, Grants, and Donations, and a Full Statement of Their Possessions, as Well Temporal as Spiritual. Ed. W. Dugdale. Six vols. in eight. London: James Bohn, 1846.

The Pipe Rolls. Multi-volume. London: Pipe Roll Society, in progress.

Les Prieurés Anglais de Saint-Florent près Saumur: Notice et Documents inedits tires de Archives de Maine et Loire. Ed. P. Marchegay. Les Roches-Baritaud: published by the editor, 1879.

Receuil des Actes des Ducs de Normandie, 911–1066. Ed. Marie Faroux. Vol. XXXVI of *Memoires de la Société des Antiquaires de Normandie.* Caen: 1961.

Statutes of the Realm. Nine vols. in ten. London: Record Commissioners, 1810–1822.

The Welsh Assize Roll, 1277–1284. Ed. J. C. Davies. Cardiff: University of Wales Press, 1940.

B. Narrative Sources

The Anglo-Saxon Chronicle, According to the Several Original Authorities. Ed. and trans. B. Thorpe. Rolls Series, Vol. XXIII in Two parts. London: n.p., 1861.

Annales Cambriae. Ed. J. Williams ab Ithel. Rolls Series, Vol. XX. London: n.p., 1860.

Annales de Margan. Ed. H. R. Luard. Rolls Series, Vol. XXXVI. London: n.p., 1864.

Annals of the Kingdom of Ireland, by the Four Masters, from the Earliest Period to the Year 1616: Edited from MSS in the Library of the Royal Irish Academy and of Trinity College, Dublin. Ed. and trans. J. O'Donovan. Seven vols. Dublin: Hodges and Smith, 1851.

The Bayeux Tapestry. London: Penguin Books, Ltd., 1943.

Brut y Tywysogion: or The Chronicles of the Princes. Ed. J. Williams ab Ithel. Rolls Series, Vol. XVII. London: n.p., 1860.

"Chronicon de Fundatoribus et de Fundatione Ecclesiae Theokusburiae, quae fundata fuit primo, anno gratiae Domini DCCXV, per Duces Merciorum," in *Monasticon Anglicamum.* . . . Ed. W. Dugdale. Six vols. in eight. London: James Bohn, 1846. II, 59–83.

Chronicon Monasterii de Bello nunc primum typis mandatum. Ed. J. S. Brewer. London: n.p., 1846.

Chronicon Petroburgense, nunc primum typis mandatum. Ed. T. Stapleton. London: Camden Society, 1849.

Chroniques Anglo-Normandes: Receuil d'extraits et d'écrits relatifs à l'histoire de Normandie et d'Angleterre pendant les XIe et XIIe siècles; publié, pour la prèmiere fois, d'après les Manuscrits de Londres, de Cambridge, de Douai, de Bruxelles et de Paris. Ed. F. Michel. Three vols. Roen: published by the author, 1836–1840.

Chroniques des Ducs de Normandie par Benoit: Publiée d'après le Manuscrit de Tours avec les variantes de Manuscrit de Londres. Ed. C. Fahlin. Two vols. Uppsala: Almquist and Wiksell, A.B., 1951–1954.

"Ex Chronico Lyrensis Coenobii," in *Receuil des Historiens des Gaules et de la France.* Eds. M. Bouquet *et al.* Vol. XII. Paris: V. Palme, 1877. P. 776.

Florence of Worcester. *Chronicon ex Chronicis, ab adventu Hengesti et horsi in Britannian usque ad M.C.XVIII. cui accesserunt continuationes duae, quarum una ad annum M.C.XLI, Altera, nunc primum typis Vulgata, ad annum M.CC.XCV. perducta. Ad fidem codicum manuscriptorum edidit.* Ed. B. Thorpe. Two volumes. London: English Historical Society, 1848.

Geoffrey of Monmouth. *The Historia Regum Britannia of Geoffrey of Monmouth.* Ed. A. Griscom. London: Longmans and Co., 1929.

—. *The Vita Merlini.* Ed. and trans. J. J. Parry. The University of Illinois Studies in Language and Literature, Vol. X, No. 3. Urbana: University of Illinois, 1925.

Gervase of Canterbury. *The Historical Works of Gervase of Canterbury, Edited from the Manuscripts.* Ed. W. Stubbs. Rolls Series, Vol. LXXIII in two parts. London: n.p., 1879–1880.

Gesta Stephani. Ed. and trans. K. R. Potter. London: Thomas Nelson and Sons, Ltd., 1955.

Gilbert Foliot. "Gilbertus Foliot, ex abbate Gloucestriae episcopus primum Herefordensis, deinde Londoniensis, epistolae et epistolae variorum ad Gilbertum et alios," in *Patrologia Latina.* Ed. J. P. Migne. Vol. CXC. Paris: Garnier Fratres, 1893. Cols. 745–1067.

Giraldus Cambrensis. *The Historical Works of Giraldus Cambrensis containing the Topography of Ireland and the History of the Conquest of Ireland.* Eds. and trans. T. Forester and T. Wright. Bohn's Antiquarian Library. London: H. G. Bohn, 1863.

—. *Opera.* Eds. J. S. Brewer *et al.* Rolls Series, Vol. XXI in eight parts. London: n.p., 1861–1891.

Historiae Normannorum Scriptores Antiqui res ab illis per Galliam, Angliam, Apuliam, Capuae principatum, Siciliam, et Orientem gestas explicantes, ab anno Christi DCCCXXXVIII, ad annum MCCXX. Insertae sunt monasteriorum fundationes variae, series Episcoporum ac Abbatum: genealogiae Regum, Ducum, Comitum, et Nobilium; Plurima Denique alia Vetera, tam ad Profanam quam ad Sacram Illorum temporum Historiam pertinentia. Ex MSS. CODD. omnia fere nunc primum edidit. Ed. A. Duchesne. Paris: n.p., 1619.

Historia et Cartularium Monasterii Sancti Petri Gloucestriae. Ed. W. H. Hart. Rolls Series, Vol. XXXIII in three parts. London: n.p., 1863.

The History of Gruffydd ap Cynan: The Welsh Text with Translation, Introduction. and Notes. Ed. A. Jones. Manchester: Manchester University Press, 1910.

Icelandic Sagas, and other Historical Documents Relating to the Settlements and Descents of the Northmen on the British Isles. Ed. and trans. G. W. Dasent. Rolls Series, Vol. LXXXVIII in four parts. London: n.p., 1887–1894.

"In Calce hujus libelli in eadem scriptura adjicitur catalogus suppeditantium naves ad expeditionem Willelmi comitis in Angliam," in *Scriptores Rerum Gestarum Willelmi Conquestoris.* Ed. J. A. Giles. London: Caxton Society, 1845. P. 21.

Iolo Manuscripts: A Selection of Ancient Welsh Manuscripts in Prose and Verse, from the Collection Made by the late Edward Williams, Iolo Morgannwg, for the Purpose of Forming a Continuation of the Myfyrian

Archaiology; and Subsequently Proposed as Materials for a New History of Wales. Ed. T. Williams ab Iolo. Llandovery: Welsh MSS Society, 1848.

Lives of the Cambro-British Saints, of the Fifth and Immediate Succeeding Centuries: from Ancient Welsh and Latin MSS in the British Museum and Elsewhere. Ed. and trans. W. J. Rees. Llandovery: Welsh MSS Society, 1853.

The Myvyrian Archaiology of Wales: Collected Out of Ancient Manuscripts, to Which Has Been Added Additional Notes upon the "Gododin," an English Translation of the Laws of Howell the Good; Also, an Explanatory Chapter on Ancient British Music. Eds. O. Jones *et al.* Denbigh: Thomas Gee, 1870.

Orderic Vitalis. "Historiae Ecclesiasticae libri XIII in partes tres divisi," in *Patrologia Latina.* Ed. J. P. Migne. Vol. CLXXXVIII. Paris: Migne, 1855. Cols. 17–984.

Saga um Jomsvikingarne: Gamalnorsk Grunntekst og Nynorsk Umseting. Ed. and trans. A. Joleik. Gamalnorske Bokverk, No. 9. Oslo: n.p., 1910.

Scriptores Rerum Gestarum Willelmi Conquestoris. Ed. J. A. Giles. London: Camden Society, 1845.

The Song of Dermot and the Earl: an Old French Poem from the Carew Manuscript No. 596 in the Archiepiscopal Library at Lambeth Palace. Ed. and trans. G. H. Orpen. Oxford: Clarendon Press, 1892.

Wace. *Maistre Wace's Roman de Rou et des Ducs de Normandie, nach den Handschriften.* Ed. H. Andresen. Heilbronn: Henninger, 1877.

Walter Map. *Walter Map's "De Nugis Curialium."* Ed. and trans. M. R. James. Cymmrodorion Record Series, No. 9. London: n.p., 1923.

William of Jumièges. "Historiae Northmannorum libri octo" in *Patrologia Latina.* Ed. J. P. Migne. Vol. CXLIX. Paris: Garnier Fratres, 1882. Cols. 779–914.

William of Malmesbury. *De gestis regum Anglorum, libri quinque; Historiae novellae, libri tres.* Ed. W. Stubbs. Rolls Series, Vol. XC in two parts. London: n.p., 1887–1889.

William of Newburgh. *Historia Rerum Anglicarum.* Ed. H. C. Hamilton. London: English Historical Society, 1856.

William of Poitiers. "Gesta Willelmi Ducis Normannorum, et Regis Anglorum a Wilhelmo," in *Scriptores Rerum Gestarum Wellelmi Conquestoris.* Ed. J. A. Giles. London: Caxton Society, 1845. Pp. 77–159.

II. Selected Bibliographic Aids

An Anglo-Saxon and Celtic Bibliography (450–1087). Ed. W. Bonser. Two vols. Oxford: Basil Blackwell, 1957.

A Bibliography of the History of Wales: Compiled for the Guild of Graduates of the University of Wales by the Welsh History Section of the

Guild. Eds. R. T. Jenkins and W. Rees. Cardiff: University of Wales Press, 1931.

The Bulletin of the Institute of Historical Research, Theses Supplements. London: Institute of Historical Research, in progress.

Calendar of Ancient Correspondence Concerning Wales. Ed. J. G. Edwards. Cardiff: University of Wales Press, 1935.

Calendar of Documents Preserved in France, Illustrative of the History of Great Britain and Ireland. Ed. J. H. Round. Rolls Series, Vol. CXLVI. London: n.p., 1899.

English Historical Documents, 1042–1189. Eds. D. C. Douglas and G. W. Greenaway. London: Eyre and Spottiswoode, 1952.

Galbraith, V. H. *The Making of Domesday Book.* Oxford: Clarendon Press, 1961. This book contains a useful bibliography.

—, and G. R. Galbraith. "A Select Bibliography of the Historical Writings of James Tait," *Historical Essays in Honour of James Tait.* Ed. J. G. Edwards. Manchester: printed for the subscribers, 1933. Pp. 437–449.

Handlist of Early Documents (Before 1500) in the Manuscript Department of the Reference Library. Cardiff: Libraries Committee, City of Cardiff Public Libraries, 1926.

Hardy, T. D. *Descriptive Catalogue of Materials Relating to the History of Great Britain and Ireland, to the End of the Reign of Henry VII.* Rolls Series, Vol. XXVI with three parts in four. London: n.p., 1862.

—. *Syllabus (in English) of the Documents Relating to England and Other Kingdoms Contained in the Collection known as "Rhymer's Foedera."* Rolls Series, Vol. CLXXVII in three parts. London: n.p., 1869–1885.

Murgatroyd, T. *Index to the First Twenty-Five Volumes of the "Bulletin of the John Rylands Library."* Manchester: Manchester University Press, 1941.

Rees, W. "A Bibliography of Published Works on the Municipal History of Wales and the Border, with Special Reference to the Published Records," in *The Bulletin of the Board of Celtic Studies,* II (1925), 321–382.

Robinson, G. W. *Bibliography of Charles Homer Haskins: Reprinted from Haskins Anniversary Essays.* Cambridge (Mass.): Houghton Mifflin Company, 1929.

Tout, M. "A List of the Published Writings of T. F. Tout," in *Essays in Medieval History Presented to Thomas Frederick Tout.* Eds. A. G. Aittle and F. M. Powicke. Manchester: printed for the subscribers, 1925. Pp. 379–397.

Tyson, M. "A Bibliography of the Published Writings of F. M. Powicke," in *Studies in Medieval History Presented to Frederic Maurice Powicke.* Eds. R. W. Hunt *et al.* Oxford: Clarendon Press, 1948. Pp. 469–491.

Warner, J. *A List of Books Illustrating the History of Caerleon in the New-*

port *Public Libraries.* Newport: Newport Public Libraries Committee, 1929.

Wheatley, H. B. "Domesday Bibliography," in *Domesday Studies.* Ed. P. E. Dove. Two vols. London: Domesday Commemoration Committee, 1891. II, 662–695.

Williams, H. F. *An Index of Medieval Studies Published in Festschriften 1865–1946 with Special Reference to Romanic Material.* Berkeley: University of California Press, 1951.

III. Secondary Sources

A. Books and Manuscripts

Armitage, E. S. *The Early Norman Castles of the British Isles.* London: John Murray, 1912.

Ashby, A. W., and I. L. Evans. *The Agriculture of Wales and Monmouthshire.* Cardiff: University of Wales Press and the Honourable Society of Cymmrodorion, 1944.

Barrow, G. W. S. *Feudal Britain: The Completion of the Medieval Kingdoms, 1066–1314.* London: Edward Arnold, Ltd., 1956.

Blair, P. H. *An Introduction to Anglo-Saxon England.* Cambridge: Cambridge University Press, 1956.

Bowen, E. G. *The Settlements of the Celtic Saints in Wales.* Cardiff: University of Wales Press, 1954.

—. *Wales: A Study in Geography and History.* Cardiff: University of Wales Press, 1952.

—. (ed.). *Wales: A Physical, Historical and Regional Geography.* London: Methuen & Co., Ltd., 1957.

Bradney, J. A. *A History of Monmouthshire from the Coming of the Normans Down to the Present Time.* Four vols. in nine. London: Mitchell, Hughes and Clark, 1907–1932.

Bund, J. W. W. *The Celtic Church in Wales.* London: D. Nutt, 1897.

Burke, B. *A Genealogical History of the Dormant, Abeyant, Forfeited, and Extinct Peerages of the British Empire.* London: Harrison, 1883.

Charles, B. G. *Old Norse Relations with Wales.* Cardiff: University of Wales Press, 1934.

Clark, G. T. *The Land of Morgan: Being a Contribution towards the History of the Lordship of Glamorgan.* London: Whiting and Co., Ltd., 1883.

—. *Mediaeval Military Architecture in England.* London: Wyman and Sons, 1884.

Cleveland, Duchess of. *The Battle Abbey Roll: with Some Account of the Norman Lineages.* Three vols. London: John Murray, 1889.

Collingwood, R. G., and J. L. N. Myres. *Roman Britain and the English Settlements.* Oxford: Clarendon Press, 1941.

Curtis, E. *A History of Medieval Ireland from 1086 to 1513.* 2nd ed. London: Methuen & Co., Ltd., 1938.

Daniel, G. E. *The Prehistoric Chamber Tombs of England and Wales.* Cambridge: Cambridge University Press, 1950.

Davies, M. *Wales in Maps.* Cardiff: University of Wales Press, 1958.

Davis, H. W. C. *England under the Normans and Angevins, 1066–1272.* 13th ed. London: Methuen & Co., Ltd., 1957.

Dictionary of National Biography. Sixty-three vols., with additional supplements, reprints, and summaries. London: Smith, Elder, and Co., 1885–1900.

The Domesday Geography of Eastern England. Ed. H. C. Darby. Cambridge: Cambridge University Press, 1952.

The Domesday Geography of Midland England. Ed. H. C. Darby. Cambridge: Cambridge University Press, 1954.

Domesday Studies: Being the Papers Read at the Meetings of the Domesday Commemoration, 1886. Ed. P. E. Dove. Two vols. London: Domesday Commemoration Committee, 1891.

Douglas, D. C. *The Norman Conquest and British Historians: Being the Thirteenth Lecture on the David Murray Foundation in the University of Glasgow, delivered on February 20th, 1946.* Glasgow University Publications, no. 67. Glasgow: Glasgow University Press, 1946.

—. *The Rise of Normandy.* London: Geoffrey Cumberlege, 1947.

—. *William the Conqueror: The Norman Impact on England.* Berkeley: University of California Press, 1964.

Dugdale, W. *The Baronage of England: or an Historical Account of the Lives and Most Memorable Actions of Our English Nobility in the Saxon's Time, to the Norman Conquest; and from Thence, of Those Who Had Their Rise before the End of King Henry the Third's Reign. Deduced from Publick Records, Antient Historians, and Other Authorities.* Two vols. London: Abel Roper, John Martin, and Henry Herringman, 1675–1676.

Dupont, E. (ed.). *Recherches Historiques et Topographiques sur les Compagnons de Guillaume le Conquérant. Repetoire de leurs lieux d'Origine. Études Anglo-Françaises.* Two parts. St. Servant: n.p., 1907–1908.

Ellis, A. S. "Some Account of the Landholders of Gloucestershire Named in Domesday Book, A.D. 1086." Unpublished. Presented to the British Museum in 1880. Number 10352.h.12.

Ellis, H. *A General Introduction to Domesday Book Accompanied by Indexes of the Tenants in Chief, and Under Tenants at the Time of the Survey as Well as the Holders of Lands Mentioned in Domesday Anterior to the Formations of That Record; with an Abstract of the Population of England at the Close of the Reign of William the Conqueror so*

Far as the Same Is Actually Entered. Two vols. London: Record Commissioners, 1833.

Ellis, T. P. *Welsh Tribal Law and Custom in the Middle Ages.* Two vols. Oxford: Clarendon Press, 1926.

Eyton, R. W. *Antiquities of Shropshire.* Twelve vols. London: John Russell Smith, 1854–1860.

Fox, C. F. *Offa's Dyke: a Field Survey of the Western Frontier Works of Mercia in the Seventh and Eighth Centuries* A.D. London: published for the British Academy by Oxford University Press, 1955.

—. *The Personality of Britain: Its Influence on Inhabitant and Invader in Prehistoric Times.* Cardiff: National Museum of Wales, 1952.

Freeman, E. A. *The History of the Norman Conquest of England: Its Causes and Results.* Six vols. Oxford: Clarendon Press, 1867–1879.

—. *The Reign of William Rufus and the Accession of Henry I.* Two vols. Oxford: Clarendon Press, 1882.

Galbraith, V. H. *The Making of Domesday Book.* Oxford: Clarendon Press, 1961.

Garnett, A. *Insolation and Relief: Their Bearing on the Human Geography of Alpine Regions.* Institute of British Geographers, Publication No. 5. London: George Philip and Son, Ltd., 1937.

Handbook of British Chronology. Eds. F. M. Powicke *et al.* London: Royal Historical Society, 1939.

Haskins, C. H. *Norman Institutions.* Harvard Historical Studies, Vol. XXIV. Cambridge, Massachusetts: Harvard University Press, 1918.

—. *The Normans in European History.* New York: Houghton Mifflin Company, 1915.

Hemmeon, M. deW. *Burgage Tenure in Medieval England.* Harvard Historical Studies, Vol. XX. Cambridge (Mass.): 1914.

Hughes, C. *Royal Wales: The Land and Its People.* London: Phoenix House, Ltd., 1957.

Janauscheck, L. *Originum Cisterciensium tomus 1, in quo praemissis congregationum domiciliis adjectisque tabulis chronologico-genealogicus, veterum abbatiarum a monachis habitatarum fundationes ad fidem antiquissimorum fontium primus descripsit L.J.* Vienna: n.p., 1877.

Jones, T. A. *History of the County of Brecknock Containing the Chorography, General History, Religion, Laws, Customs, Manners, Language, System of Agriculture, Antiquities, Sepulchral Monuments and Inscriptions, Natural Curiosities, Variations of the Soil, Stratification, Minerology, Lists of Rare and Other Plants and Birds, Parliamentary History, Names and Biographies of Sheriffs and Mayors of Brecknock, Also the Genealogies and Arms of the Principle Families Properly Coloured and Emblazoned, Together with the History of Every Parish, and the Names of the Patrons and Incumbents of All Livings.* Four vols. in two. First published in 1809. Brecknock: Blisset, Davies and Co., 1909–1911.

Kendrick, T. D. *A History of the Vikings*. London: Methuen & Co., Ltd., 1930.

Laws, E. *The History of Little England beyond Wales and the Non-Kymric Colony Settled in Pembrokeshire*. London: George Bell and Sons, 1886.

Lewis, A. R. *The Northern Seas: Shipping and Commerce in Northern Europe*, A.D. *300–1100*. Princeton: Princeton University Press, 1958.

Lewis, H. *The Ancient Laws of Wales: Viewed Especially in Regard to the Light They Throw upon the Origin of Some English Institutions*. London: Elliot Stock, 1899.

Lewis, S. *A Topographical Dictionary of Wales: Comprising the Several Counties, Cities, Boroughs, Corporate and Market Towns, Parishes, Chapelries, and Townships, with Historical and Statistical Descriptions; and Embellished with Engravings of the Arms of the Bishoprics and the Arms and Seals of the Various Cities and Municipal Corporations*. Two vols. London: S. Lewis and Co., 1849.

Lieberman, F. *Die Gesetze der Angelsachesen*. Three vols. Halle: n.p., 1898–1916.

Lloyd, J. E. *A History of Carmarthenshire*. Two vols. Cardiff: The London Carmarthenshire Society, 1935.

—. *A History of Wales from the Earliest Times to the Edwardian Conquest*. Two vols. 3rd ed. London: Longmans, Green and Co., 1912.

—. *The Story of Ceredigion (400–1282)*. Cardiff: University of Wales Press, 1937.

Loomis, R. S. *Wales and the Arthurian Legend*. Cardiff: University of Wales Press, 1956.

Maitland, F. W. *Domesday Book and Beyond: Three Essays in the Early History of England*. 2nd ed. Cambridge: Cambridge University Press, 1907.

Margary, I. D. *Roman Roads in Britain*. Two vols. London: Phoenix House, Ltd., 1955.

Masseville, L. de. *Histoire Sommaire de Normandie*. Six vols. Rouen: Antoire Maurry, 1691–1704.

Matheson, C. *Changes in the Fauna of Wales within Historic Times*. Cardiff: The National Museum of Wales and the University of Wales Press, 1932.

Morris, J. E. *The Welsh Wars of Edward II: A Contribution to Medieval Military History, Based on Original Documents*. Oxford: Clarendon Press, 1901.

Nash-Williams, V. E. *The Early Christian Monuments of Wales*. Cardiff: University of Wales Press, 1950.

—. *The Roman Frontier in Wales*. Cardiff: University of Wales Press, 1954.

Nichols, Thomas. *Annals and Antiquities of the Counties and County*

Families of Wales . . . . Two vols. London: Longmans, Green, Reader, and Co., 1872.

North, F. J. *The Evolution of the Bristol Channel: with Special Reference to the Coast of South Wales.* Cardiff: The National Museum of Wales, 1955.

Ordnance Survey, *Map of Britain in the Dark Ages.* Southampton: Ordnance Survey, 1935.

—. *Map of Monastic Britain.* Chessington: Ordnance Survey, 1950.

Orpen, G. H. *Ireland under the Normans, 1169–1216.* Five vols. Oxford: Clarendon Press, 1911.

Owen, G. *Prooffes Out of Auntient Recordes, Writings and Other Matters That the Lordshipp of Kemes is a Lordshippe Marcher, Baronia de Kemeys, from the Original Documents at Bronwydd.* Cambrian Archaeological Association. London: J. Russell Smith, n.d.

Pezet, M. *Les Barons de Creully: Études Historiques.* Bayeux: La Société Académique, 1854.

Poole, E. *The Illustrated History and Biography of Brecknockshire from the Earliest Times to the Present Day: Containing the General History, Antiquities, Sepulchral Monuments and Inscriptions, with the History of the Principal Families, Institutions, and Societies of the County, Together with the Parochial History of All of the Parishes in the Said County, to Which Is Added a Biographical Record of Eminent Inhabitants, History of the Borough and County Parliamentary Representatives, with a Roll of High Sheriffs to the Present Times, Mayors of Brecknock, and Many Useful Tables of County Information.* Brecknock: published by the author, 1886.

Poole, R. L. *Chronicles and Annals: a Brief Outline of Their Origin and Growth.* Oxford: Clarendon Press, 1926.

Powel, D. *The Historie of Cambria Now Called Wales: a Part of the Most Famous Yland of Britaine, Written in the Brytish Language Above Two Hundred Yeares Past. Translated into English by H. Lhoyd, Gentleman, Corrected, Augmented and Continued Out of Records and Best Approoved Authors by David Powel.* First published 1584. London: reprinted for John Harding, 1811.

Rees, W. *An Historical Atlas of Wales from Early to Modern Times.* Cardiff: University of Wales Press, 1959.

—. *South Wales and the March, 1284–1415: A Social and Agrarian Study.* Oxford: Oxford University Press, 1924.

Rhys, J., and D. Brynmor-Jones. *The Welsh People: Chapters on Their Origin, History and Laws, Language, Literature and Characteristics.* 4th ed. London: T. Fisher Unwin, Ltd., 1923.

Rodd, Lord Rennell of. *Valley on the March: A History of a Group of Manors on the Herefordshire March of Wales.* Oxford: Oxford University Press, 1952.

Round, J. H. *The Commune of London and Other Studies.* Westminster: Constable and Co., 1899.

—. *Family Origins and Other Studies: Edited with a Memoir and a Bibliography by William Page.* London: Constable and Co., 1930.

—. *Feudal England: Historical Studies on the XIth and XIIth Centuries.* London: Swan Sonnenschein and Co., Ltd., 1909.

—. *Studies in Peerage and Family History.* Westminster: Constable and Co., 1901.

Royal Commission on Land in Wales and Monmouthshire. London: n.p., 1896.

Seebohm, F. *The English Village Community, Examined in Its Relations to the Manorial and Tribal Systems and to the Common or Open Field System of Husbandry: An Essay in Economic History.* 4th ed. London: Longmans, Green and Co., 1905.

Southall, J. E. *Wales and Her Language: Considered from a Historical, Educational and Social Standpoint, with Remarks on Modern Welsh Literature and a Linguistic Map of the Country.* Newport: published by the author, n.d.

Stenton, D. M. *English Society in the Early Middle Ages, 1066–1307.* Vol. III of *Pelican History of England.* London: Penguin Books, Ltd., 1959.

Stenton, F. M. *Anglo-Saxon England.* Oxford: Clarendon Press, 1943.

—. *The Development of the Castle in England and Wales.* The Historical Association, leaflet No. 22. London: The Historical Association, 1910.

—. *The First Century of English Feudalism: Being the Ford Lectures Delivered in the University of Oxford in Hilary Term, 1929.* 2nd ed. Oxford: Clarendon Press, 1961.

Stokes, G. T. *Ireland and the Celtic Church: A History.* 2nd ed. London: Hodder and Stoughton, 1888.

A Survey of the Agricultural and Waste Lands of Wales. Cahn Hill Improvement Scheme. London: Faber and Faber, Ltd., 1936.

Tout, T. F. *Mediaeval Town Planning: A Lecture.* Manchester: Manchester University Press, 1934.

—. *The Study of Mediaeval Chronicles.* Manchester: Manchester University Press, 1922.

Trent, C. *The Changing Face of England: The Story of the Landscape through the Ages.* London: Phoenix House, Ltd., 1956.

Vinogradoff, P. *The Growth of the Manor.* 2nd ed. London: George Allen and Co., Ltd., 1911.

Wade-Evans, A. W. *The Emergence of England and Wales.* 2nd ed. London: W. Heffer and Sons, Ltd., 1959.

Wheeler, R. E. M. *Prehistoric and Roman Wales.* Oxford: Clarendon Press, 1925.

Williams, A. H. *An Introduction to the History of Wales.* Vol. II, Part I. Cardiff: University of Wales Press, 1948.

Williams, G. J. *Iolo Morgannwg, a Chywyddau'r Ychwanegiad.* London: National Eistedfodd, 1936.

Williamson, H. R. *The Arrow and the Sword: An Essay in Detection, Being an Enquiry into the Nature of the Deaths of William Rufus and Thomas Becket, with Some Reflections on the Nature of Medieval Heresy.* 2nd ed. London: Faber and Faber, Ltd., 1955.

Wood, J. G. *The Lordship, Castle and Town of Chepstow, Otherwise Striguil, with an Appendix on the Lordship of Caerleon.* Newport: Mullock and Sons, Ltd., 1910.

B. Articles

Ashby, A. W. "The Place of Cereal Growing in Welsh Agriculture," in *The Welsh Journal of Agriculture*, II (1926), 36–46.

Baddeley, St.C. "Notes on Portions of a Late and Secondary Roman Road System (*c.* A.D. 220–390) in Gloucestershire," in *The Transactions of the Bristol and Gloucestershire Archaeological Society*, LII (1930), 151–185.

Banks, R. W. "The Castles of Grosmont, Skenfrith and Whitecastle," in *Archaeologia Cambrensis*, Series IV, Vol. VII (1876), pp. 229–311.

—. "Herefordshire and Its Welsh Border During the Saxon Period," in *Archaeologia Cambrensis*, Series IV, Vol. XIII (1882), pp. 19–40.

Bateson, M. "The Laws of Breteuil," in *The English Historical Review*, XV (1900), 73–78, 302–318, 496–523, 754–757; XVI (1901), 92–110, 332–345.

Beeler, J. H. "Castles and Strategy in Norman and Early Angevin England," in *Speculum*, XXXI (1956), 581–601.

Bishop, T. A. M., "The Norman Settlement of Yorkshire," in *Studies in Medieval History Presented to Frederic Maurice Powicke*. Eds. H. W. Hunt *et al.* Oxford: Clarendon Press, 1948. Pp. 1–14.

Bromberg, E. I. "Wales and the Medieval Slave Trade," in *Speculum*, XVII (1942), 263–269.

Carlyon–Britton, P. W. P. "The Saxon, Norman and Plantagenet Coinage of Wales," in *The Transactions of the Honourable Society of Cymmrodorion for 1905–1906*, pp. 1–30.

Clark, G. T. "The Appeal of Richard Siward to the Curia Regis from a Decision in the Curia Comitatus in Glamorgan, 1248," in *Archaeologia Cambrensis*, Series IV, Vol. IX (1878), pp. 241–263.

—. "Bronllys Castle," in *Archaeologia Cambrensis*, Series III, Vol. VIII (1862), pp. 81–92.

—. "The Castle of Builth," in *Archaeologia Cambrensis*, Series IV, Vol. V (1874), pp. 1–8.

—. "The Castle of Ewyas Harold," in *Archaeologia Cambrensis*, Series IV, Vol VIII (1877), pp. 116–124.

—. "Coyty Castle and Lordship," in *Archaeologia Cambrensis*, Series IV, Vol VIII (1877), pp. 1–21.

—. "Glamorgan Adventurers in Ireland," in *Archaeologia Cambrensis*, Series IV, Vol. III (1872), pp. 210–211.

—. "The Lords of Avan, of the Blood of Jestyn," in *Archaeologia Cambrensis*, Series III, Vol. XIII (1867), pp. 1–44.

—. "The Manorial Particulars of the County of Glamorgan," in *Archaeologia Cambrensis*, Series IV, Vol. VIII (1877), pp. 249–269; Vol. IX (1878), pp. 1–21, 114–134.

—. "Tretower, Blaen Llyfni and Crickhowell Castles," in *Archaeologia Cambrensis*, Series IV, Vol. VII (1876), pp. 276–284.

—. "Wigmore," in *Archaeologia Cambrensis*, Series IV, Vol. V (1874), pp. 97–109.

Conway, R. P. "The Black Friars of Cardiff: Recent Excavations and Discoveries," in *Archaeologia Cambrensis*, Series V, Vol. VI (1899), pp. 97–105.

Corbett, W. J. "The Development of the Duchy of Normandy and the Norman Conquest of England," in *The Cambridge Medieval History*. Eds. J. R. Tanner *et al.* 2nd ed. reprinted. Eight vols. Cambridge: Cambridge University Press, 1957–1959. V, 481–520.

Davis, H. W. C. "The Anarchy of Stephen's Reign," in *The English Historical Review*, XVIII (1903), 630–641.

Douglas, D. C. "The Ancestors of William Fitz Osbern," *The English Historical Review*, LIX (1944), 62–79.

Drinkwater, C. H. "Translation of the Shropshire Domesday," in *The Victoria Histories of the Counties of England: Shropshire*. Vol. 1, Ed. W. Page. London: Archibald Constable & Co., Ltd., 1908. Pp. 309–349.

Easterling, R. C. "The Friars in Wales," in *Archaeologia Cambrensis*, Series VI, Vol. XIV (1914), pp. 323–356.

Edwards, J. G. "The Normans and the Welsh March," in *The Proceedings of the British Academy*, XLII (1956), 155–177.

Fleure, H. J., and T. C. James. "Geographical Distribution of Anthropological Types Found in Wales, in *The Journal of the Royal Anthropological Institute*, XLVI (1916), 35–153.

Fleure, H. J., and W. E. Whitehouse. "Early Distribution and Valley-Ward Movement of Population in South Britain," in *Archaeologia Cambrensis*, Series VI, Vol. XVI (1916), pp. 101–140.

Fox, A. "Dinas Noddfa, Gelligaer Common, Excavations in 1936," in *Archaeologia Cambrensis*, Series VII, Vol. XCII (1937), pp. 247–268.

—. "Early Welsh Homesteads on Gelligaer Common, Glamorgan, Excavations in 1938," in *Archaeologia Cambrensis*, Series VII, Vol. XCIV (1939), pp. 163–199.

—. "Excavations on Gelligaer Common," in *The Bulletin of the Board of Celtic Studies*, IX (1937–1939), 297–299.

Fox, C. F. "Dinas Noddfa, Gelligaer Common, Glamorgan," in *The Bulletin of the Board of Celtic Studies*, IX (1937–1939), 295–297.

Freeman, E. A. "Was Roger of Montgomery at Senlac?" in *The Palatine Notebook for 1882*, pp. 141–143.

Freeman, T. W. "The Early Settlement of Glamorgan," in *The Scottish Geographical Magazine*, LII (1936), 12–33.

Glover, R. "English Warfare in 1066," in *The English Historical Review*, LXVII (1952), 1–18.

Goskar, K., and A. E. Trueman. "The Coastal Plateaux of South Wales," in *The Geological Magazine*, LXXI (1934), 468–477.

Gould, I. C. "Ancient Earthworks," in *The Victoria Histories of the Counties of England: Hereford*. Vol. 1. Ed. W. Page. London: Archibald Constable & Co., Ltd., 1908. Pp. 199–262.

Graham, R. "Four Alien Priories in Monmouthshire," in *The Journal of the British Archaeological Association*, new series, XXXIV (1928), 102–121.

Grimes, W. F. "A Leaden Tablet of Scandinavian Origin from South Wales," in *Archaeologia Cambrensis*, Series VII, Vol. LXXXV (1930), pp. 416–417.

Haskins, C. H. "Knight–Service in Normandy in the Eleventh Century," in *The English Historical Review*, XXII (1907), 636–649.

—. "Normandy under William the Conqueror," in *The American Historical Review*, XIV (1909), 453–476.

—. "The Norman 'Consuetudines et Iusticie' of William the Conqueror," in *The English Historical Review*, XXIII (1908), 502–508.

Hirshberg, R. I., and J. F. Hirshberg. "Meggers' Law of Environmental Limitation of Culture," in *The American Anthropologist*, LIX (1957), 890–892.

Hollister, C. W. "The Norman Conquest and the Genesis of English Feudalism," in *The American Historical Review*, LXVI (1961), 641–663.

Hope-Taylor, B. "The Norman Motte at Abinger, Surrey, and its Wooden Castle," in *Recent Archaeological Excavations in Britain*. Ed. R. L. S. Bruce-Mitford. London: Routledge and Kegan Paul, 1956. Pp. 223–249.

Howorth, H. H. "The Family of Montgomery," in *The Palatine Notebook for 1881*, pp. 185–187.

—. "The First and Second Roger de Montgomery," in *The Palatine Notebook for 1882*, pp. 27–31.

—. "Roger II de Montgomery," in *The Palatine Notebook for 1882*, pp. 76–80.

Hunt, W. H. "Bernard de Neufmarche," in *The Dictionary of National Biography*. Eds. L. Stephen and S. Lee. Twenty-two vols. London: Oxford University Press, 1908–1909.

Jones, W. L. "Walter Map," in *The Transactions of the Honourable Society of Cymmrodorion for 1905–1906*, pp. 161–188.

Jones-Pierce, T. "The Age of Princes," in *The Historical Basis of Welsh Nationalism*. Cardiff: Plaid Cymru, 1950. Pp. 42–59.

Lewis, E. A. "The Development of Industry and Commerce in Wales during the Middle Ages," in *The Transactions of the Royal Historical Society*, new series, XVII (1903), 121–173.

Lewis, H. "Ancient Trackway from England to West Wales," in *Archaeologia Cambrensis*, Series VI, Vol. XX (1920), pp. 283–285.

Lloyd, J. E. "Wales and the Coming of the Normans (1039–1093)," in *The Transactions of the Honourable Society of Cymmrodorion for 1899–1900*, pp. 122–164.

–. "The Welsh Chronicles," in *The Proceedings of the British Academy*, XIV (1928), 369–391.

Maitland, F. W."Northumbrian Tenures," in *The English Historical Review*, V (1890), 625–632.

Marshall, G. "The Norman Occupation of the Lands in the Golden Valley, Ewyas, and Clifford and Their Motte and Bailey Castles," in *The Transactions of the Woolhope Naturalists' Field Club for 1936–1938*, pp. 141–158.

Meggers, B. J. "Environmental Limitation on the Development of Culture," in *The American Anthropologist*, LVI (1954), 801–824.

Miller, A. A. "The 600-foot Plateau in Pembrokeshire and Carmarthenshire," in *The Geological Magazine*, XC (1953), 148–159.

Morgan, O. "Report on the Discovery of an Ancient Danish Vessel," in *The Archaeological Journal*, XXXV (1878), 403–405.

Nash–Williams, V. E. "Further Excavations at Caerwent, Monmouthshire, 1923–1925," in *Archaeologia*, LXXX (1930), 228–237.

Nichols, J. G. "The Battle Abbey Roll," in *The Herald and Genealogist*. Ed. J. G. Nichols. Eight vols. London: n.p., 1863–1874. I, 192–208.

O'Doherty, J. F. "Historical Criticism of the Song of Dermot and the Earl," in *Irish Historical Studies*, I (1938–1939), 4–20.

Otway-Ruthven, A. J. "The Constitutional Position of the Great Lordships of South Wales," in *The Transactions of the Royal Historical Society*, Series V, Vol. VIII (1958), pp. 1–20.

Owen, H. "The Flemings in Pembrokeshire," in *Archaeologia Cambrensis*, Series V, Vol. XII (1895), pp. 96–106.

Paterson, D. R. "The Scandinavian Settlement of Cardiff," in *Archaeologia Cambrensis*, Series VII, Vol. LXXVI (1921), pp. 53–83.

–. "Scandinavian Influences in the Place-Names and Early Personal Names of Glamorgan," in *Archaeologia Cambrensis*, Series VI, Vol. XX (1920), pp. 31–89.

Planche, J. R. "On the Norman Earls of Shrewsbury," in *Collectanea*

Archaeologia: Communications made to the British Archaeological Association, I (1861), 67–78.

Prothero, R. M. "The Bristol Channel Coastlands: Early Cultural Contacts," in *The Scottish Geographical Magazine,* LXV (1949), 44–54.

Rees, W. "Medieval Gwent," in *The Journal of the British Archaeological Association,* New Series, XXXIV (1928), 189–207.

–. "The Medieval Lordship of Brecon," in *The Transactions of the Honourable Society of Cymmrodorion for 1915–1916,* pp. 165–224.

Round, J. H. "The Family of Clare," in *The Archaeological Journal,* LVI (1899) (Series II, Vol. VI), 221–231.

–. "Introduction to the Herefordshire Domesday," in *The Victoria Histories of the Counties of England: Hereford.* Vol. I. Ed. W. Page. London: Archibald Constable & Co., Ltd., 1908. Pp. 263–307.

–. "Introduction to the Worcestershire Domesday Book," in *The Victoria Histories of the Counties of England: Worcester.* Vol. I. Ed. H. A. Doubleday. Westminster: Archibald Constable & Co., Ltd., 1901. Pp. 235–280.

–. "Richard de Clare, or Richard Strongbow," in *The Dictionary of National Biography.* Eds. L. Stephen and S. Lee. Twenty-two vols. London: Oxford University Press, 1908–1909. X, 390–393.

Seaton, Rev. Prebendary. "History of Goodrich," in *The Transactions of the Woolhope Naturalists' Field Club for 1901–1902,* pp. 212–215.

Slack, W. J. "The Shropshire Ploughmen of Domesday Book," in *The Transactions of the Shropshire Archaeological Society,* L (1939), 31–35.

Sollas, W. J. "Paviland Cave: An Aurignacian Station in Wales," in *The Journal of the Royal Anthropological Institute,* XLIII (1913), 325–374.

Stenton, F. M. "The Road System of Medieval England," in *The Economic History Review,* VII (1936–1937), 1–21.

Stevenson, W. H. "A Contemporary Description of the Domesday Survey," in *The English Historical Review,* XXII (1907), 72–84.

Tait, J. "Introduction to the Shropshire Domesday Book," in *The Victoria Histories of the Counties of England: Shropshire.* Vol. I. Ed. W. Page. London: Archibald Constable & Co., Ltd., 1908. Pp. 279–307.

Taylor, C. S. "The Norman Settlement of Gloucestershire," in *The Transactions of the Bristol and Gloucestershire Archaeological Society for 1917,* pp. 57–88.

Tout, T. F. "Robert Fitzhamon," in *The Dictionary of National Biography.* Eds. L. Stephen and S. Lee. Twenty-two vols. London: Oxford University Press, 1908–1909.

Turner, F. J. "The Significance of the Frontier in American History," in *The Turner Thesis.* Ed. G. R. Taylor. Boston: D. C. Heath and Company, 1956. Pp. 1–18.

Waddington, H. M. "Games and Athletics in Bygone Wales," in *The Trans-*

actions of the Honourable Society of Cymmrodorion for 1953, pp. 84–100.

Warner, R. H. "Eardisley and Its Castle," in *The Transactions of the Wool-hope Naturalists' Field Club for 1903*, pp. 256–262.

Webb, W. P. "The Frontier and the 400 Year Boom," in *The Turner Thesis*. Ed. G. R. Taylor. Boston: D. C. Heath and Company, 1956. Pp. 87–95.

Wheeler, R. E. M. "A New Beaker from Wales," in *The Antiquaries' Journal*, III (1923), 21–23.

Williams, D. T. "Gower: A Study of Linguistic Movements and Historical Geography," in *Archaeologia Cambrensis*, Series VII, Vol. LXXXIX (1934), pp. 302–327.

INDEX

abbeys: 56, 85, 101, 163
Aberafon (borough): 109
Aberdovey (castle): 125
Abereinion (castle): 125
Abergavenny: 122, 163
Aber Llech: 91
Aberllyfni: 92
Aberystwyth: town, 37; castle, 122
Ada (child of Herluin of Heugeville): 83
Adeliza (wife of William Fitz-Osbern): 29 n.
Adrian IV (pope): 133 n.
Aelfgar (English noble): 17, 18
Agnes (wife of Bernard of Neufmarché): 85
agreement of 1081: See treaties
agriculture: limits on, 7, 9; of Welsch, 7–8, 9; in Wales, 70, 71, 92, 107–109 *passim*, 182, 183; of Cambro-Normans, 93, 182; and feudalism, 123; in Normandy, 166; mentioned, 68, 111
Alençon: 66, 118
Algeria: 176
Alretone: 68, 69
Amiera (wife of Warin the Bald): 67
Angevins: 22, 152
Anglesey, isle of: 112, 113, 118
Anglo-Normans: military of, 121, 139, 140; culture of, 125, 152, 159, 178, 182; mentioned, 160. See also Normans
Anglo-Saxons: 14–15, 74, 168. See also Mercians
Anglo-Saxon Chronicle: 27, 36
Anjou: 28
Annales Cambriae: 37, 91
Annals of Margan: 103, 104
Annals of the Four Masters: 146
Archenfield (Erging): 32, 74
archers: 138, 139, 144

Argentan: 68, 118
Arnulf (brother of Robert of Bellême): 118–120 *passim*
Arques, William of: 83
Arthur (British king): 4, 172
Arundel: 66, 118, 120
Arwystli: 94
Aufay (town): 83
Aufay family: 83, 84
Avene family: 109
Avon (region): 106, 109, 178
Avon River: 108, 109

Bach, manor of: 72, 86
Bailleul-en-Gouffern: 67
balance of power. See power, balance of
Barri, Robert of: 138
bastides: 167
Battle Abbey: 84–85, 163; cell of, 84–85, 90
Battle Abbey Roll: 97
Bayeux: 96, 100
Bayeux, Odo of: 26, 27, 81
Beauvais: 84
Becket, Thomas à: 133, 136
Bellême: 66
Bellême, Robert of: 99, 118–121
Benedictines: 163
Berkeroll (knight): 102
Berkeshire: 72 n.
Bernard (bishop): 164
Bernard of Neufmarché. See Neufmarché, Bernard of
Beryngton (estate): 86
bishops: 47
Black Death: 183
Black Mountains: 73
Blackwell (estate): 56
Blaen Llyfni (fortress): 91, 92
Bleddyn (Welsh king): 28
Bleddyn (king of Powys): 82